Roman Archa

MW01088722

Roman Archaeology for Historians provides students of Roman history with a guide to the contribution of archaeology to the study of their subject. It discusses the issues with the use of material and textual evidence to explain the Roman past, and the importance of viewing this evidence in context. It also surveys the different approaches to the archaeological material of the period and examines key themes that have shaped Roman archaeology. Throughout, the author argues for the need for greater understanding between archaeologists and ancient historians in order to form a full picture of the Roman past.

Roman Archaeology for Historians provides an accessible guide to the development of archaeology as a discipline and how the use of archaeological evidence of the Roman world can enrich the study of ancient history, while at the same time encouraging the integration of material evidence into the study of the period's history. This work is a key resource for students of ancient history, and for those studying the archaeology of the Roman period.

Ray Laurence is Professor of Roman History and Archaeology at the University of Kent, UK. He has published extensively on the Roman Empire, with titles that include: *The Roads of Roman Italy: Mobility and Cultural Change* (1999), *Roman Pompeii: Space and Society* (2007), and *The City in the Roman West c. 250 BC–c. AD 250* (2011).

Approaching the Ancient World
Series Editor: Richard Stoneman

The sources for the study of the Greek and Roman world are diffuse, diverse and often complex, and special training is needed in order to use them to the best advantage in constructing a historical picture. The books in this series provide an introduction to the problems and methods involved in the study of ancient history. The topics covered range from the use of literary courses for Greek history and for Roman history, through numismatics, epigraphy and dirt archaeology, to the use of legal evidence and of art and artefacts in chronology.

Roman Archaeology for Historians

Ray Laurence

Routledge
Taylor & Francis Group

LONDON AND NEW YORK

First published 2012
by Routledge
2 Park Square, Milton Park, Abingdon, Oxon OX14 4RN

Simultaneously published in the USA and Canada
by Routledge
711 Third Avenue, New York, NY 10017

Routledge is an imprint of the Taylor & Francis Group, an informa business

British Library Cataloguing in Publication Data
A catalogue record for this book is available from the British Library

Library of Congress Cataloging-in-Publication Data
Laurence, Ray, 1963–
    Roman archaeology for historians / Ray Laurence.
        p. cm. – (Approaching the ancient world)
    Includes bibliographical references and index.
    1. Archaeology and history–Rome. 2. Rome–Antiquities. I. Title.
    DG77.L38 2012
    937–dc23
                        2011049385

ISBN: 978-0-415-50591-8 (hbk)
ISBN: 978-0-415-50592-5 (pbk)
ISBN: 978-0-203-11548-0 (ebk)

Typeset in Baskerville and Gill Sans
by Taylor & Francis Books

Contents

Illustrations

Preface

You do not need to be an archaeologist to read this book. It is intended to be a book that will allow students of ancient history to understand how the subject of Roman archaeology arranges itself, its preoccupations and some of its history, and to provide a knowledge base for engagement with archaeologists. Archaeology is an exciting subject and mostly presented to the public as discoveries, but the academic discipline of archaeology is far more exciting, developing innovative interpretations and presenting new perspectives for ancient historians to engage with. Archaeology is a vast subject and there is no pretence of covering it all in this book. Instead there is an overview with case studies or academic developments that I feel are significant for ancient historians. There is much more to discover by delving into the references and bibliography. The fact of new discoveries via fieldwork means the discipline of archaeology has a subconscious or even conscious focus on the possibility of alteration of our understanding that crosses over into interpretation – so statements in this book are very much those of 2011 (or even a bit earlier) and will be subject to change in the future as perspectives on the Roman past shift.

To my embarrassment, Richard Stoneman commissioned this volume some ten years ago, on hearing about a conference session at the Theoretical Archaeology Group (TAG) annual conference on the subject of the disciplinary boundary between ancient history and archaeology. The session organizer, Eberhard Sauer, efficiently produced a book of those papers entitled *Archaeology and Ancient History* published by Routledge in 2004 and in November 2011 a conference at the University of Leicester revisited the issues. Ancient history is entwined with archaeology in undergraduate degree programmes. In research, there is a cross-over between information being developed in both disciplines, but I have a sense that ancient history may be becoming more open to archaeology as a discipline and has incorporated the material dimension into its historical narrative.

Today, in departments of archaeology in the UK, there are more undergraduate students taking joint honours degrees in ancient history and archaeology than there are in single honours archaeology. Let us be absolutely clear: the majority of students taking archaeology are also taking ancient history. There is something of a conundrum though: most universities in the UK maintain a separation between their archaeology staff and their Roman history staff – placing them in respective departments of archaeology and classics. These departments create degree programmes with a primary focus on a syllabus for their single honours students of a single discipline and develop quite different local applications of their university's policies and practices on a variety of logistical issues for the teaching of undergraduates – from deadlines to marking criteria. For ancient history and archaeology students, these are features that are bemusing and have to be accommodated. What is perhaps more startling for ancient historians is that Roman archaeology is academically quite a distinct discipline that draws on the work of Roman historians, but develops in quite a different way.

Surprisingly, there is no textbook for the subject of Roman archaeology and this causes something of a problem for students of ancient history, who wish to look into the possibilities and potential of the use of archaeological evidence. There is a good essay question to be written on the character of Roman archaeology as seen in say the last ten volumes of the *Journal of Roman Archaeology* representing a decade of disciplinary endeavour filtered by the editor of the journal, referees and the editorial committee, plus the authors who choose to send their papers to the journal for publication. This book tries to set out a basic introduction for history students of why Roman archaeology matters, as well as its characteristics. The book does focus more on the view from the UK and its tradition of the study of Roman archaeology. This is somewhat different from that found in North America, Australia or nearer to home in France, Germany, Spain, Italy, Morocco, Tunisia and Libya. There is not space here to discuss the full variety of national traditions of the subject. What I do offer in this slim volume is a viewpoint from ancient history into the subject area of Roman archaeology; it is not a textbook for Roman archaeology – that will need to be written from within the discipline of archaeology – but instead points to debates and subject matter for discussion that I feel are of interest to the subject of ancient history.

I was once an undergraduate and, at the end of my first year, I was persuaded to change the subject of my degree course and take a new programme in ancient history and archaeology. It was a single honours course involving two departments: classics and archaeology. Like most joint academic ventures, it drew on existing degree structures but added a core module in years two and three. In year two, archaeology brought to the programme a compulsory unit in method and theory, while classics produced a compulsory module in sources for ancient history. These two modules in many ways defined the differences between the two constituent departments: ancient history was founded on the interpretation and evaluation of sources, whereas at the very heart of archaeology was not just methodology, but a range of theoretical approaches that were regarded as highly valued assets. Innocently, as a student, I would apply what I was taught by archaeologists in essays set by my tutors who were classicists. This did not always go down well, and revealed the academic distance between the two subjects that comprised my BA in Ancient History and Archaeology. Later, as a personal tutor to students at the University of Reading, I was told by ancient history and archaeology students that there is a way to write essays successfully for the classics department and quite another for the archaeology department. Their experience as undergraduates, as recently as 2005, was not so different from my own; their degree in ancient history and archaeology was delineated more thoroughly with marking criteria (two sets, subtly different, provided by each department), but as students they were facing the same undefined challenge: how to bridge a gap between two quite different academic cultures. This phenomenon is not unique to the UK and can be found in North America and in most European universities (Patterson 1995 for in-depth historical analysis of a similar situation in the USA; Andrén 1998: 1–36 on the European tradition) and is also seen in parallel disciplines including Byzantine studies (Rautman 1990).

For more than 20 years, I have had the pleasure of facing the challenge of using both textual evidence, the bread and butter of ancient history, and archaeological material (or should I say archaeological theory?) with a view to producing, not so much an integrated view, but at least a different view of the Roman past (compare Andrén 1998; Morris 2000; Moreland 2001; Foxhall 2004; Laurence 2004; Rankov 2004; Sauer 2004a; 2004b; Martinón-Torres 2008). This approach is archaeological in two senses: first, it includes evidence that has been discovered and published (or not) by archaeologists, and second, my interpretations are derived from a body of theoretical perspectives valued by archaeologists. The latter is important: the largest archaeology meeting held on an annual basis in the UK is the Theoretical Archaeology Group's conference or TAG and is a venue in which ideas have been debated, argued and feuds have even developed. Few Roman archaeologists attended TAG 20 years ago, but those who did realized the potential of what was happening in their discipline and a new generation of Romanists, who had themselves as undergraduates taken courses in archaeological method and theory (later theory and method or even just theory), saw an opportunity to place a greater emphasis on the role of theory in Roman archaeology. In 1990, Eleanor Scott convened a conference on Theoretical Roman Archaeology at the University of Newcastle and each subsequent year a meeting of what is known as TRAC (Theoretical Roman Archaeology Conference) has been held. There was also a sense that 'the young' of the time shared a belief in change and utilized theory to achieve change (there was a degree of 'anger can be power'). Years later, some of the young have become mid-career academics. My point is that when we are to discuss archaeology, we are not just looking at archaeological evidence, but also at an academic approach that places an explicit emphasis on the use of theory. Also, radicals become established and ideas that were radical become mainstream and in need of questioning.

For ancient historians, this emphasis on theory might have seemed a little unusual in the 1980s or 1990s but today, if we were to look at the respective reading lists of social historians and those of social archaeologists, we would find considerable convergence in their reading, if not in the nature of the use of these works in the construction of arguments with regard to the past. A new generation of ancient historians in the late 1980s and 1990s were looking at areas neglected by the UK-based discipline of archaeology – notably the Mediterranean – with a view to mining not just the data neglected by archaeologists in the UK, but also the methodologies associated with the discipline of archaeology as practised in the UK. Located as postgraduates and early career lecturers in classics departments during the 1980s and 1990s these scholars built bridges with departments of archaeology but were also acutely aware of the activities of literary critics in their own department who were deploying a slightly different set of theoretical approaches from those cherished by the discipline of archaeology. However, there was much common ground and certainly an undefined core reading list of Pierre Bourdieu, Michel Foucault and Anthony Giddens with the latter being more important to archaeologists than to classicists. My point is that the disciplines of ancient history and of archaeology are far closer together today than they were in the 1980s or the 1990s, but most undergraduates taking a course in ancient history and archaeology will have experience of the different emphases within these two disciplines.

As an undergraduate, I gained access to the subject from staff both in an archaeology department and a classics department over the course of three years. Frequently, in writing this book, I found myself returning to books that were new from that time and came to realize how cutting edge my lecturers were. Barry Burnham, Rob Young and David Austin, in their very different ways, set out the vibrancy of archaeological theory and its relevance to the study of the past. This book owes much to them and their colleague in the classics department, Keith Hopwood, who sadly died in 2009. Keith's open-minded and clever critique of ideas derived from archaeology combined with a lecturing style that was just different, as well as an enthusiasm for encouraging students in the development of ideas, needs to be remembered. Coincidentally, in 2009, I finally visited archaeological sites in southern Turkey that Keith had explored and delivered lectures on a quarter of a century previously. In so doing, at Aspendos and Perge, memories of Keith's lectures on epigraphy, the city, bandits and the exploitation of the landscape of Cilicia under the Roman Empire came back to me.

Over the course of the ten years that this book has taken to write, I have benefitted from the sound judgements and wisdom of colleagues and students who have aided my endeavour to bring archaeology to the attention of Roman historians, and to ensure that we really can capture the totality of the evidence about the past – however imperfectly the balance may be in any book. I owe thanks to many wonderful colleagues at the universities of Reading, Birmingham and, more recently, Kent. Special thanks are due to colleagues who have supported the interaction of archaeology and ancient history and also those colleagues who have revealed the complexities of doing so: Martin Bommas, Megan Brickley, Leslie Brubaker, John Creighton, Janet DeLaine, Ken Dowden, Michael Fulford, Vince Gaffney, Paul Garwood, Roberta Gilchrist, Helen King, Csaba La'da, Luke Lavan, Niall McKeown, Stephen Oakley, Gillian Shepherd, Diana Spencer, Ellen Swift, Elena Theodorakopoulos, Francesco Trifilò, Andrew Wallace-Hadrill, Chris Wickham, Steve Willis and Maria Wyke. My understanding of museums and issues that surround their use and even survival has been enhanced by conversations over the last two to three years with Paul Bennett, Penny Bernard, Martin Crowther, Peter Davies, David Ford, Rhiannon Harte, Joanna Jones, Charles Lambie, Janice McGuinness and Céline Murphy, as well as other members of the Canterbury Heritage Partnership. Lloyd Bosworth went beyond the call of duty to produce many of the illustrations. There are many others who should also be acknowledged who I have discussed the nature of archaeology with, not least those who participated in the British School at Rome's Tiber Valley Project, including especially John Barrett, David Mattingly, Martin Millett, Louise Revell, Rob Witcher and Simon Keay, and others who I have met regularly at the bi-annual Roman Archaeology Conference – a snapshot into the subject of archaeology for any Roman historian. A special thank you needs to be given to colleagues with whom I have written and edited books with: Mary Harlow, Simon Esmonde Cleary, Gareth Sears and David Newsome. The process of writing and editing those books delayed the writing of this book but also contributed to the content in many quite different ways. The final acknowledgement is to Teresa Chacon who acted as a non-academic reader/proofreader. All misconceptions (and mistakes) are, of course, my own.

Chapter 1

Questions of Evidence

To understand archaeology as a discipline, the evidence that it produces and the interpretations it puts forward, we need to begin with a matter that divides archaeologists from historians – the use of evidence and the combination of evidence texts and archaeological data. These are subjects that can cause scholars to get a little hot under the collar. Some have even suggested that combining these forms of evidence is only desirable after both sets of evidence have been studied independently (see Allison 2001). Part of the problem is caused by a belief that texts surviving from antiquity can be regarded or treated as data. What I wish to do for much of this chapter is to examine how texts need to be read, treated and analysed in the context of their production and consumption – i.e. the time when they were written and read – and how the time of production of a text reveals a temporal point that can be seen to be a context, or a point from which we may integrate the content with the archaeological record of the same time.

The problems raised in discussion of how we read and combine texts and material evidence may be embedded within the institutional power struggles that established the modern discipline of archaeology – that will be a focus of Chapter 2 of this book, but needs to be introduced here. To create a modern discipline of archaeology in the mid–late 20th century, it was seen as essential for archaeology to assert its place as much more than the 'handmaiden of history'. In so doing the discipline developed an emphasis on the independent study of material culture mostly without reference, if possible, to texts – the province of historians. The teaching of historical archaeology in UK universities at times appears to feature a deliberate attempt to avoid an engagement with textual evidence, and to focus solely on the analysis of archaeological data. This may be pragmatic; after all few single honours archaeology undergraduates will be versed in textual analysis, but any joint honours student taking ancient history will find the avoidance of textual evidence baffling, and will be even more confused when their use of this evidence in essays is not rewarded. As

Anders Andrén (1998) stresses, there are archaeologists who do not wish to engage with any textual sources and instead derive their conclusions entirely from the archaeological data (see examples discussed in Sauer 2004a). There are also some archaeologists who still wish to use the archaeological record to 'prove' that the textual evidence is simply wrong or a misrepresentation of the past (Allison 2001). These approaches are similar to those of the historian, who sees no value in archaeology and suggests that archaeology can only show you what you knew already from your texts – all such practitioners are missing the point. As Andrén (1998: 4) points out, the two types of evidence, texts and artefacts, are two different human discourses. Relating these together can be straightforward or down-right impossible. The key to success in this area is keeping a wary eye on the contexts, dates and type of materials that are being integrated from these two quite different discourses.

Part of the problem for ancient historians in dealing with archaeology is that we have read the texts that seem to describe the places that survived as archaeology. We cannot disaggregate or completely lose our knowledge of texts prior to evaluating a piece of archaeological evidence. Nor would such a process be desirable, since texts can aid the development of archaeological knowledge. For example, in approaching the archaeology of King Herod's new city at Caesarea most scholars will have read Josephus' description of the new city (Josephus *Wars* 410–13; *Antiquities* 15.331–38). Caesarea, like Augustus' Rome, was rebuilt in marble and its buildings were seen by Josephus to have been worthy of the person from whom the city gained its name, Caesar (Augustus). Josephus' harbour at Caesarea is the size of the Piraeus in Athens. What we see here is a rhetoric that praises the city and its builder/monarch (compare the later writer Menander Rhetor's *How to Praise a City*). However, what can be identified in the archaeological record coincides with the rhetorical description of the harbour itself, but there are monuments within Josephus' text that have yet to be identified (see Vann 1992). This is an example of a text aiding archaeology to formulate a strategy for investigating a site – Josephus' two accounts aid the fieldwork on site. Importantly, in this example, the texts of Josephus and the archaeological site are broadly contemporary. In effect, both the text and the archaeological data are derived from a very similar (if not congruent) context: the 1st century AD – hence in this example the convergence of the two sets of source material is less problematic.

Texts and archaeology in context

The relationship between texts referring to historical phenomena and the archaeological investigation of sites or even landscapes associated with those phenomena becomes far more complex when the historical writers are distanced by years or even centuries from the events themselves. Here, I wish to illustrate how the inappropriate reading of texts and archaeological evidence from different contexts can cause a disjuncture in the evidence and reduce the value of archaeology aiding historical analysis. Most students of Roman history will come across the land reform of Tiberius Gracchus in 133 BC. The basis of much of our knowledge of the motivations for these reforms comes from passages in the biography of this man by Plutarch (*c.* AD 50–120), *Tiberius Gracchus*, and Appian's historical narrative: *The Civil Wars*. Interestingly, Appian (*c.* AD 95–165) was an author who inspired Karl Marx, and with good reason, because he offers the modern reader some of the rare instances of socio-economic analysis that survive from antiquity. To quote some of the text to provide a flavour of Appian's work:

> The rich getting possession of the greater part of the undistributed lands (ager publicus), and emboldened by the lapse of time to believe that they would never be dispossessed, absorbing adjacent strips and their poor neighbours' allocations, partly by purchase under persuasion and partly by force, came to cultivate vast tracts instead of single estates, using slaves as labourers and herdsmen, lest free labourers should be drawn from agriculture into the army. At the same time the ownership of slaves brought them great gain from the multitude of their progeny, who increased because they were exempt from military service. Thus certain powerful men became extremely rich and the race of slaves multiplied throughout the country, while the Italian people dwindled in numbers and strength, being oppressed by debt, taxes and military service. If they had any respite from these evils, they passed their time in idleness, because the land was held by the rich, who employed slaves instead of freemen as cultivators.
>
> (Appian *Civil Wars* 1.7, Loeb translation).

What is difficult to see in this superb piece of persuasive and coherent analysis is the question of when all this was occurring. Appian in some ways suggests that it refers to the time at which the *Lex Licinia* was passed in 367 BC and in other ways suggests the process was also occurring closer to 133 BC (App. *BC* 1.8). Perhaps, what is most logical is that Appian is suggesting that the process took place prior to 367 BC and over the 234 years since 367 BC and the passing of the *Lex Licinia*. It is a long-term phenomenon that would seem to lead to Tiberius Gracchus' legislation. In contrast, Plutarch (*TG* 8), suggests that on a journey to Spain through Etruria, Tiberius Gracchus saw a large deserted landscape populated only by slave herdsmen and it was the end result of the long-term process that inspired his legislation. Again the passage is worth quoting:

> When the rich began to outbid the poor by offering higher rentals, a law was passed [the Lex Licinia presumably] which forbade any one individual holding more than 500 *iugera* of land. For a while this law restrained the greed of the rich and helped the poor ... But after a time the rich men in each neighbourhood by using the names of fictitious tenants, contrived to transfer many of these holdings to themselves, and finally they openly took possession of the greater part of the land under their own names ... The result was a *rapid* decline of the class of free small-holders all over Italy, their place being taken by gangs of foreign slaves, whom the rich employed to cultivate the estates from which they had driven the free citizens ... His brother Gaius Gracchus has written in a political pamphlet that while Tiberius was travelling through Etruria on his way to Numantia, he saw for himself how the country had been deserted by its native inhabitants, and how those who tilled the soil or tended the flocks were barbarian slaves introduced from abroad and it was this experience which inspired the policy.
>
> (Plutarch *Life of Tiberius Gracchus* 8, Loeb translation)

Plutarch, unlike Appian, is linking the result of the process to a specific instance in the life of Tiberius Gracchus. Obviously, we are dealing with two writers who are shaping their material for consumption more than two centuries after the legislation of Tiberius Gracchus. The authors are producing literature at a distance from the events themselves, rather than documenting observations contemporary with the legislation of 133 BC. Is it possible for archaeology to prove or disprove the veracity of their reporting? Can archaeology help us untangle what was the author's invention (*inventio*) or the invented tradition of the Gracchan legislation associated with Roman society in the late 1st and 2nd centuries AD and what can be seen as the preservation of the 'facts' from the 2nd century BC?

To provide answers to these questions, we need to provide compatible archaeological data. The large-scale landscape surveys in South Etruria and the Middle Tiber Valley identified sites dated by the evidence of pottery picked in the field (see Chapter 4 for further discussion of survey evidence). What we find associated with the 2nd century BC is a populated landscape quite unlike that described by Plutarch in the passage above (Lloyd 1986 based on Potter 1979). Perhaps we should not be surprised at a disjuncture of the two types of evidence. Plutarch reports a process via the personal recall of the subject of his biography. More importantly, his source – a pamphlet of Gaius Gracchus – served a rhetorical and political purpose and was far from objective. It was a piece of propaganda and as such we should expect exaggeration or a rather economical approach to the ideal that we associate with the truth. In other words, to expect a replication of this text on the ground is misguided and archaeology aids us in seeing our textual sources for what they are: in the case of Plutarch, literary construction of a life of a man from the past that places a firm emphasis on the subject of the biography and his experiences as sources for his political motivations. We also need to recognize that archaeological evidence cannot be precisely dated to coincide with the decade associated with 133 BC. What archaeology is far better at doing is providing us with data for the long-term change that might be seen to coincide with the processes that Appian and Plutarch seem to be referring to from the 4th to the 2nd centuries BC. The recent reassessment, including substantial re-dating of the pottery, has produced an overall pattern of long-term change in the settlement patterns of the Middle Tiber Valley up to approximately 50 miles north of Rome, and has produced a powerful model of landscape continuity over the long term. The data are presented in Figure 1.1. What we see in black are sites that have continuity from one broad period to another and in grey are the new sites that appear during each broad period. Mapping this data onto the texts of Plutarch and Appian demonstrates some convergence between the two types of evidence. In the period c. 500–350 BC (Classical in Figure 1.1), there is a marked drop in the number of sites from the earlier period – this

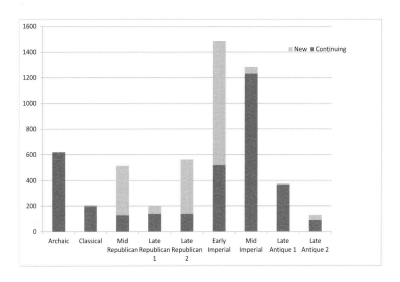

Figure 1.1 Sites in the Tiber Valley over time (provided by Rob Witcher)

might have some convergence with the need to pass the *Lex Licinia* that may have been behind the overall expansion in the number of sites in the Mid-Republican period down to the middle of the 3rd century. Following this period, Late Republican 1 (down to the end of the 2nd century BC), there was a contraction in the number of sites – perhaps coinciding with some of the conditions suggested by Plutarch and Appian (see Patterson et al 2004 for details and discussion). However, there are other striking questions of the data-set reproduced in Figure 1.1. Not least, the massive expansion of the number of settlements in the region in the Early Imperial period that is sustained through to c.250 AD. This was the stable landscape seen by Plutarch and Appian under the emperors and is the point of comparison for their discussion of the Agrarian legislation of the past – it was a landscape whose population had expanded under the empire and had become stable (see Chapter 4 for further discussion). Looking back into the past, Appian and Plutarch created a landscape of chaos caused by the greed of the rich and the presence of slavery. What archaeology does here is provide us with an understanding of the landscape of these two authors' present time and relates it back to the earlier phases of settlement geography. Seen in this context, Appian and Plutarch were making sense of the cultural memories of an Italian landscape that was fundamentally different from what they themselves experienced (see Witcher 2006a on the subject of memory and field survey).

I feel this aspect, that the textual sources are shaped by their time of production, needs to be re-emphasized once again with reference to Plutarch on the subject of Gaius Gracchus. What presents Romanists with a greater challenge than historical archaeologists working on later periods is the nature of the textual sources. These are inherently, for the most part, produced by a literary elite producing narratives in various genres – often at considerable distance from the historical phenomena that they are attempting to represent. In reading these texts, we need to be well aware of the context of production and recognize that the texts may actually say rather more about the author's time than about the activities of those in the past that are represented in their texts (Andrén 1998: 147; Scott 1993 for discussion). Hence, the passages of Appian and Plutarch quoted earlier in this chapter represent a view of Greek writers under the rule of the Roman emperors examining the flaws of the Roman Republic. There is an implicit comparison between the social divisions and greed of the rich of the Republic with the contemporary efforts of the emperors and the elite in Italy to support the poor via the *alimenta* (Laurence 1999b: 49–51). The positive values found in these texts associated with the Gracchi written by Plutarch engage with a rhetoric used to praise the emperor:

He [Gaius Gracchus] also introduced legislation which provided for the founding of colonies, the construction of roads, and the establishment of public granaries. He himself acted as director and supervisor of every project and never flagged for a moment in the execution of all these elaborate undertakings. On the contrary, he carried out each of them with extraordinary speed and power of application, as if each concern were the only one he had to manage, so that even those who disliked and feared him most were amazed at his efficiency and his capacity to carry through every enterprise to which he set his hand. As for the people, the very sight of Gaius never failed to impress them, as they watched him attended by a host of contractors, craftsmen, ambassadors, magistrates, soldiers, and men of letters, all of whom he handled with a courteous ease which enabled him to show kindness to all his associates without sacrificing his dignity, and to give every man consideration that was his due.

(Plutarch *Life of Gaius Gracchus* 6, Loeb translation)

When Plutarch describes the landscape created by Gaius Gracchus, he is not representing the landscape of the past, but instead is describing the contemporary landscape of Italy in the late 1st and early 2nd century, which we can identify in the archaeological record and again engages with the praise of emperors as road builders (see, for example, Statius *Silvae* 1.5). The passage is worth quoting:

The construction of roads was the task into which he threw himself most enthusiastically, and he took great pains to ensure that these should be graceful and beautiful as well as useful. His roads were planned to run right across the country in a straight line, part of the surface consisting of dressed stone and part of trampled down gravel. Depressions were filled up, watercourses or ravines that crossed the line of the road were bridged, and both sides of the road were levelled or embanked to the same height, so that the whole of the work presented a beautiful and symmetrical appearance. Besides this he had every road measured in miles ... and stone pillars erected to mark the distances.

(Plutarch *Life of Gaius Gracchus* 7, Loeb translation)

Interestingly, very few milestones survive from the Republican era whereas these are relatively common monuments from the late 1st and early 2nd centuries AD (Black et al 2009). Equally apparent is the description by Plutarch of the road surface of dressed stone that is familiar to us today from the archaeological record – but was an innovation that caused Statius to see the building of the new Via Domitiana as a suitable subject to use to praise the emperor Domitian (*Silv.* 1.5). Appian (*BC* 1.23) highlights how the action of road-building caused many contractors and craftsmen to be indebted to the builder – a statement about the legitimation of emperors in the 2nd century AD as much as it is an analysis of the power base of Gaius Gracchus.

Viewing these texts in their context of production, we gain new insights into the landscape of Italy that helps us to explain and interpret the archaeological remains associated with inscriptions commemorating the emperor as road builder or restorer. That landscape found in the 1st and 2nd centuries AD, as we can see from Figure 1.1, has been shown archaeologically to have been at its most densely populated and at its most stable – presenting the greatest number of cases of continuity of occupation from period to period. Plutarch is describing this developed landscape of Italy found under the emperors, rather than that created by Gaius Gracchus in the 2nd century BC.

The archaeological report

Archaeological evidence has, since the late 19th century, been published (although often much remains unpublished, particularly in the Mediterranean) in the form of reports that present things in a sequence: introduction, description, the finds, discussion and appendices. There is an appearance of objective and even scientific rigour and there is a profound absence of personal pronouns (see Hodder 1989 for discussion, also Dyson 1995). The report appears to be definitive and the interpretation of the site to be relatively uncontroversial. Discussion of site reports cannot exist in a vacuum and here I wish to discuss a recent report of an archaeological survey of Falerii Veteres published in 2007 by a team assembled by Simon Keay and Martin Millett as part of their Arts and Humanities Research Board-funded exploration of the towns of the Tiber Valley (Carlucci et al 2007). For students, the first thing to notice about the report is that it is long, almost 100 pages, and heavy on the detail of what was found. However, the point of the report is that it does make known all the data found. The report is divided into sections:

The Introduction sets out the aims of the piece of work – to collect as much data from the site without excavating it – as well as a topographical survey, geophysical survey, geo-chemical analysis of soil samples and surface collection of pottery and other small finds. In addition, the report will include a report on the archives of earlier excavations.

The Archaeological and Historical Background refers to earlier discoveries and the overall chronology of the site from the earliest Bronze Age finds down to the textual evidence for the destruction of the town in 241 BC (Polyb. 1.65; Livy *Per.* 20; Zonaras 8.18).

The Archival Sources reports on the discovery of the notebook of Raniero Mengarelli's excavations at the end of the 19th century.

The Fieldwork sets out what was done on site. Magnetometry was used as the main geophysical method, because it was quick and effective in detecting topographical features. The language of the report can turn off many students. It is full of 'anomalies', 'negative features' that are located with reference to numbered plans. Resistivity was only used selectively (due to length of time to gain results) and the results seem rather inconclusive. There then follows a lengthy section on the geo-chemical survey – partly because in surveys of other sites this technique had not been used. This technique aids with the determination of the 'use of space' and 'identifies zones of activities' – alas undated. The report then moves onto field walking that was conducted with a view to gaining a sense of chronology. The research was hindered by poor conditions of visibility, because the site was mostly turned over to pasture and not ploughed. Distribution maps of types of pottery are given and particular note is made of a find in a modern field wall of architectural terracottas. The find of these sculptural and architectural terracottas produces the next section of the report, an independent *Interpretation of the Excavated Terracottas* by one member of the team, and is related to the presence of temples on the site. Comparisons are made with finds at other sites and this enhances our understanding of the temples of Apollo Soranus and Minerva at this site.

General Discussion then follows, beginning with problems of interpreting the evidence. Erosion disrupts the data-set and a long history from the Bronze Age down to the 3rd century BC makes the association between features difficult. The discussion then moves onto the sanctuary and highlights how the survey had identified the relationship of the sanctuary to a previously unknown orthogonal grid of streets. This is where the authors present the significance of the work and in some ways is the section for ancient historians to read first, prior to examining the earlier sections that detail the evidence that leads to this discussion. Most significantly, perhaps, is the point made by the team that both the temple of Apollo Soranus and the temple of Minerva were abandoned in the 3rd century BC – the latter known to be so from Ovid *Fasti* 3.843–46, but the abandonment of the former does not appear in any text that we have. Other temples, such as that of Juno Curitis, continued to be utilized (Ovid *Amores* 3.13).

There is a final *Afterword* on some initiatives for the archive of documentation of the site.

It is undeniable that this work contributes to the understanding of earlier excavations and the overall understanding of the topography of this important site, known from textual sources to have been destroyed by Rome in 241 BC. But how do ancient historians use this information? There is important data here for the relationship of the sanctuaries to the phenomenon that we call urbanism. What is also striking is the prominence in the use of texts by this archaeological team in the discussion of change at the sanctuary and the identification of a 'ritual boundary' associated with the east–west passage of the sun identified spatially with an east–west communications artery. The *General Discussion* does allow for some synthesis of what was found, but that synthesis is limited to the evidence from this site. There is no sense of how urbanism as seen from this survey might conform to that found at other sites across the Tiber Valley. This criticism is one that is often made by historians of the work by archaeologists (Hopkins 1978: 71; Lloyd 1986: 42). The problem here is not just that the synthesis is limited, but also that as Ian Hodder (1989) has observed the report itself, including the *General Discussion*, is presented as a single voice that is cautious. The caution might be caused by field training that emphasizes positivism and fears the possibility of ridicule and humiliation in the future, if another archaeologist were to excavate or re-evaluate the evidence (Dyson 1995: 43). Although this is perhaps not what we expect, it presents an opportunity for historians: we have all the data presented to us in the report, but what is not there is a full discussion of the implications of the work for a wider reading of urbanism prior to 241 BC. Others will make their own conclusions about the discoveries in the report. In so doing, inevitably perhaps, historians might over-interpret the data or use the data in ways unintended by those writing the report. However, the nature of these reports is that there is only limited discussion of the wider implications of the discoveries made – hence, we have to accept that the discussion of these implications will occur in other works of synthesis that will in turn be debated. The important thing to realize is that archaeological reports will present the data and make, in most cases, guarded deductions from the data.

The combination of evidence

As we have seen from the Falerii Veteres report, archaeologists do use textual evidence in the discussion of their findings. Texts are cited and the dating point for the destruction of Falerii Veteres derived from these texts is accepted: Livy (*Per.* 20) informs his Augustan readership that the revolt of the Faliscans was suppressed in a matter of six days and they were permitted to surrender and Polybius (1.65) stresses that Falerii Veteres was captured after a siege lasting three days. This hardly makes the settlement a threat to Rome. However, it is clear by the time of an Augustan readership that the city was known as a place whose walls had been torn down (Ovid *Amores* 1.13). The text that says the most about the settlement history is that of the 12th century AD Byzantine compiler Zonaras who adds that the population was moved from this site to Falerii Novi. This comment in Zonaras has become a key text for the understanding not just of the history of this site, but also for the construction of a general model of Roman intervention in the settlement history of Italy (Terrenato 2001 for discussion). A view echoed by members of the team set up to undertake a geophysical survey of the site of Falerii Novi (Keay et al 2000: 1–3; 84–86). Seven years on, the work of the team seems to use these same textual sources for the investigation of the destruction of Falerii Veteres. Whereas earlier in their 2000 publication, careful attention had focused on the critique of textual sources, in 2007 the emphasis on this aspect had disappeared and was replaced with an acceptance of the sources.

In the discussion of religious sites, the Augustan discussion of the capture of a Faliscan goddess is found in Ovid's *Fasti* (3.843–46), but this needs to be connected to Ovid's account of his own experience of the ruined walls found in the *Amores* (3.13) and a procession on the site to the temple of Juno Curitis. Strikingly, Ovid suggests that it was Camillus in 394 BC who destroyed the walls of the city, rather than associating their destruction with the revolt of 241 BC. Certainly, it is at this point in the history of the city that most authors refer to the impregnability of Falerii Veteres (Livy 5.26–27; Val. Max. 6.5.1; Plu. *Camillus* 10). It is only in the much later writers that we find any reference to the confiscation of territory (Eutropius 2.28) or the relocations of population (Zonaras 8.18). Hence, perhaps, Ovid and the other Augustan writers clarify what the geophysics is, accounting for a ruined city that continued to have an existence in the landscape of Roman Italy as a place of the Faliscan revolt that was so easily crushed by Rome. It is a city that was not rebuilt, that lost some of its gods to Rome, but others were maintained. Interestingly, what is searched for by archaeologists investigating Falerii Veteres is not the landscape of a destroyed town but the nature of urbanism prior to that destruction by Rome. What we can do with this archaeological evidence is to relocate it into a different textual context from that of the archaeologists' interpretations found in their report that had a focus on the city prior to its destruction by Rome. This is a natural tendency among ancient historians and is part of our dialogue with archaeologists (compare Dyson 1995). However, the textual and archaeological evidence points to a later temporal phase and the memory of earlier events that shaped the landscape of Falerii Veteres in contrast to the impulse to chart change and urban development from limited evidence (see Millett 2007b for an approach to geophysical evidence and change).

Ancient historians re-evaluate findings of archaeologists and re-appropriate their data for their own purposes – in my case, presenting an understanding of a city whose walls had been destroyed by Camillus in 394 BC within an Augustan context of seeing the landscape of Italy. The original writers of the archaeological report may not appreciate having the two sets of evidence re-combined in a new way to produce a new understanding of the site, but this is what a dialogue across disciplines leads to. To enable that dialogue, as we saw in the case of the agrarian reforms of the 4th to 2nd centuries BC, we need to re-contextualize the textual evidence so that it can address questions of long-term history or what is known as the *longue durée* with a view to understanding an embedded and re-invented cultural memory of the historical landscape that we sometimes simply identify with a period called 'Roman', which covers a chronological range from 300 to 1,200 years.

Chapter 2

Dialogues of Academic Difference
The Present Past of Roman Studies

There are very broadly two historical strands to Roman archaeology. One that was firmly rooted in the traditions of travel, found in the 18th century Grand Tour, saw in at least some, if not all, things associated with antiquity a set of aesthetic and moral values (Andrén 1998: 10). Another tradition, founded on local history, formed the basis for the documentation of the spread of Roman culture. These two strands have caused sculptural objects from the Mediterranean to be highly valued and to have an artistic and/or moral value in line with the first tradition but for similar objects found in the northern provinces to be less valued by this tradition and not associated with a similar set of values by the second tradition (Henig 2004). I do not want to delve too deeply into the past with reference to these traditions, but wish to note that most forms of archaeology involve travel, viewing, some form of assimilation or analysis and then publication. What distinguishes the two traditions is the distance travelled, further to the Mediterranean or less far in Britain. It is not possible here to create a narrative that accounts for the development of Roman archaeology in all countries or at all times. Instead, I wish to set out an English perspective that demonstrates the continuities of intellectual thought from the turn of the 20th century to the present day. As we shall see, we may think today that the discipline of archaeology, as practised in the UK, might have little in common with its past; yet, underpinning nearly every approach and concept, we find at its root an articulation that is entrenched in the age of an imperial Britain (see Hingley 2000, 2008; Freeman 2007; Stray 2010).

Archaeology in the Edwardian age

In 1893, a young man whose family had lived in Rome for the last three years, arrived in Oxford and encountered his tutor at Christchurch College. The young man was Thomas Ashby and his tutor was Francis Haverfield.

These two men were to shape the discipline of Roman archaeology and to create a set of values that continue to underpin the subject down to the present.

Today, Francis Haverfield is better known for his work on Roman Britain and in particular his work *The Romanization of Roman Britain* – yet that is only half of the picture. He was an international scholar, who travelled widely and was conscious of the need for collaboration between scholars – the impetus perhaps for the foundation of the Society for the Promotion of Roman Studies in 1910 (see Macdonald 1924 for a biography of Haverfield). Anyone going back to the actual text of Haverfield's books, whether *Ancient Town Planning* (1913) or *The Romanization of Roman Britain* (1915 for 3rd edition), will be startled by what they read. These are books from a different time, an age when Britain had an Empire, and was about to fight a war in Europe – yet this was also a time when archaeology as a discipline was developing a new international confidence. What is so fascinating is that Haverfield in the opening pages of *The Romanization of Roman Britain* seeks to set forth a praise of the Roman Empire – an action he sees as unusual compared with the works of other historians who damned the Roman Empire 'as a period of death and despotism' (see Stray 2010; and Freeman 2007). What he replaces this image with in his own work, including that on Town Planning, is a sense of the 'practical' Romans advancing civilization both qualitatively and quantitatively with the spread of Roman material culture to places beyond the Mediterranean (Haverfield 1915: 7–22). These notions of cultural change were informed by the English experience of ruling a British Empire – it needs to be noted that the English could feel superior to the autocratic Romans in a certainty of their parliamentary democracy for all male adult citizens (Hingley 2000: 111–29). Underpinning the entire thesis was a conviction that the imperial power might civilize the conquered barbarian and create a unified culture. Invasion leads to cultural change within Haverfield's conception of Romanization. This causes the recovery of Roman archaeological materials in Britain to cease to be of just local or antiquarian interest and to create a greater importance for such archaeological finds – these become part of a grand-narrative on the nature of the Roman Empire and integrates the most local or even the most meagre Roman assemblage from Britain with the historical trajectory of the entire Roman imperial project (Andrén 1998: 10). This is not a unique phenomenon associated with Britain. A Belgian professor, Franz Cumont, was creating a very similar narrative based upon archaeological sources that was explicitly defined as an historical essay (Cumont 1914). Of course, Cumont and Haverfield were not disconnected and this points to the need to see the development of Romanization as a phenomenon that did not occur in isolation in Britain, but was a European intellectual phenomenon with its roots leading back to the German historian Theodor Mommsen (Hingley 2000: 113–14). What Romanization did for the archaeology of the Roman provinces was to transform its data-set from a subject of interest at a local level into a valuable asset for the study of cultural change in response to imperialism.

What of Haverfield's student, Thomas Ashby? He was to learn his trade as a professional archaeologist at the excavations conducted by Haverfield at Caerwent (Hodges 2000 for biography of Ashby), but it was in Rome and its environs that he was to learn another art: the recording of ruins or standing remains, and his teacher was Rodolfo Lanciani. Another of Ashby's Oxford professors, Henry Pelham, was instrumental in setting up the British School at Rome in 1901 (see Hodges 2000: 46–47; Wallace-Hadrill 2001). Ashby was the first student at the school and in 1901, it was announced that a book on the Roman roads of the Campagna was to be published by him – in reality the work was published in the first volume of the *Papers of the British School at Rome* in 1902. It is a 160-page article, illustrated with 23 figures and eight maps, that was followed four years later by part II, a further 198 pages – sadly this second article did not include the black and white photographs that characterized the first part (Ashby 1902, 1903). To undertake the work, Ashby walked in the company of others out of the city along the ancient public highways. What he saw in this rural landscape was a spread of the city into the countryside in antiquity (Hodges 2000: 35–36) and all was to be noted, mapped, photographed, written up and published. It is possible today to follow Ashby's published notes, but you will find that the suburbs of modern Rome have once again spread across this area that had been countryside. There is much more to Ashby's work than simple recording though; he looks at what was an almost deserted landscape and wonders about the population density in antiquity (a subject recently discussed by Witcher 2005) while at the same time he can compare the presence of side-roads in antiquity with their absence in his own day (Ashby 1902: 135–36). Ultimately, he sees a future when the countryside around Rome will be repopulated and a new landscape would emerge. A hundred years on, we would describe what Ashby was doing as landscape archaeology or an evaluation of heritage sites. In Britain, Ashby's work was not viewed positively and at the time was seen as having no great importance (Hodges 2000: 77), whereas in Italy he was seen as a valued expert practitioner of archaeology. Perhaps the death of Haverfield in 1919 had caused a shift in the view of this type of work and a move back towards art history and text-based histories in Britain. His work, it has to be said, was highly appreciated and understood in Rome, where it enthused a new generation of scholars – some visiting the British School (for example, Ian Richmond) and others who were Italian (such as Giuseppe Lugli 1931). This is still true today; students in Italy are more likely to have heard his name than those in the UK. More will have come across his book on aqueducts (Ashby 1935) than his numerous articles on roads and settlement patterns (Hodges 2000: 116–27 for a bibliography of Ashby's works). What Ashby did was to systematize the study of topography with a view to creating a documentary record that was fully referenced to earlier studies and was carefully mapped.

British archaeology in Italy in the late 20th century

An academic death in a road accident on 14 July 1980 was obviously a sad loss, but also created some discussion of the perspective of the dead man – a 49-year-old called Martin Frederiksen (Brunt 1980; Harris 2005). This was a man remembered for two things that are relevant for this book: using both texts and archaeological data in the writing of history and taking account of both Anglophone and Italian scholarship (Harris 2005: VII). In his twenties, Frederiksen had a scholarship to make a study of new men in the Roman senate from 100 BC to the death of the emperor Trajan, but once in Rome became involved in a more archaeological venture and dropped his original project – with some deep disquiet expressed back at his college in Oxford (Wallace-Hadrill 2001: 107). With John Ward-Perkins, the Director of the British School at Rome, Frederiksen became directly involved in the recording of the landscape of South Etruria. The project explicitly extended the range of Ashby's earlier topographical studies by looking to the north of Rome with a mission to record the evidence that was being unearthed by ploughing (Ward-Perkins 1955). Roads and standing remains were identified on the ground with the aid of the aerial photographs taken by the RAF during the Second World War. Frederiksen accompanied Ward-Perkins in his work and published an Appendix to the report on the inscriptions that were recorded (on Ward-Perkins see Wilkes 1983). The project was to develop in its next phase as a two-pronged operation, with Ward-Perkins organizing the recording of roads and monuments in the vicinity of the Via Amerina and Falerii Novi; and Frederiksen working to the east focusing on the area around Città Castellana or Falerii Veteres. Their joint report on the road systems of the Ager Faliscus was published on a scale to rival the earlier work of Ashby (Frederiksen and Ward-Perkins 1957). The authors of the report had upped their game and included six-figure grid references to standing remains that they came across – so that there was a record of the remains for the future in the face of the destruction of the archaeological record, the aim of their work. However, there was much more than objective recording to this work. The authors were working towards another goal: the understanding of the historical landscape that was altered when Rome resettled the Faliscans at Falerii Novi (discussed in Chapter 1). The techniques of recording were to be used for the publication of a survey of the area within the walls of the city of Veii (Ward-Perkins 1961) and refined further by Barri Jones and others to include not just standing remains but also finds of pottery that could provide dating evidence for the sites identified (Jones 1962, 1963) and culminated in the publication of the survey around Veii (Kahane et al 1968). What these surveys revealed were landscapes of the Roman Republic that were quite distinct from the image of Roman agriculture found in Cato the Elder's treatise *On Agriculture*. This was something that Frederiksen (1970–71) highlighted in an article presented in English at a conference in Italy and published in the newly founded Italian journal – *Dialoghi di Archeologia*, a classic combination of British and Italian academic cultures that facilitated the integration of archaeological data within a historical context. The co-founder of the South Etruria survey could see in the development of data-collection techniques by others, that moved away from simply recording standing remains, a dynamic narrative of landscape change that could inform historians about the nature of the Italian landscape associated with the reforms of the Gracchi. However, in doing so, he stepped away from the narrative that began with the texts and disassociated himself from ancient historians and classicists who could not comprehend that archaeological data can provide information with regard to systems of land-tenure (a view that had circulated in Oxford for at least 60 years; see Haverfield 1911a: xviii). This shift towards an understanding of Latin texts as the thought systems of the Romans about their past (Frederiksen 1970–71: 332) – that, if depended upon without recourse to archaeological material, would 'reproduce or even magnify the distortions with which the Romans saw their past' – led Frederiksen towards a twin-track approach in which archaeology could produce, via field surveys, a landscape history. Running through the methodology is a validity of archaeology in bringing light onto questions that arose in textual sources (for example, in Potter 1979). It seems obvious for those who have read Peregrine Horden's and Nicholas Purcell's *The Corrupting Sea*, which includes a section based on this evidence from South Etruria (Horden and Purcell 2000). However, there are still accounts of the Gracchan crisis that pay little or no attention to any archaeological evidence and continue to proclaim as a truth those distortions Frederiksen identified in the texts that survive from antiquity (for example, Lintott 1994: 62–85). What is clear though is that there has been a shift in the ancient historian's relationship with archaeological material (see most recently Launaro 2011).

Back to Roman Britain

In 1910, the Society for the Promotion of Roman Studies was founded and with it came into existence the *Journal of Roman Studies*. An inaugural lecture was presented by Francis Haverfield, in which he set out a need for the study of Roman history and archaeology to 'up its game', and become more professional and research-orientated (Haverfield 1911a). In the same lecture he discussed the work of the Royal Commission of Ancient and Historic Monuments of England and also the explosion of data associated with the new discipline of Roman history, as established by Theodor Mommsen in the late 19th century – 'more difficult, more full of facts, more technical'. He saw the development of an integrated body of knowledge of the Roman Empire that could combine the archaeologist's knowledge of a single site. His example was York, with not just the historian's knowledge of Roman military history or colonial settlement but also with knowledge of other archaeological sites from Italy and the provinces of the Roman Empire. He concluded his lecture with an appeal for the universities in Britain to take much more seriously the study of Roman Britain. In so doing, he notes that one university was permitting the substitution of a course (or 'module' in modern education speak) in Latin Prose with one on Roman Britain. This was seen as an interesting development but caused the rebuke: 'It is of no use to know about Roman Britain in particular unless you also know about the Roman Empire' (Haverfield 1911a: xx). Something would seem to have changed by the end of the 20th century, when students, lecturers and professors could review a divide between the study of Roman archaeology (perhaps more specifically Roman Britain) and Roman history. Underlying this change in attitude is what Chris Stray (2010) has documented as an attempt in the middle of the 20th century to contain archaeology within the wider discipline of Roman studies and to limit the ambition of archaeology. Times change, of course, but there is a tension between archaeology and ancient history and/or classics revealed in the history of the Society for the Promotion of Roman Studies that led to the foundation of a separate journal for the study of Roman Britain – *Britannia* (Stray 2010). Those tensions, in all likelihood, persist among the Council of the Society even today.

Britannia was set up as a journal of the same magnitude as the *Journal of Roman Studies*, perhaps reflecting the importance of the study of Roman Britain at least to a large constituency within the Society for the Promotion of Roman Studies (Stray 2010). *Britannia* set out to be the place for the notice of new discoveries and a place for academic discussion and can be compared to similar European journals such as *Gallia*, first published in 1943. Contact was to be maintained with developments in the wider Roman Empire through the Society for the Promotion of Roman Studies and its *Journal of Roman Studies*. Unlike its sister journal, *Britannia* included an editorial section that reported on the state of the subject each year and can be read as a commentary on the development of Roman Archaeology in the UK (with a focus exclusively on the province of Britannia). Volume 2 contains an exhortation by the editor for the use of up-to-date excavation techniques and recording; volume 3, in the face of accusations of insularity, featured an editorial admonishing students of Roman Britain not to neglect the broader background of the Western Provinces; such matters were not the remit of the *Britannia*, and it was noted that the *Journal of Roman Studies* was the place for such articles. Volume 4 pointed up the appointment of two new lectureships in Roman archaeology in 1973: A. J. Parker to a post in Roman art and archaeology at the University of Bristol and T. W. Potter to a lectureship in Romano-British matters at the University of Lancaster, and so on.

Running through the editorials over more than 30 years to the close of the 20th century are some recurring themes relevant to our discussion here: the relationship between professional/academic archaeologists and amateurs; and the understanding of Roman Britain not in isolation but within the context of an archaeology of the Roman Empire (see the editorial of 2003 for a recent instalment). Strikingly, the contents of *Britannia* by 1989 – in the view of the journal's editor Malcolm Todd – were becoming skewed, with few contributors venturing 'discursive or problem-oriented' papers and, instead, playing it safe with 'descriptive' pieces. This was a theme taken up by the prehistorian Richard Bradley in a review in the same journal of the Britannia Monograph: *Research on Roman Britain 1960–89*. The reviewer observed a distance between work on Roman Britain and developments in theory and methodology that had been so effective in altering the nature of the study of prehistory over a similar period of time (Bradley 1990). There was an important observation: Romanists had and still have a far larger body of evidence to work with, but would seem to have resisted what many saw as the temptation of theory that was regarded as the reserve of archaeologists studying prehistory (confirmed by the editorial of *Britannia* in 1993). It has to be said that relatively few publications in *Britannia* move from the 'descriptive' through to the 'problem-oriented' and onto the 'theoretical' mode of communication – perhaps because, as the editor observed in 2005, *Britannia* could only publish the papers it received and authors of papers on Roman Britain perceived *Britannia* to be a journal of a certain type – the subtext was that the journal only received papers that were descriptive rather than theoretical.

The editorials of *Britannia* towards the end of the 20th century give the impression that a secure world was under siege. A number of developments might have justified this. In 1988, a new journal appeared with the stated purpose of concerning itself with 'Italy and all parts of the Roman world from about 700 BC to about 700 AD' (excluding the prehistoric period, but including the 'Etruscan period'). This journal was called the *Journal of Roman Archaeology* – perhaps in recognition of the fact that the *Journal of Roman Studies* published few articles on Roman archaeology. Embracing the fact of its existence and a greater awareness of the wider context of Roman archaeology, in 1995 the Society for the Promotion of Roman Studies established a Roman Archaeology Conference to be held biannually, with what was described in the editorials of *Britannia* as a 'menu of themes' within which there was a place for Roman Britain – although that was not the total focus of the conference. A year on from this first conference (1996), the editor was commenting on a 'malaise' in archaeology of Britain in the Roman period that was seeing a decline in the number of post-graduate researchers and in 1999, the editor could conceive of a time when the study of Roman Britain was pushed to the margins with an increased concentration of research skill shifting from the study of Roman Britain towards the study of the Roman Mediterranean or other areas of archaeology.

The concerns expressed prompted the Society for the Promotion of Roman Studies to conduct a survey in 2000 that revealed a decline in the teaching of courses in Roman Britain to undergraduates, and an overall decline in the number of lecturers and professors in Roman archaeology. The results of the survey were discussed at a conference in 2002 entitled 'Whither Roman Archaeology?' There was much discussion of what had happened, but a realization that the rather insular world of Roman Britain could not continue and there was what might be seen as a blip in which the concentrations of staff in Roman archaeology were shifting (see summaries by Gardner 2003 and James 2003). What we see here is a shift in the balance between the study of Roman Britain and the study of the wider archaeology of the Roman Empire. In 1970, the establishment of *Britannia* marked the apogee of the study of the province as a firm focus for all students and staff in UK universities. However, 15 years on (c. 1985), there was a marked and sustained increase in joint degree programmes in ancient history and archaeology that naturally led to a shift in focus towards a wider constituency that focused on the Mediterranean. Roman Britain, the editor of *Britannia* was to note in 2003, was not an area that postgraduate students found attractive.

The rise of theory

As a response to the critique of Roman archaeology in the late 1980s as lacking a theoretical basis and disengaged from the developments of the subject, in particular in prehistory (see Reece 1989; Scott 1989 reviewing Todd 1989), Eleanor Scott held a conference at the University of Newcastle in 1990 that had a very specific agenda: to discuss the role of theory and the development of the use of theory in Roman archaeology (Scott 1993, 2006). The response was followed by a second and a third Theoretical Roman Archaeology Conference (TRAC) that established an annual series that is now beyond its 21st birthday. The early years of the conference attracted what has become referred to as the 'TRAC generation', who were undertaking or had recently completed PhD theses in the 1990s. As undergraduates, these scholars had taken courses or modules on archaeological theory and closely followed developments at the Theoretical Archaeology Group's (TAG) meetings, within which a new agenda was being formulated for prehistory. TRAC was the venue for the explicit discussion and introduction into the discipline of a number of key authors whose thinking underpins so much of archaeological interpretation in the Roman period, notably that of Michel Foucault, Anthony Giddens and Pierre Bourdieu, as well as the application of their thought by prehistory, for example by John Barrett, Richard Bradley, Ian Hodder, Michael Shanks and Chris Tilley. Importantly, papers from these meetings were published and readers can examine these to see what the preoccupations were at the close of the 20th century and into the first decade of the 21st century (see also Laurence 1999a, 2006; Gardner 2006; and Scott 2006 for overviews). In 1993, the US archaeologist, Stephen Dyson, saw the impact of the trend in the UK, of which TRAC was part of: in short, the formation of a postmodern discipline (Dyson 1993).

For some Roman archaeologists, the significance of the 'T' for *Theory* in TRAC was not fully understood or was played down. The 1997 editorial in *Britannia* noted the seventh meeting of TRAC would be held alongside the second meeting of the Roman Archaeology Conference (RAC). The comment is worth quoting: 'Under the auspices of TRAC, younger contributors can offer the fruits of fresh research, as well as reviews of recent work and new approaches in individual provinces and regions of the Empire, including the work of Roman Britain.' Seven years on from its inception, TRAC was still associated with the 'younger' scholar with 'new approaches' – the word 'theory' was still controversial. So what had happened to the original 'TRAC generation', now seven years older? They had moved on to organizing panels of speakers in the biannual Roman Archaeology, with the first meeting in 1995. The panels at RAC (and for that matter at TRAC) had, and still have, rather less explicit reference to theory but there is an underlying structure that is based in theory and the development of an explicit theoretical basis that was discussed and developed in TRAC during the 1990s. In short, 'TRAC won' (*pers. comm.* Martin Millett) and the establishment of RAC in 1995 demonstrated the strength of TRAC. The young scholars of the early 1990s, some 20 years on, have now moved on to mid-career positions in academia and in museums. This progression has positioned theory at the core of the discipline and caused Roman archaeology today to be very different from 20 years ago, characterized by Richard Reece as like 'stamp collecting' and with a disciplinary 'death-wish' (Reece 1989).

Roman archaeology in the 21st century

There is no textbook that tells you what Roman archaeology is, and there is no book that covers the archaeology of the Roman Empire – the nearest equivalent being Kevin Greene's *The Archaeology of the Roman Economy* (Greene 1986). This would seem quite strange, if not bizarre – Roman archaeology, if it is an academic discipline (or sub-discipline), does not have one of the most basic tools that we associate with other university-level disciplines. Yet this reflects the nature of the discipline: it is fragmented into a set of specialist areas – something that Greg Woolf identified in 2003 (Woolf 2003). These divisions are most apparent geographically. Many studies and most syntheses tend to focus on a single province or number of provinces of a similar nomenclature: Germany, Gaul, Britain, Spain or a geographical region composed of provinces: the Balkans, or North Africa, or simply that space known as Italy – divisions that made sense in the Edwardian age but bear little utility for the study of archaeological phenomena in the 21st century and the cultural context of globalization. Scholars have specialized in their region of the Roman Empire and seldom step out of this comfort zone to synthesize material from other provinces, even though they might seek parallels for material objects in other provinces. Identifying a pattern within the archaeological record in one of these areas of specialism needs to be explained within a wider perspective that also accounts for the phenomenon in other areas of the Roman Empire.

However, the fragmentation does not end there. As Woolf (2003: 420–21) points out, even theory is separated through the creation of TRAC, a necessity as we have seen in 1990, but perhaps a problem some 20 years later. Mention should also be made of institutional division between Roman archaeologists located in wider disciplinary divisions associated with classics and archaeology/anthropology. Such disciplinary boundaries create differences and allow for statements, such as 'as an archaeologist, I have a problem with that approach' or 'as an historian I don't think that works with the evidence we have', and a sense of academic identity based on the articulation of difference and characterization of people within the disciplines as potential friends and enemies. For students, undergraduate or graduate, an awareness of these divisions needs to be borne in mind.

Often, I was located in classics departments over the course of my career where colleagues have regarded the archaeology department and archaeology as 'the other' and at times 'the enemy' (it also works in reverse formation from the perspective of those within archaeology departments). These are tensions felt at the highest level as well as by undergraduates (Stray 2010). This also explains in part the need for this volume that is about Roman archaeology but is aimed at a readership composed of ancient historians. It has to be said that, now more than ever before, we are beginning to see the integration of these two subjects that logically meet via an interest in the explanation of very similar phenomena in the past.

These divisions exist and, I would suggest, will continue to exist in the future, because they are part of the disciplinary history and structure of Roman archaeology. I do not think a sudden paradigm shift will resolve these issues of academic differentiation and, if Woolf (2003) is right, they are in fact likely to become more apparent in the face of the increase in information availability and communication in the future. The problem is in part that the subject is big and complicated (Woolf 2003: 426) and can only be addressed through direct collaboration to produce a fully engaged synthesis of a key subject, something that I have engaged with on the subject of the city (see Laurence et al 2011). At the student end of things, the problem of the fragmentation of the subject of Roman archaeology might be most effectively addressed through the examination of phenomena with reference to case studies that come from separate areas of the Roman Empire, rather than seeking a supervisor for a dissertation or a thesis who is an expert on x in y province or region (for other examples of divisions to be overcome see Woolf 2003: 425–26). As a consequence, in this book readers will find examples and case studies drawn from both the Mediterranean, mostly Italy, and from Britain. They are interspersed to demonstrate that we ought to seek a means to understand what it was to inhabit the Roman Empire, whether in the Mediterranean or in the province of Britain. The inter-regional approach to Roman culture has its resonances also in Roman archaeology (Millett 2007b: 325–26).

Chapter 3

From Topography to Archaeology
Revealing the Roman Forum

There is a question voiced by some ancient historians about archaeology that is often articulated as a wonder whether all the effort in terms of human and financial resources involved in archaeological projects is really worth the results produced. To answer this question, I wish to set out to evaluate the impact of archaeological projects on our understanding of the most central space of Roman cities – the forum. The chapter begins with an examination of the use of texts for the study of topography and then moves onto an examination of archaeological investigations in the Forum Romanum in Rome, before examining the survey and excavation of fora elsewhere. What I wish to demonstrate is that the archaeologist's attention to detail reveals and adds to our understanding of these central areas of the Roman city as revealed in texts and through the study of the standing remains of buildings. In so doing, I will present at the end of the chapter a new understanding of the forum based on this evidence.

What is the study of ancient topography? How does it work?

Topography is about the search for certainty. It seeks to match the excavated remains of the city of Rome or parts of the Roman Empire with our knowledge of such places derived from ancient literature. This produces names for excavated monuments, but only does so if they are mentioned in ancient literature. Not surprisingly, it is in the study of the city of Rome that we see the full application of topographical methodologies. These named monuments can be found in the topographical dictionaries. The first was published by Samuel Platner and Thomas Ashby in 1929 and has been updated with a newer version by Lawrence Richardson (1992) in English and a six-volume and multi-language edition edited by Margaretta Steinby (1993–2000) with a similar project under completion for the suburbs of Rome (La Regina 2001–6). Only monuments or excavated remains for which we know the names can be included within this framework; anonymous items do not merit inclusion. At the very heart of topography is the intersection of textual evidence and material culture, but it needs to be recognized that it is the texts that are in the driving seat, as can be seen from the entries in the recent volume entitled *Mapping Augustan Rome* (Haselberger et al 2002), which is a map of textual knowledge.

The ancient texts that are the bread and butter of the historian's diet include numerous names of places within the city of Rome, in Italy and in the provinces of the Roman Empire. These texts provide the naming of the parts of the Roman Empire and the city of Rome that are the framework for the study of archaeological finds. Yet, we need to recognize that the textual evidence does not simply, like a guidebook, inform us of the names of all parts of the city. Indeed, the evidence that can be quarried from these texts produces testimony about a subject. For example, Donald Dudley (1967: 81–83) in a sourcebook for the city of Rome presents the information on the Golden Milestone or *Miliarium Aureum*. He cites the setting up of the milestone by Augustus that appears in Dio Cassius (54.8) and then presents the accounts of Otho's accession to the imperial throne in 69 AD given by Plutarch (*Galba* 24) and by Tacitus (*Hist.* 1.27). It is these last two texts that provide us with an account of the relative topography of the Golden Milestone. Both Plutarch and Tacitus state that Otho left the Domus Tiberiana on the Palatine Hill and went down to the Forum and was hailed *Imperator* by 23 soldiers at the Golden Milestone, with Plutarch adding that he went down through the Velabrum and that the milestone was next to the Temple of Saturn. The standing remains excavated in the 1950s near the temple of Saturn would appear to be the remains of the Golden Milestone – see Figure 3.1, position B (Kähler 1964: 58–59). However, visitors to the Forum today are presented with a location between the imperial *rostra* and the senate house or Curia that is firmly labelled as the Golden Milestone on the basis of Pliny's *Natural History* (3.66) which says that the location was *in capite Romani fori* – at the head of the Forum and coincided where the *Umbilicus* or centre of the city was located – see Figure 3.1, position A. The problem here is that the surviving texts do not give one answer but two, and the material evidence that is available between the temple of Saturn and the Curia can support either of them without actually discounting either location as more or less likely. Faced with this situation, Filippo Coarelli (the true master of the topographer's art) posited a solution that there were two centres of Rome – one the centre of the city, the Umbilicus, on one side of the imperial *rostra* and on the other side the centre of the Empire, the Golden Milestone (Coarelli 2007: 64). This does not resolve the textual issue of disagreement, but instead uses the disagreement to

Figure 3.1 Rome: Forum Romanum – standing remains open to interpretation: where is the Golden Milestone?

create a new form of knowledge and the idea of two centres for Rome. Archaeology has played only a minor role: it is now time to turn to how archaeology can shift the nature of our understanding of topography.

This chapter will first examine an example of the workings of topography in the city of Rome and then examine how archaeological excavation can contribute to the development of this knowledge base with reference to the Forum Romanum, prior to moving onto a similar discussion of topography outside Rome. The key question to be asked is how does archaeology contribute to our understanding of the subject matter, apart from giving an evocative sense of place via the viewing of ruins from the reading of texts that mention topographical locations?

The stratigraphy of the Forum Romanum

Over the course of the 19th century, Rome's Forum was excavated. It began in the first half of the century with the removal of the medieval and modern buildings that had grown up around the ancient structures of the Arch of Septimius Severus and the temples of Castor and Pollux, Concordia, Saturn, and Vespasian and Titus. This work created isolated monuments that were to be connected up by excavations down to a consolidated level associated with the travertine pavement that can be

Figure 3.2 Rome: Forum Romanum – the Travertine paving

seen today (Figure 3.2). The monuments exposed were identified via the associated inscriptions and the topographical method set out above. The final phase of this work that began at the turn of the century did not radically alter the known topography of the forum. With some relief, Rodolfo Lanciani (1988) reported in March 1900 that these excavations 'have revealed nothing concerning the general topography of the famous district'. For excavation to have done so would have caused a shift away from the emphasis on a text-based explanation of monuments within the forum.

However, the excavators were also concerned with the development of a clearer understanding of the chronology of the forum. Sequences of earlier levels were discovered in a well in front of the Republican *comitium* (senate house) and the stratigraphic excavations conducted in the area of the *comitium* were published (Boni 1901, see Burton-Brown 1905: 87–92 or Baddeley 1904: 7–24 for a summary in English; for a reassessment see Ammerman 1996: 124–26). However other soundings undertaken by Giacomo Boni were to remain unpublished. The excavations that were published and presented as sections of up to 24 layers from natural sub-soil to the travertine pavement (Boni 1901) provide us with information of what lies below the level we see today. Everything beneath the travertine paving was regarded as Republican in date and created a five-metre deep sequence that could be matched with evidence from texts; for example, the fifth layer was full of ashes and bones and was explained with reference to a passage from Plutarch's *Life of Tiberius Gracchus* (15) referring to the sacredness of tribunes (Boni 1901: 319). The connection between the archaeological layer and this discussion is at best tangential. However, what was established was a relative sequence of layers that included levels of beaten earth, compacted gravel and burnt levels. Forty years later, the Swedish archaeologist, Einar Gjerstad, excavated a five-metre long section in the *comitium* that revealed eight pavement levels (Figure 3.4), combined with the sections established earlier – a relative chronology of development was established that via the pottery sequences could be dated to create an absolute chronology (Gjerstad 1941: 123–58). The first paving was dated to the 6th century, with the second aligned to a period prior to the sack of Rome by the Gauls in 390 BC, and the third dating from after 390 BC down to about 200 BC. Things get tricky after this. Dating for the fourth pavement is provided with a *terminus ante quem* of Sulla, but its origins are sought in the literary record referring to fires and paving (Liv. 26.27.2–4, 27.11.16, Plin. *NH* 19.1 (96). 24) ranging from 210 to 174 BC. After Sulla, the fire of 52 BC is referred to – however, in all this there is a fundamental difficulty: we do not know if these events known from texts affected the paving of the forum. What these excavations do is to bring into the discussion of topography additional information, which needs to be harmonized with existing knowledge (Van Deman 1922) and based on texts and standing remains of ancient structures.

The problem of the unpublished material was addressed, in part, by an excavation undertaken by Gjerstad after the Second World War to the southwest of the statue base associated with the *Equus Domitiani* (Figure 3.3). An area, previously investigated by Boni, 5.9 by 3.4 metres was excavated from the travertine pavement down to natural or virgin soil. Twenty-three distinct layers were identified (Figure 3.4 from *Antiquity* article). This allowed Gjerstad to map onto the 23 levels the chronology of Rome from its foundation in the 8th century BC. The results were first published in Italian (Gjerstad 1952a) with a summary in English (Gjerstad 1952b) and were controversial: the earliest paving of the forum took place in 450 BC; a burnt level was associated with the Gallic sack of Rome (387/6 BC) and a new forum pavement; the third forum pavement was found to be dated to 335 BC; above this lay a fourth forum pavement dated by pottery to c. 200 BC; the fifth pavement was that of Sulla; the sixth was dated to the late 50s BC; and finally there was the travertine pavement of the Augustan period. Below the first pavement lay a series of what Gjerstad termed 'pre-urban' or hut levels and tombs that he associated with the expansion of the city from the hills down into the valley of the forum under the kings.

Figure 3.3 Rome: Forum Romanum – excavations through the Forum paving

The sequence established by Gjerstad was broadly accepted until the issues were re-investigated by Albert Ammerman (1990). He disputed the existence of the earliest sequence that considered a series of huts being replaced by the paved forum. Rather than seeing the full chronological sequence for the occupation of Rome from the time of Romulus in the sections excavated by Boni and Gjerstad, he, instead, proposed that the sequence needed to be assessed with reference to the hydrology of the area. A series of cores were taken across the forum to produce a profile of the natural soils on which the forum is constructed (Ammerman 1990: 634). This resulted in the observation that the original ground level was as little as seven metres above sea level that formed a natural basin into which flowed three sources of water. Given that the Tiber annually rises to a level higher than ten to 13 metres above sea level, the original area on which the forum was built was subject to annual flooding or formed a seasonal lake. This observation led to a re-interpretation of the lower levels of the sequence of layers set out by Gjerstad (1952a, 1952b). The region was simply not suitable for habitation and the lower levels of the stratigraphic sequence (levels 23–28) represent attempts at land recla-mation onto which was constructed the pavement of the forum. To do this the ground surface was raised by two metres, requiring the deposition of 10,000m^3 of material (Ammerman 1990: 642–43). The material utilized for this purpose also contained domestic rubbish that can be dated to between 650 and 575 BC (Ammerman 1990: 643). Ammerman goes on

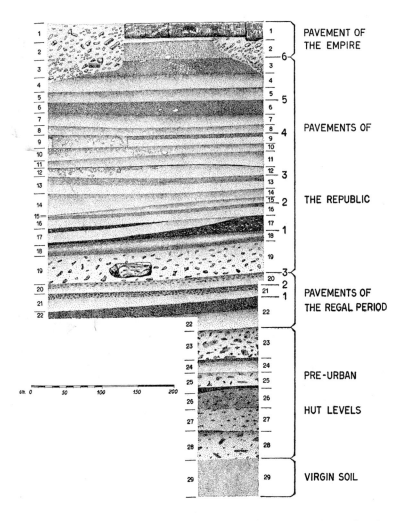

Figure 3.4 Rome: Forum Romanum – excavated section relating phases of paving to chronology of the Forum by Gjerstad (by permission of the journal *Antiquity*)

to show that there is a massive significance to this simple observation: towards the end of the 7th and in the beginning of the 6th centuries BC, the population devoted considerable resources to the transformation of their landscape that had previously been associated with the burial of the dead (Vaglieri 1903 for evidence). The effort involved and the change in the value system associated with this archaeologically-attested event produced the first forum in Rome. In a subsequent article, Ammerman (1996) demonstrated that the original *comitium* lay above the flooded zone that later became the forum and importantly that the *comitium's* pavement was cut out of the outcrop of bedrock explaining in part why no earlier pottery to the late 7th century BC has been found. These investigations from the early 1990s cause a complete reappraisal of the historical narrative of the early occupation of Rome that can be found in volume seven of the second edition of the *Cambridge Ancient History* published in 1989 (for example, Momigliano 1989: 66–68). However, the implications of this research for the Forum as an area difficult to inhabit may not appear in key textbooks on early Rome that are sympathetic to archaeological material, even if recognized in endnotes (for example, Cornell 1995: 55, 73, 94 with note 36). The story of Rome begins differently if we start with the natural topography that is associated with the place that became the *comitium*, which overlooked an area subject to seasonal flooding or lake that became the Forum Romanum. This is the beginning of the story, but the major change is the action of large-scale landscape transformation that is identified archaeologically under the Etruscan Kings.

Subsequent investigations by Ammerman and Filippi (2004) confirmed that the valley between the Capitoline and Palatine hills from the Tiber across to the later Forum of Augustus was composed of a region that was wet in winter and dried out in summer, which lay less than nine metres above sea level (Ammerman and Filippi 2004: 12). The coring that was involved (15 metres in depth) in discovering the shape of this valley also located a major clay source, and established via petrographic analysis that this was the clay source for the first tiles used in Archaic Rome from the 7th century onwards (Ammerman et al 2008). There is a further implication of this: in the Velabrum of the late 7th century BC (i.e. between the Forum Romanum and the Tiber) lay not a swampy wasteland, but an industrial zone. It was at this location that a new building technology developed the production of tiles that roofed the new buildings of the city of Rome (Ammerman et al 2008: 26–27). This was the area that became the *Vicus Tuscus* – an area associated with production and commerce which was rather different from the marshes associated with the region in later Latin texts that have shaped our perspective of the Velabrum in Archaic Rome (compare Coarelli 1983: 263 figure 75; Coarelli 1988: 11; see Ammerman 2006).

The pavement of the Forum Romanum

Anyone who has taken part in an excavation in the past 50 years will have experience of the recording of what was excavated via photography and drawing of the surfaces in plan (Figure 3.2). It comes as something of a surprise that the pavement of the Forum Romanum remained unrecorded in these formats in any systematic way until the 1980s. The project set up in the late 1970s set out to make amends for this omission, regarding the paving of the forum as a series of archaeological contexts. Some were recent, such as the relaying of the paving in front of the *rostra*. Others dated back to the medieval period and were associated with a lime kiln in which blocks of marble, travertine and limestone were reduced to a powder. There was a concern to identify which blocks of paving were original and thus in context, and which were restorations or re-use. A key element in determining whether a block was original or not was to identify the presence of a metal clamp linking the block to a neighbouring block – a technique found in other excavated Roman forum pavements. As a consequence, we are able to examine the central paved area of the forum as a defined architectural space that may date back to the 2nd century BC (Giuliani and Verduchi 1987 for final publication of the project).

The pavement of the forum, known as the '*area*' or in Italian '*l'area*' is a defined space extending from the Augustan Rostra for a distance of 187 metres. It is defined on its longer sides by roads and is delineated by *crepidines* between the roads paved with grey basalts and the white limestone/ travertine paving of the *area* (Figure 3.3). To enter the *area* involved a step up or a step down from the adjoining roads and a sense of change in position from outside to within the *area*. This delineation of space defines the *area* as a monument. Simply the fact that it is not a building should not remove the *area* from consideration as a monument in a similar way and of similar importance as, for example, the Basilica Julia. However, unlike the Basilica Julia, the *area*'s history can only be revealed archaeologically.

The *area* is not a level surface. Those standing nearest to the Augustan Rostra were more than a metre to two metres higher than those at the far end of the *area* (rising from 12.16 to 14.2 metres above sea level). Intriguingly, this observation was made with another that the *rostra* (including the so-called *Rostra Vandalica*) in the forum were contemporary with the paving (Giuliani and Verduchi 1987: 46). This observation in association with the intersection of the *rostra* and pavement with the arch of Septimius Severus provides a date for the final pavement post-203 AD (Giuliani and Verduchi 1987: 46–50). This provides us with a new dating point for the pavement for which there is no textual attestation and that challenges the established view that the pavement was Augustan in date – confirmed by the pavement inscription with the name Lucius Naevius Surdinus, who was praetor in 9 BC (*CIL* VI. 148). Instead, we now have two clear phases. The Augustan date is confirmed by the pottery fill of the passages beneath this phase of the paving (Giuliani and Verduchi 1987: 54–59) that are seen to be associated with an earlier phase. It is suggested by the investigators to date to the Sullan era and the text of Festus (416L) that refers to Aurelius Cotta (Giuliani and Verduchi 1987: 53–61) repairing the previous century's paving (Plin *NH* 19.24), and which was associated with gladiatorial games in the forum (see Welch 2007 for discussion). The original observation that the *area* was not a level surface reveals the need to see the remains that we have today as at least three different phases. At the same time, it reveals a continuity for the *area* as a monumental space that was maintained across four centuries from Cato through to the Severans (if we accepted the attestation of Pliny *NH* 19.24 that Cato paved the forum for the first time). The more regular quadrilateral forms of the paving in the Forum Romanum associated with the Augustan and Sullan phases have much in common with those found elsewhere at Terracina and Pompeii. However, the vast majority of the paving belongs, not surprisingly, to the final phase of the *area* that was associated with repairs undertaken from the time of Septimius Severus (Giuliani and Verduchi 1987: 61–66).

The authors of this project set themselves in opposition to the standard topographical methods that gave preference to the textual identification of monuments and the definition of archaeologically determined events with reference to a series of texts (Giuliani and Verduchi 1987: 18, 23). This sets the work apart from that of Coarelli's extensive discussion of the Forum Romanum from a much more philological perspective, which relies so heavily on the interpretation of the representation of the Forum in texts. Certainly, the detailed mapping and study of the intersection of the paving of the *area* creates a new body of knowledge that can be integrated with the textual evidence for the republican phases. However, the intention is to engage with the historians' texts and in places to use them. What is perhaps different is that the study begins with the archaeology and seeks to explain that in its own terms, rather than seeing the archaeology as an extra dimension for the explanation of the representation of the forum in the texts of classical authors (compare Coarelli 1983: 211–33 for reassertion of these).

Forum pavements elsewhere

Relatively few pavements from Roman forums survive from other cities across the Roman Empire. Where they do survive, they show a strong convergence with the paving of the Forum Romanum at Rome. At Segobriga in Spain, the excavation of the pavement of the Forum in 2000 and 2001 revealed not just the paving of the forum, but also the way the space of the pavement was subdivided (Figure 3.5). What was discovered was a space for a large statue base (c. 7m by 7m) in the paving in front of

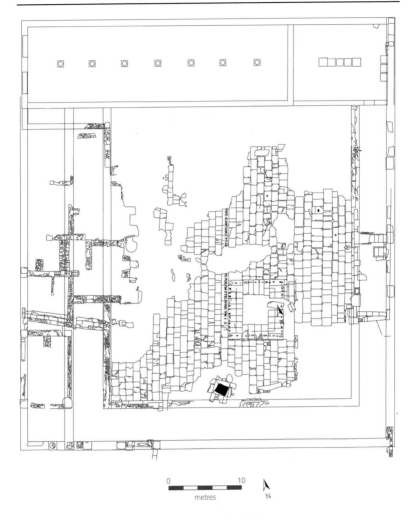

Figure 3.5 Segobriga: pavement with paving inscription

which was an inscription in bronze letters set into the paving reading: [Proc?]ulus Spantamicus La[c?]us forum sternendum d(e) s(ua) p(ecunia) or 'Proculus Spatamicus Lacus paved the forum from his own money' (Abascal et al 2001, 2002). A person reading the inscription from left to right would begin reading the letters and walk across the paving and would end up in front of the statue base, where the letters terminated. The person would look up and see the statue; if they were to turn to the left they could look back along the line of the letters that was aligned with the second column at the entrance of the basilica. This, looking at the plan of the forum, was not accidental. The inscription and position of the statue base were firmly aligned with reference to the basilica. Indeed, it replicates the division of space within the basilica, in which the eastern end of the basilica was set apart for the setting up of statues, some of which have been recovered dressed in togas. There is also a fragmentary inscription. These remains can be interpreted in combination with a head of Agrippina and an inscription to Tiberius from the site as a place in which the town honoured members of the imperial family, probably after their deaths (Abascal et al 2001, 2002). The statue in the forum was also orientated with reference to both the temple and the road running along the edge of the forum in front of the temple. The statue in the middle of the forum was at the centre of view within the *area* that had been created as a level paved space through the construction of galleries beneath the basilica. The excavators date the construction of the forum in this case to the Augustan period, when Segobriga became a *municipium*, or in the period shortly after that emperor's death. The design and use of space in the forum at Segobriga as set out based on these excavations demonstrates how archaeology reveals the orientation and use of what may at first sight appear to be an empty space.

However, in no way should we make a general statement from this example to all forums found in the Roman Empire. Looking at the paving and position of statue bases within the *area* of another forum shows how variable the approach taken to the use of space in the *area* was. In Italy, visitors to Terracina can see in the main Piazza of the old city the Via Appia and adjacent to it the limestone paving of the Augustan forum (Figure 3.6). The pavement has not been excavated but instead, like that of the Forum Romanum in Rome, subject to a careful survey by Maria Rosaria Coppola (1984). This, like the forum at Segobriga, was a level space created through the use of vaults to build out from the existing hillside to create a rectangular space that is dominated today by the Cathedral – originally a Roman temple. A series of short columns on the edge of the *area* separated the forum from the Via Appia and its traffic, adjacent to which were a number of small statue bases (Figure 3.7). More significantly, bisecting the forum was a bronze inscription set into the paving: A. Aemilius A.F. Stravi(t) or 'Aulus Aemilus son of Aulus paved [the forum]' (*CIL* 10.6306). The inscription is in front of a large statue base (c.6m by 6m). The inscription cuts the *area* in half creating a division of the rectangular space into two zones, one between the temple and the statue and one behind the statue base. Unlike at Segobriga, the letters of the pavement inscription do not end at the statue base, instead the statue base is orientated to be precisely in the centre of the *area* and at the point

Figure 3.6 Terracina: the Forum is paved in white limestone cut into rectangles, whereas the Via Appia is paved in grey basalt polygonal blocks

which if a person was reading the letters they would have read Aulus Aemilius' name (Figure 3.7). There were other additions orientated with reference to the inscription: a fountain and another statue base were set up to the east of the word 'stravit' (he paved). In many ways, the orientation here is precisely the opposite that we find at Segobriga. Yet there are things in common: there are two points of orientation in both cases; at Terracina the inscription is at a right angle to the Via Appia and faces the temple, whereas at Segobriga the inscription is at a right angle to the basilica and is orientated towards the road and temple. These two examples of pavement inscriptions from forums are not unique. We know of them from Pompeii, Atena in Lucania, Velleia, Saepinum and Juvanum in Italy and at Madauros and Ippona in North Africa (Romanelli 1965; see Coppola 1984: 359 for bibliography; also Jouffroy 1986 *passim*). Hence, we should anticipate that these inscriptions would have been marking or creating the major division of space so often seen in plans of 'the forum' as an empty undivided space surrounded by public monuments. The positioning of the pavement inscriptions as we have seen varies, but for the most part is located at a central point on the longer axis of the forum (Figure 3.8), dividing the rectangular space into two – as is found in the well-preserved example at Velleia, where the bronze letters show that the magistrate, a *duumvir*, Lucius Lucilius paved the forum at his own expense (Aurigemma 1940: 8–11, *CIL* XI.1184). Perhaps, more

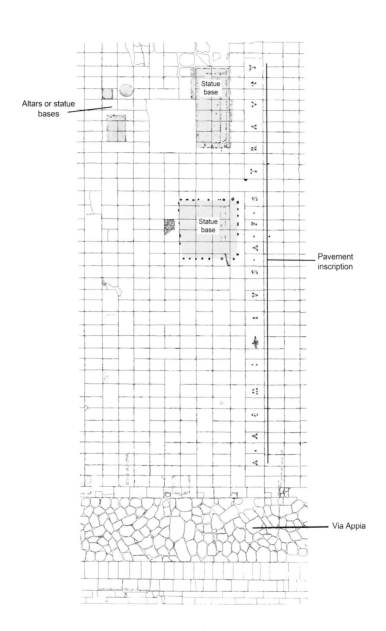

Figure 3.7 Terracina: The Forum showing the placement of pavement inscription in relation to statue bases

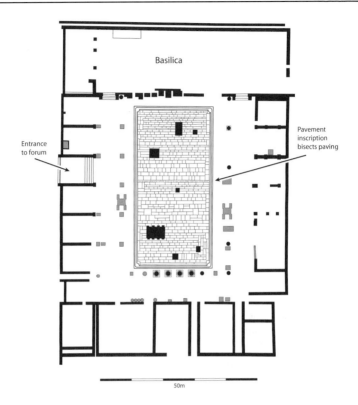

Figure 3.8 Velleia: the Forum with the pavement inscription dividing the central piazza area into two sections

importantly, the paving of the forum as a space with white stone was not just a feature of 2nd century BC Rome; it can also be identified in the paving of the forum at Pompeii in the 2nd century BC (Sogliano 1925: 253–57; for lettering see van Buren 1918: 70–71; 1925: 104–5) and we should note that the forum at Velleia was laid out prior to the Roman conquest of that region. In both the cases of Velleia and Pompeii, the final format of the paving inscription divided the rectangular paved space into two halves or two squares.

These examples either excavated or surveyed by archaeologists provide historians with a greater range of information, when compared to what we find in texts. Inscriptions refer to the paving of *fora* (*CIL* 5.7427, 10.5416, *ILAfr* 558), but it is those inscriptions, identified as inscribed onto the actual pavements of a forum that, though rare, provide the clearest evidence for the marking of space by the person who paid even 200,000 sesterces to provide a paved space at the centre of their city (*ILAlg.* 1.2120) or 300,000 to include a temple (*AE* 1926: 143). Due to the fact that often only a letter or a few letters are inscribed on each stone of the pavement, these pavement inscriptions are often lost due to the individual stones being reused in quite different locations. For example, the pavement inscription published in the 1950s from the forum in Saepinum in Italy that was reused in the *proscaenum* of the theatre (*AE* 1959: 276; Cianfarani 1959: 375–76; Jouffroy 1986: 72) and was reconstructed from six pieces of stone each containing at the most three letters. Equally, these pavements can be built over and even if excavated the letters can be hard to read. For example, the forum at Assisi was excavated in the 19th century and a museum was constructed over a section of the forum pavement. Those excavations neglected to publish the pavement inscription that was also excavated. It was only in the 1970s, when Gianfranco Binazzi was in this museum to study other inscriptions, that he happened to notice in the floor of the museum (the pavement of the forum) a series of letters that were in a line between the tribunal and the monument of the Dioscuri. He published the inscription and today visitors to the Museum of the Forum can view the letters that had been excavated in the 19th century but had never been published and had become obscured (*AE* 1981: 317; Binazzi 1981). Today, visitors to Assisi can view the 13 blocks of this 7.4-metre long inscription. Stray finds of bronze letters also occur in other paved areas; for example at Terracina a second forum was identified on the basis of the find of some bronze letters (*NSc* 1886: 277; De La Blanchère 1887; *Eph Epig.* 8.635). One wonders how many such inscriptions there might have been, and should we see the pavement inscription as a fundamental aspect of the spatial design of the Roman forum?

What is a Roman forum in light of this archaeological research?

The history of the Roman Forum is bound up with the development of urbanism on the site of the city of Rome. This involved the reclamation of land and the development of a central space that was overlain with gravel in the space that was to become the Forum Romanum. It should be seen as part of a series of monumental changes that were also associated with the development of tile-making, using clays from the nearby Velabrum. The gravel surface of the forum was paved at some point, certainly by the end of the 2nd century. This development of a central paved space was not unique to Rome and it can also be found at Pompeii, prior to the establishment of a Roman colony there under Sulla in the 1st century BC.

For the period from the point at which the forum becomes a paved space, we need to shift our attention from seeing just an architectural space – defined by Vitruvius in the case of Italian towns as a rectilinear space for the reason that the Italians had a tradition of watching gladiatorial contests in the forum (Vitr.5.1). It is also a place, for Vitruvius, to be associated with *tabernae* (usually translated as shops). The dimensions of the short to the long sides of the forum, according to Vitruvius, should have been 2:3 with the forum itself varying in actual size according to the number of people using the space. What Vitruvius sets out to define is a space surrounded by colonnades, to which is joined a basilica. As we have seen in this chapter, this rectilinear space was broken up not just by statue bases built over the pavement of the forum but also by an inscription cutting across the space to create a division to the space.

This is an important observation, because many fora are found that are divided into two. For example, the forum at Brescia is traversed by a major road that separates a section associated with the major temple from another section associated with shops and the basilica (Figure 3.9). What the pavement inscription at Pompeii does is to create a similar division between an area in front of the temple and another associated with basilica, government buildings and shops – a similar form of organization can be found at Terracina. Even within the forum at Velleia with no temple within it, we find the inscription aligned so that not only does it bisect the forum, but it is also aligned so that the attention of a person entering the forum is drawn to the lettering that informs them of who paved the space. Contrary to the many plans of a forum from numerous cities reproduced in books on Roman architecture or the Roman city, the forum was not an empty space. It was a written space within which the writing of the name of the person responsible for paying for the paving was prominent and the letters of this person's name became a linear feature. The letters of that person's name became a reference point for the construction of statue bases that could cause a line of letters in the pavement to take on a three-dimensional form – containing movement within the area in front of the pavement inscription and the statue bases behind it. This could cause the main area of activity in a forum to be contained not in the rectilinear space defined by Vitruvius but in a square space that he associated with Greek *agora*.

The use of archaeological material to test the applicability of textual ideas in this manner is not always popular with historians. The certainties that were falsely associated with a text and elucidated with reference to numerous plans of a forum from many sites across the Roman Empire are not easily given up. However, most will have already come to terms with the fact that the houses of Pompeii do not conform to the houses

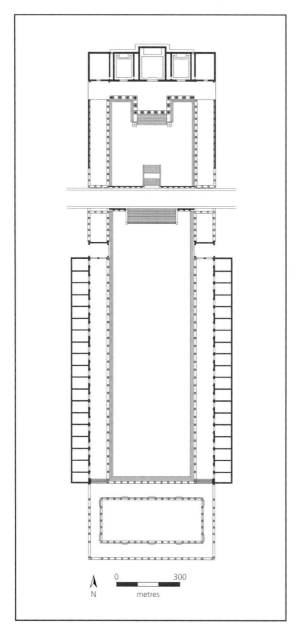

Figure 3.9 Brescia: the Forum is divided into two sections by the major road running through the city

found in the text of Vitruvius. Such testing of the representation of architectural and material forms in texts via the archaeological remains that we have is necessary. It should not be a destructive process: no one's evidence is better than anyone else's, but instead such studies reveal the difference between the representation of reality in texts that we have and the use of the city. This enriches both the discipline of archaeology and that of history. We can begin to make sense of how Roman culture represented in textual forms three-dimensional realities of considerable complexity.

Chapter 4

From the City to the Country
Archaeological Excavation and Field Survey

Looking over the literature produced at the interface between the disciplines of archaeology and ancient history, there lies a preoccupation with the subject of 'the city and the country'. Often these are seen as almost discrete entities interacting with each other, but that are fundamentally separate. Michael Rostovtzeff, as a Russian exile, saw this as a dichotomy that made sense of his homeland in the early 20th century, but it is also a dominant mode of discourse within European culture. It is a discourse that is implicit in the model of the consumer city familiar to ancient historians from the work of Moses Finley and a generation of scholarship that includes both Wim Jongman's discussion of Pompeii and Neville Morley's discussion of Rome and its hinterland (Morley 1996), while also encapsulating perspectives of towns and the countryside in Roman Britain (for example, Rivet 1964 or papers in Miles 1982). The centrality of the relationship of the city and countryside was established in the first ever social and economic history of the Roman Empire, which was written by Rostovtzeff originally in the 1920s and then re-issued through to the end of the 1950s. At the heart of the discussion lie two paradigms: one a conception of history based on the experience of the end of the 19th and early 20th centuries, and second, the use of archaeological evidence. The latter had been a feature of Tenney Frank's earlier work, in which 'large-scale factory methods' and 'industrial capital' were incorporated into the interpretation of garum and textile production in Pompeii (Frank 1918: 233–34) and a comparison between the Eumachia building and the Blackwell Hall in medieval London with an associated cross-comparison of the *collegia* of Pompeii with the guilds of the Middle Ages – a subject that was duly developed by Moeller (1976) more than half a century later – a study anticipated by Rostovtzeff (1926: 514–15).

Rostovtzeff's conception of the economy involved a rise of a bourgeoisie that underpinned a form of city-capitalism in the manner of an urban middle class in opposition to the peasants of the countryside, who suffered a 'rapid decline in material wealth' and a decline in their 'purchasing power' that resulted in the stagnation of the economy under the emperors (Rostovtzeff 1926: xi-xii and set out 125–79). Underpinning the development of this model was a conception of the development of capitalism in Italy with the spread of slave production in the 2nd century BC, and the development of new markets for goods in Gaul, Spain and Africa (Rostovtzeff 1926: 21), a view substantiated by the spread of Roman material culture. In Italy, the owners of production (big capitalists and the rich municipal bourgeoisie) were located in the villas that had been excavated in the vicinity of Pompeii, Stabiae and Herculaneum (Rostovtzeff 1926: 31). Prosperity under Augustus could be evaluated with reference to the ruins of cities in Umbria (Rostovtzeff 1926: 59). Literary evidence is also used: Horace's references to his Sabine farm run by a slave-manager, *vilicus*, locates Horace as an example of the urban population exploiting the countryside for profit that becomes 'a characteristic feature of Central Italy' (Rostovtzeff 1926: 61). However, it is the exchange of manufactured goods as exemplified by finds in the archaeological record that prevails across the text and creates the visual imagery found in museums, such as that in Aquileia, on which Rostovtzeff's model of the economy is based (Rostovtzeff 1926: 71). Importantly, he rejected the use of literary evidence to characterize the city and the country and instead looked to archaeology for elucidation of the problem that he saw as vital for the understanding of social and economic history (Rostovtzeff 1926: 180–305). He surveys the evidence province by province over the course of more than a 100 pages to try to elucidate what the relationship was between the minority living in towns and the majority of the population living in the countryside and involved in agricultural production. What writers in the early 20th century saw was a resolution of a contemporary debate over the nature of the Roman economy as either fundamentally undeveloped or characterized by the language of the 'intricate industrial system of modern times' (Frank 1927: 219). Part of the problem of the nature of this debate was a lack of data and a reliance on literary sources. The proponents for resolution staunchly advocated the use of archaeological evidence, particularly that from Pompeii, the only excavated city with adequate remains if poorly published data. The power of the arguments developed at the beginning of the 20th century based on archaeology would create an orthodoxy of a capitalist Roman Empire that would survive until it was challenged by Moses Finley in the 1970s with the development of the new orthodoxy of the ancient economy. What this material reveals is how Roman historians have manipulated the archaeological record to produce conclusions that are often a reflection of their own ideological positions in the present. Following on from this discussion, the chapter moves on to recent excavations of villas within the vicinity of Rome and discusses how the evidence has been interpreted and how it might engage with current debates over the nature of the city and the landscape that borders the city.

The villas of Campania: a dreamtime of Roman capitalism?

Rostovtzeff (1926: 496–97) saw the potential of studying the villas destroyed by the eruption of Vesuvius and the need for a proper survey. Most of the sites had been excavated in the 1890s, notably those at Boscoreale. The finds from these sites were sold, significantly the treasure to Baron E. Rothschild who donated part of it to the Museum of the Louvre, and dispersed elsewhere, with frescoes being displayed in the Metropolitan Museum in New York and numerous finds in the Field Museum of Natural History in Chicago (De Cou 1912). The excavation of these villas allowed Roman historians to view the material culture at first-hand for the first time from the 1890s onwards. The most graphic example is probably that of the Villa Della Pisanella at Boscoreale (Pasqui 1897 for full report), whose plan is frequently reproduced (Figure 4.1). The structure is dominated by production with a large wine cellar (Q) and both a wine press (P) and an olive press (T). There are also three mosaic-inlaid rooms that provided the owners with a small bath suite of changing room (M), warm room (N), and hot room (O), while elsewhere in the villa two large bronze bathtubs (1.75m in length) were found in the peristyle (A), alongside cupboards in which other materials were stored. Presumably the bathtubs provided for immersion in water, whereas the bathing rooms provided a steam bath. Rooms around the peristyle included bedrooms (B and D), a dining room (F) and another room that contained 23 agricultural tools (G), ranging from spades and picks through to hammers and sickles. There was a kitchen close to the baths (H) and the furnace for heating the water (L) – a feature of the villa is its evidence of water tanks and plumbing for the baths. There is also evidence of an upper storey that was residential. The 409 finds recorded in the excavation report from 1897 provide some insight into the material wealth of the villa, but what we lack is adequate comparisons to other sites.

For Tenney Frank (1918: 236–37; incorporated into Frank 1923: 404–5), this villa was iconic and provided evidence of 'a practical farmer' and 'a man of urbane breeding', who was engaged with a 'world of commerce and industry' rather than a 'domestic economy'. This villa was seen to be owned by a man producing wine for the market and 'to him the land was a factory for the production of a special article from the profits of which he could make a living' (Frank 1918: 238) and also to consume a high

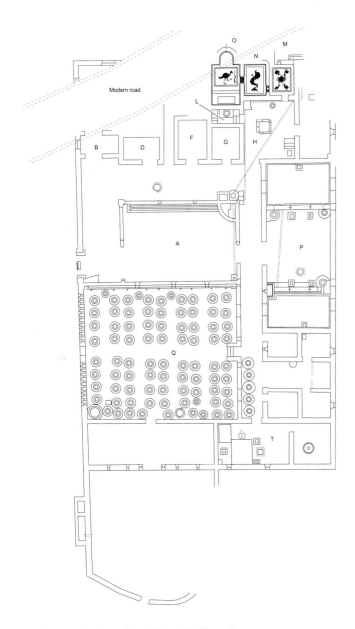

Figure 4.1 Boscoreale: plan of the Villa della Pisanella

quality of resources depending on the skill of the urban tradesman: plumbing and silver-smithing being notable (Frank 1918: 237). City and country
were seen to join together and Frank saw in Pompeii and its hinterland
'the whole system of industries appear[ing] in all stages of development
toward capitalistic production' (Frank 1918: 240). In this discussion, we can
see a problem. Frank looks at a few selective examples for the simple
reason that the evidence from Pompeii had not been fully published and
he calls for a 'republication of Pompeii by social and economic historians'
(Frank 1918: 226; c.f. Carrington 1931: 110). The same villa features in
John Day's survey of agricultural life of Pompeii, onto which the texts
from agricultural writers could be mapped to discuss diversification in
agriculture. He provides a calculation of the value of the wine from the
villa to have been 48,000–144,000 sesterces depending on the quality of the
wine involved (Day 1932: 180–81 – no real detail of the calculation is
provided; calculation incorporated into Frank 1940: 264). Although other
villas had not been so fully excavated, this villa at Boscoreale becomes
seen as typical of all others (Day 1932: 182–88). As a student of Rostovtzeff, Day (1932) constructs his interpretation within this framework of
a diversifying bourgeoisie composed of freed slaves, alongside a wealthy
aristocracy of wine producers. A view of the aristocracy that was supported by Mary Gordon's (1927, see also 1931) study of the *Ordo* of Pompeii and included the incorporation of descendants of freedmen into the
aristocracy. Another study of the villas by R. C. Carrington (1931: 115–16)
draws on Rostovtzeff's typology of villas: (a) luxurious summer residences;
(b) farm-houses inhabited all the year round; and (c) agricultural 'factories'
run by slaves. The survey concludes with an allusion to modern debates
over the nature of the city and an antithesis between the newly planned
Garden Cities of the 20th century and the industrial city of the 19th
century: 'Pompeii and its vicinity was no garden city or suburb, but the
scene of an intense industrial activity' (Carrington 1931: 190). Interestingly,
the research undertaken by Day and Carrington with respect to the
interpretation of this villa was incorporated by Frank into his fifth volume of
the *Economic Survey of Ancient Rome* published in 1940, but little had changed
from his original publication of 1918 more than 20 years earlier – affluence
was derived from production with the 'landholder adapting his scale of
life to the production of his farm' (Frank 1940: 265).

The problem of interpretation of archaeological remains seen here is
that the evidence is fitted into a preconceived pattern; in the case of
Rostovtzeff, Frank and others at the beginning of the 20th century, this
reinforced their position to ensure the dominance of an interpretation
of the Roman economy that reflected modern capitalist conceptions. It
was a model that lasted until the onslaught of Finley in the 1970s, who

created – via a swathe of seminal works of his own and via the work of his students in Cambridge – a conception of the economy that was primitivist, in which production was embedded in the social structure of society and economic rationality did not exist (Finley 1973; 1985; discussed most effectively by Jongman 1988: 30–55). Finley did not utilize archaeological material, but one of his students did. Wim Jongman engaged directly with the evidence that Rostovtzeff, Frank and others had used to build their model of a capitalist economy and sharply focused his discussion on town-country relations. Within his complex argument, Jongman developed a position that viewed the economic conditions of the 1st century AD as unique and within which models of modern or pre-modern economies needed adjustment. Effectively, this divorces his work from both Finley's and Rostovtzeff's positions. It is also interesting to note that, in 1918, Frank was estimating the population of Pompeii at 25,000, whereas for Jongman in 1988 it was between 8,000 and 12,000. The excavated villas have a limited role to play in his argument for the reason that he considered them to be poor indicators of land-use given how much of the 79 AD landscape remains unexcavated and also that the villas' location may be dictated by the network of roads leading from the gates of Pompeii (Jongman 1988: 112–23). Moreover, Jongman is wary of older excavation reports from the end of the 19th and early 20th century in terms of reliability, when compared to more recent published excavations that include full consideration of planting patterns and greater focus on publication of all the finds (see Jashemski 1987, 1993: 288–91; De Caro 1994). There is resistance here to the compelling nature of single examples from which a micro-economic model of villa production might be determined and, instead, Jongman (1988: 131–37) puts forward a macro-economic model of production based on the carrying capacity of the Pompeian hinterland. What this macro-economic model provides for is an understanding of the individual villa that is excavated. Hence, what has occurred is that the model based on capitalism is replaced with another derived specifically for the historical situation of antiquity through which we may interpret any archaeological excavated remains.

Cynically, the Roman historian might suggest on this basis that the entire enterprise of villa excavation does not alter the model – since any one villa will always be interpreted within the framework of macro-economic theory. At the same time, archaeologists can protest that the evidence 'should speak for itself' prior to incorporation into the historians' models of interpretation. The problem with the latter is that the relationship between evidence and interpretation within archaeology is not as divorced as this, and theories of interpretation are necessary for establishing significance. To conclude this chapter, I wish to turn now to three recent archaeological projects that have sought to elucidate the relationship between the city of Rome and its hinterland. These shift our focus away from economics and towards the development and phenomenology of landscape with a view to understanding long- and short-term landscape change. These studies perhaps reflect far more the potential of archaeology to engage directly with Roman history and to produce interpretations that directly arise from the archaeologists' emphases on change and the environment.

A villa three miles north of Rome

In 1995, in anticipation of development of the new music Auditorium, an excavation took place that revealed a villa close to the ancient line of the Via Flaminia as it approached the Mulvian Bridge to the north of the city of Rome. The villa that was excavated was located close to the Tiber at some 13 metres above sea level and less than three Roman miles from the Forum in the city of Rome (papers in Carandini et al 2006 are essential for what follows here. See Figure 4.2A–D for phase plans), and not far from the location of the sacred spring of Anna Perenna. The low-lying nature of the site might be one of the explanations for its rebuilding in the 2nd century BC and its abandonment from the 2nd century AD, the former a period associated with major flooding (Oros. 4.11.6; Aug. *Civ. Dei.* 3.18) and the latter a time when we witness the raising in level at urban sites close to the Tiber, including within the Campus Martius in Rome and at Ostia. The site can be dated back to the 6th and 5th centuries BC; hence it is one of the key sites for understanding the nature of settlement close to the metropolis of Rome over the *longue durée* (Figure 4.2). A courtyard structure was gradually developed on the site from the 5th to the 3rd centuries BC (Figure 4.2A, 4.2B). In the late 3rd to 2nd centuries, the complex was redeveloped with a recognizable *atrium* (courtyard – Figure 4.2C). This development was followed by further rebuilding in the late 2nd century or 1st century BC through to the 1st century AD (Figure 4.2D), and was followed by the abandonment of the site in the 2nd century AD. Subsequently, these phases were buried under almost a metre of alluvial material. The villa was located on marginal land right on the floodplain of the Tiber, perhaps owing part of its location to its proximity to the route to the shrine of Anna Perenna. However, this region was not just associated with agriculture – nearby, close to the third milestone on the Via Flaminia, a tile manufacturing centre has been excavated. Such manufacturing was a characteristic of many agricultural settlements and should be associated with what we might term Roman land management that did not differentiate between manufacture and

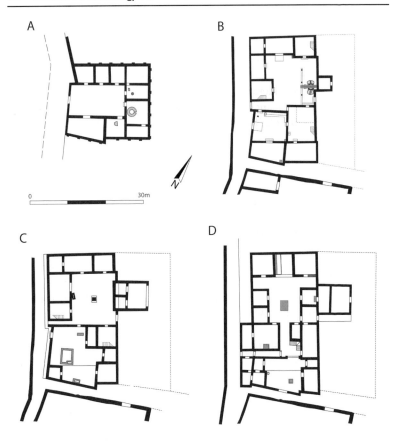

Figure 4.2 North of Rome: villa at the site of the Auditorium (Rome) A – 550–500 BC;
B – 500–350/300 BC; C – 225–150 BC; D – 150–80 BC

agriculture. Such diversification may have been necessary given the uncertainty of undertaking agricultural production on marginal land subject to flooding.

The development of the villa is instructive of the changing nature of settlement at the site and needs to be outlined to set out an overview of chronological change at a settlement site close to the city of Rome. What the villa also demonstrates is the diffusion of olive production, since the villa contained an oil press within the second phase of rebuilding (i.e. c. 500–350/300 BC, Figure 4.2B). Another adjacent complex, described as a 'servile quarter' in the publication by Andrea Carandini and his team (2006: 150–89) contained areas for habitation, including ovens and a well, and interestingly two infant burials. What is suggested is that a number of these rooms were for slaves. Obviously, there is an assumption here: in a building complex of less sophistication than the villa, it is assumed that slaves were housed and that the building was not simply that of a neighbour who had not redeveloped his property. These structures suffered a destruction phase associated with a considerable amount of pottery found in this phase and that of the rebuilding and the reoccupation of the villa in the following period (c. 300–225 BC). The orientation was not so different from that found in the earlier structure but, importantly, one of its two courtyards was arranged around an *impluvium* and there was a second courtyard, at the centre of which was an altar in front of a small temple or shrine that would have housed two deities (Figure 4.2C). The excavators associated the first courtyard with a section of the house dedicated to production and a slave family under its *vilicus*, whereas the section of the second court-yard, with its altar and shrine, was seen as part of the house associated with the free family. What the excavators are doing is imposing onto the archaeological plan the text of Cato the Elder, *De Agricultura*. This would seem a little unjustified, since the spatial formation could be open to other forms of social organization than those envisaged by a senator living later in the 2nd century BC. What we are seeing though is a separation of the villa into two sections.

The villa was completely redeveloped over the course of the 3rd and 2nd centuries BC (Figures 4.2B and 4.2C) and the division of the building into two separate sections was obliterated as space was expanded for the inclusion of two dining rooms and a formal atrium off which were placed rooms including a *tablinum* with some form of archive or library, as well as rooms on a first floor. Significantly, the largest room was the kitchen. The courtyard previously associated by the excavators with slaves was considerably reduced in area. What has happened here is that the villa has been adapted to conform to the new architectural ideals of what has become known in the literature as the atrium house – most famously found in Pompeii. It is this structure, with some modifications, that increased the storage capacity of the villa and survived until its abandonment some two centuries later. The final phase of the villa includes an intentional destruction of the villa in the 3rd century and the burial of the dead close to the former site of habitation.

The story of the development and destruction of the villa has some importance for our comprehension of the chronology of rural architecture, but far more significant for our discussion are the finds and, in particular, those of amphorae used for transporting liquids in the late Republic and Imperial periods. The vast majority of these vessels were used for the transportation of wines produced in Italy and in southern Gaul. But, there are other products: garum (or fish sauce) from the Spanish provinces of Baetica and Lusitania, wines from the Aegean and the Greek East, and olive oil from the African provinces (Carandini et al 2006: 447–53). This pattern of consumption reveals the linkage between this rural site and the city. However, when compared with the villas at places such as Stabiae on the bay of Naples: the villa found in the building of the new Auditorium in Rome is modest, it does not have a bathing facility. Perhaps, the inhabitants made the short journey to the city to avail themselves of these facilities. Eventually, of course, the cemeteries of the city encroached on the site itself.

The Villa of Livia at Prima Porta

Six miles to the north of the villa excavated during the construction of the new Auditorium lies the Villa of Livia at a place simply known as Ad Gallinas at the ninth milestone of the Via Flaminia some 50 metres above sea level (see papers in Messineo 2001; Reeder 2001 provides a description in English). It was here that the famous statue of Augustus at Prima Porta was found, which is now displayed in the Vatican Museums. It has also been the subject for the recreation of the villa within a virtual reality format of second life (see papers in Forte 2007; www.vhlab.itabc.cnr.it/ flaminia/index02.html). The archaeological investigation of the villa and its garden reveals the context for this famous statue, which is used as an iconic representation of the age of Augustus on book covers and for undergraduate classes.

The villa was located on a hill at the point where the Via Flaminia and Via Tiberina joined together. It was in a position both to command views across the Tiber Valley and to be seen from afar. Perhaps its location is given more meaning by a reported portent that when Livia was betrothed to Augustus in 37 BC, an eagle dropped an unusually white chicken holding laurel berries in its beak into her lap; these berries were then planted at the villa, which became known as Ad Gallinas. It was from here that the laurels worn at the triumphs of emperors were gathered until the trees died in 68 AD (Suet. *Galba* 1; Plin. *NH* 15.136–37; Dio 48.52; Obseq. *Lib. Prodig.* 131). It should be remembered that two laurel trees were planted in front of Augustus' house on the Palatine in 27 BC, ten years after the planting of the laurel seeds at the villa of Livia (Dio 53.16.4; Kellum 1994: 211–13). When discussing this portent, we should bear in mind that Livia was not only betrothed to Augustus: she was also pregnant and due to give birth to the future emperor Tiberius. Therefore, perhaps we should read the portent as a justification for the succession of Tiberius as much as a prophecy of the future greatness of Augustus and Livia. This is particularly significant when we view the imagery of the statue of Augustus

Prima Porta as a *posthumous* statue created after Augustus' death in 14 AD. There has been much debate over where this statue of Augustus stood within the Villa of Livia, but the most compelling argument put forward is that the statue stood in the atrium of the villa and was set up after 14 AD (Figure 4.3). Hence, the posthumous statue of the emperor greeted visitors to the villa in an action of *ad locutio* (Klynne and Liljenstolpe 2000a), and its imagery features Tiberius at the centre of the breastplate. Importantly, the statue remained here for visitors that included the Julio-Claudian emperors, who came to gather laurel leaves for their own triumphs.

Of particular interest for our discussion of villas and the city is the so-called 'Garden Room' at the villa of Livia, that Barbara Kellum describes as 'much more than a simple decorative landscape' and suggests that within the painting there is a 'system of ordering that creates a convincing spatial illusion of an outdoor garden within the parameters of a subterranean room' that was 11.7 by 5.9 metres (Kellum 1994: 215; Gabriel 1955 for full description). Within the landscape represented, there is a fence in the foreground with grass receding from it to a stone, parapeted above which are plantings described by Kellum (1994: 215–17) as 'a lush, tangled thicket of flowering plants, bushes and trees', which she associates with the landscape of Virgil's *Georgics* and the decoration of the lower register of the Ara Pacis. The presence of birds reminds Kellum of the text of Varro (*RR* 3.5.9–17), in which an aviary is represented and can be connected to the presence of a birdcage in the Garden Room at the Villa of Livia. What we have on the walls of the room is a representation of plants that were present in gardens in Italy. They are mundane rather than exotic, yet the modes of representation found in Augustan poetry allow us to read into the mundane an ideological significance (Kellum 1994 discusses this relationship in more depth, also Gabriel 1955).

The question remains, what was the relationship of this landscape of shrubs and trees, including laurels, to the actual gardens of the Villa of Livia? The paintings do not display trees towering over shrubs and bushes, but low-level plantings. The gardens of the villa were subject to a full investigation by the Swedish Institute in Rome during the 1990s. This included a geophysical survey of the main garden (75 by 75 metres, Figure 4.3 for location) and excavation of both this garden and the smaller gardens associated with the villa itself (Liljenstolpe and Klynne 1997; Klynne and Liljenstolpe 2000b). It is not so much the structures that these excavations revealed that are significant here, but the detailed information derived from the study of environmental data. Ezequiel Pinto-Guillaume (2002) published a full account of all the snails identified inhabiting the garden areas that were excavated. The large open-terraced garden revealed few snails in its central area in contrast to the areas that were at

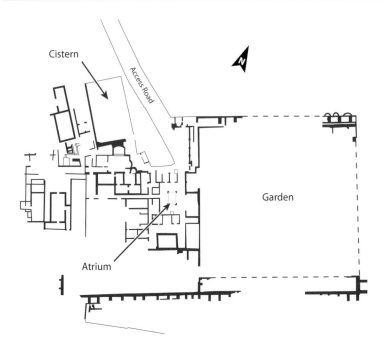

Figure 4.3 North of Rome: the Villa of Livia at Prima Porta

the edge of this open area. The latter would correspond to the view in the distance from the villa, whereas the open area was in the foreground. This area was understood by the excavators to have been a 'hanging garden' with a water-channel or *euripus* that was in front of the planting area and dated to 50–75 AD. Land snails (*H. Aspersa, H. Aperta, C. nemoralis, C. virgata*) were consumed by people living at the villa, as were some marine species. One form of land snail (*R. decollata*) may have been used for the control of pests (including other snails). Other species that were found (*P. Elegans, C. nemoralis, H. Aspersa, C. acicula, R. pura*) are associated with planting areas and tend to live in damp and shady conditions. This would imply that the plantings formed a low-level woodland canopy with shrubs and herbs, which can be connected to the landscape of Rome in book eight of the *Aeneid* (Virg. *Aen.* 8.91–100; Pinto-Guillaume 2002: 55–56) and to the paintings found in the Garden Room of the villa itself. The garden landscape revealed by archaeology is a created landscape, just as those found in the frescoes of the villa and in the text of Virgil are created landscapes. What we can begin to see though is how the representations of landscape in image and text can be directly related to the three-dimensional landscapes that existed in the Augustan and Julio-Claudian periods at the Villa of Livia. When combined with the knowledge of portents predicting Augustus'/Tiberius' rise to power, this villa becomes transformed into a public memorial and an ideological signifier for imperial rule in the 1st century AD.

The Tiber Valley

As we saw in Chapter 2, after the Second World War, the British School at Rome embarked on a major project to record the archaeological remains of South Etruria. This initiative was followed up by others in the same region on the part of Italian scholars (Patterson and Millett 1998). Material was recorded and pottery was collected from sites right across the region, with 850 square kilometres investigated by the British School. A synthesis of the project was published by Tim Potter in 1979, but it was not until 1997 that a team of pottery experts was assembled to re-evaluate the material and to conduct a full investigation of all the material from the Tiber Valley. This was underpinned by a geographical information system (GIS) and can be combined with other surveys, including those of the coastal region of Etruria (Witcher 2006a). This facilitates the comparison of trends in the settlement pattern between regions and the isolation of significant variables. The key disadvantage is that there are numerous biases of collection methods, dating horizons and, not least, a lack of precise dating to within a range of five to ten years (Patterson 2006 and Witcher 2006b discuss these problems in depth). Instead, what we have are some very broad periods. For the Tiber Valley project these are defined as (Patterson et al 2004):

Archaic 600–500 BC
Classical 500–350 BC
Mid-Republican 350–250 BC
Late Republican 1 250–150 BC
Late Republican 2 150–1 BC
Early Imperial 1–100 AD
Mid-Imperial 100–250 AD
Late Antique 1 250–450 AD
Late Antique 2 450–550 AD

The material found is evaluated under a general rubric of sites, and patterns of continuity and discontinuity are recorded over time and represented graphically. This points to periods of expansion in the period 350–250 BC, followed by contraction over the course of the next period, 250–150 BC, representing a reduction in the number of sites by more than 50 per cent; from 150–1 BC there is considerable expansion back to the levels experienced in the period 250–150 BC. However, it is in the 1st century AD that we find a massive expansion in the number of sites by more than 100 per cent; an expansion that is largely sustained through the next century, but is reduced down to a much lower level after 250 AD. Looking at the overall trend, this would suggest that we should expect rural settlement patterns to be inherently unstable and displaying considerable discontinuity over long periods of 100 years or more (compare evaluation by Patterson et al 2004). However, what is remarkable is the scale of continuity found from the 1st century into the 2nd century AD. The density of settlement and continuity of settlement pattern is remarkable, but perhaps we should point to an instability in this pattern – during the 2nd century AD, few new sites were created. This might suggest that the expansion in density of sites and thus also of population was achieved in the 1st century AD. It has to be said that historians have tended to focus far more on the crises of the Republic or of Late Antiquity, rather than seeking an explanation of the increase in agricultural settlement. What the Tiber Valley Project has done is to bring this problem into clearer focus.

Looking at the broad period of 200 BC through to 200 AD (Figure 4.4), we can identify a quite different settlement history for the Tiber Valley when compared to the other regions of Etruria (Witcher 2006a). This history involves a huge leap in the number of settlement sites in the period from 25 BC through to the end of the 1st century AD. In short, the density of settlement in the Tiber Valley more than doubles and is then maintained at this level to the end of the 2nd century AD. This would suggest that the carrying capacity of the landscape, in terms of population, was increased. The generator for this increase is likely to have been the growth and development of Rome as a capital city of empire under the first emperors, with the result that the hinterland could, by association with the capital, support a higher level of population. This factor of itself causes us to realize that the landscape can be reshaped and reconfigured by forces other than those of environmental determinism. As an aside, looking at Figure 4.4, it should be noted that the reduction in the number of sites in coastal Etruria occurs long after Tiberius Gracchus was said by Plutarch to have viewed a deserted landscape (*TG* 8; Witcher 2006a: 112). The collapse of the town of Cosa associated with the Ager Cosanus might in some way explain the overall decline of population in this city's hinterland. The association of the fortunes of the city with those of the countryside causes us to question the validity of maintaining the city and country in antithesis to each other, because the city extended into the countryside and the two elements were part of a single socio-economic system (Witcher 2005 for

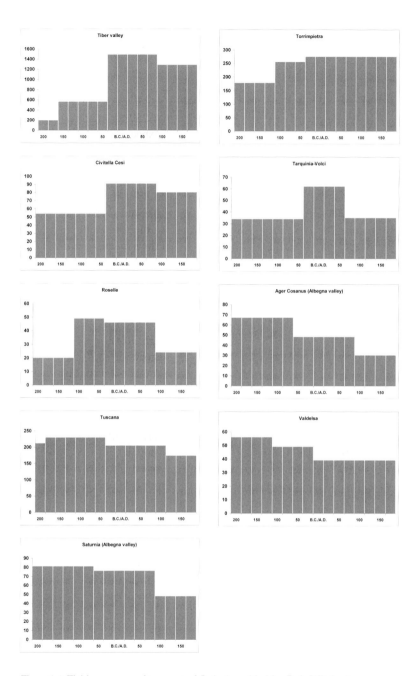

Figure 4.4 Field survey results – central Italy (provided by Rob Witcher)

reconstruction of population figures). This is something that is also suggested in the material culture found at the Villa at Rome's Auditorium and at the Villa of Livia at Prima Porta.

After the city and country

At the beginning of the 21st century, we are conceiving of the city-country relationship in a quite different way to the opinion of 100 years ago. Perhaps, more significantly, the shift in our thinking about this relationship has only changed very recently. After all, for Finley (1985) the city was a consumer city that was separated from the countryside that sustained it. Today, we do not see the city and its influence ceasing at the gates and that outside these stood a separate realm. Within the field of archaeology, cities have been the focus of investigation. However, with the advent of time-efficient forms of geophysics (a trend that will continue), there is the possibility of investigating the entire landscape of the Roman city and to insert all archaeological data to a GIS. Projects of this magnitude have been begun, for example at Wroxeter (Gaffney et al 2007) and more recently at Silchester (Creighton 2006). These tend to be termed 'hinterland studies' and are conducted after excavation and geophysical investigation in the city is well underway. In some ways, this is a hangover from the 20th century, when city and country were seen as separate archaeological entities. The two are converging into what might be described as an urban process, by which the city and its hinterland are both considered. It makes sense: the elite moved from urban residence to productive villa and chose to commemorate their dead relatives at either location according to choice and fashion (Mouritsen 2005). Shifting away from the past's separation of city from country (see Wallace-Hadrill 1991), we find an increasing body of data in relation to surveys of the countryside or 'hinterland' of the city – I prefer 'landscape' of the city – but what is less clear is how this material should be integrated with excavations within the city to form a full understanding of the archaeology of an urban process that varied chronologically. However, what it does create is an essential truth for Roman historians: archaeology and archaeologists cannot be simply ignored; they have data that will impinge on all historical interpretations of the Roman past.

Chapter 5

From Italy to the Provinces
Imperialism and Cultural Change

If there is one thing that ignites Roman archaeologists it is the subject of cultural change, or what has become known as 'Romanization'. It owes its origin to Francis Haverfield's book *The Romanization of Roman Britain* published in 1906, a book that owes its inspiration to Theodor Mommsen and historical scholarship from the 19th century (Freeman 2007). For Roman historians delving into Roman archaeology, there is a need to step carefully when it comes to discussing Romanization. It is a topic that will produce strong opinions, groans of depression and frustration, and an understanding that draws on Roman historical research but sets itself apart from it. This chapter seeks to set out some (but certainly not all) of the key areas of debate regarding Romanization and to relate these to the concerns and conceptions of historians. It should be noted at the very outset that this is a two-way street – archaeologists are deeply influenced by the work of ancient historians and may implicitly or explicitly reproduce concepts developed by ancient historians. In fact, in this chapter, I would suggest that the work of Moses Finley, setting out an economy at diametric odds to the work of Michael Rostovtzeff (discussed in the previous chapter), underpins the modern conception of Romanization (see Greene 1986 for a view of Finley's work from within archaeology prior to 1990, and Greene 2000 for a view ten years on from the publication of Millett's 1990a *The Romanization of Britain*).

In discussing archaeologists' debates over the nature of cultural change, the focus will be on the discussion of Roman Britain, a province on the periphery of the Roman Empire but at the very centre of the debate over the nature of Romanization. Not all positions, nor every reference to the debate, can be encapsulated within this chapter (see Revell 2009 for an alternative view from within the discipline of archaeology). What is included here is an overview of conceptions and an analysis of the relationship of these positions to debates within Roman history. I see the articulation of the modes of explanation put forward over the last 20 years or so to be embedded in the debate from the 1970s over the nature of the ancient economy, which was very much part of the undergraduate curriculum in Roman archaeology in the 1980s and can be identified in various edited volumes published as British Archaeological Reports (BARs) over the course of the late 1970s and 1980s (for example, Miles 1982), as well as in Kevin Greene's (1986: 14–16) textbook *The Archaeology of the Roman Economy*. I am not suggesting that 1990 marks a sea-change in the study of cultural change, but instead wish to suggest that the articulation of that subject in Martin Millett's *The Romanization of Britain* draws together earlier themes and provides a text for the discussion of the subject matter, both in the teaching of undergraduates and at conferences, for the next decade and continues to define discussion implicitly if not explicitly. What is less well understood and seldom discussed is the convergence of Millett's (1990a) discussion with Finley's conception of the ancient economy.

From Moses Finley's *Ancient Economy* to Martin Millett's *Romanization of Britain*

More than 80 years on from Haverfield's original publication came Millett's (1990a) book with a similar title – *The Romanization of Britain*. It is an 'essay in interpretation' of archaeological evidence and has provided archaeology with a synthesis of the evidence and a 'modern commentary on the social and economic development of the province' of Britannia (Millett 1990a: xv). It was a timely publication because it arrived at a point when the preoccupations of Roman archaeology were subject to some fierce criticism (see Chapter 2) and it appeared in the same year that the first Theoretical Roman Archaeology Conference (TRAC) was held in Newcastle. More than 20 years on, it might be hard to imagine quite how different this book was from what students had read before, such as Sheppard Frere's third edition of *Britannia* (1978) and Peter Salway's *Roman Britain* (1981). At the heart of the book was a conception of Romanization utterly different from that of Haverfield's; it was a 'two-way process of acculturation', in which the results were not always initiated by outside influences of a Roman elite, but also by the inhabitants born in the province (Millett 1990a: 2).

A striking feature of *The Romanization of Britain* is that it is a book that in its first chapter drew on the ideas of ancient historians, particularly Finley and his students (see Chapter 4 for discussion), to create an overview of the Roman economy and relate this field to that of Roman imperialism (Millett 1990a: 2–8). The emphasis on acculturation as a two-way process causes Millett's conception of Roman imperial rule to be decentralized and at a low level of control, with a consequence that the material gain to Rome was also low, in which the empire was 'a federation of diverse peoples under Rome, rather than a monolithic and uniformly centralized block' (Millett 1990a: 8). This conception is in a direct counterpoint to a concept of 'any emergence of systematic economic imperialism', but does not deny a flow of wealth between core and periphery with the potential of economic growth in municipalities that controlled taxation (Millett 1990a: 8). This viewpoint shapes the argument, for example in discussion of the import of Roman goods into pre-Roman Iron Age Britain, to reject the use of imports by the social leaders of south-east Britain to maintain power through the monopolization of the use of exotic imports and other raw materials, not on grounds of the material evidence but on that of the scale of supply and the observation that 'a highly exploitative economic network is inappropriate for the Roman empire' (Millett 1990a: 38). Instead, the economic trade in such goods was embedded in the social relationships (including kin, clientship and diplomacy) between south-east Britain and Gallia Belgica, with a degree of profit-making. Strikingly, this aligns the book with the thinking put forward by Finley in *The Ancient Economy* and re-writes the scale of analysis from that of the city into the context of diplomatic relations between those within the Roman Empire and those at its edge.

There is a consistency in *The Romanization of Britain* that maintains a low impact of empire on the overall pre-Roman Iron Age economy. It is argued, for instance, that the impact of the arrival of 40,000 Roman soldiers was minimized with an intention 'not to over-exploit the supply base' yet, as Millett (1990a: 56) admits, the Boudiccan revolt did happen. The overall impact in terms of food production is calculated at 2 per cent, but was not evenly distributed. Mention must be made here of another impact of these 40,000 soldiers, that of the change in the sex ratio of society. Millett suggests that the soldiers formed relationships with native women, effectively removing a large number of younger women. This had the effect of destabilizing native practices on the one hand and, on the other, Romanizing the women, who he sees as potentially becoming 'a very significant force in the acculturation of the remainder of the native population over whom they had a fundamental influence' (1990a: 60). Credible or not, at a theoretical level this proposal embeds social relations of conquering soldiers and natives into a model of non-exploitative power relations (or an economic relationship embedded within social relations) within which both sides have agency to shape the future in terms of acculturation (contrast this position with that of Mattingly 2006: 175–76; 195, who characterizes the relationship via the supply of prostitution).

What I am arguing for is that *The Romanization of Britain* is a book whose vision is driven by a conception of the Roman Empire derived from the work of ancient historians working in the 1970s and 1980s following the publication of Finley's *The Ancient Economy*. There is, however, an important adjustment: the cities or *civitates* of Britain may have had some public buildings but this did not mean that the pre-Roman Iron Age economy was necessarily developed or altered via the conquest by Rome (Millett 1990a: 65–101). Hence, the economy of Roman Britain was embedded in the social system to a far greater extent than was found in the Mediterranean and only stimulated through taxation in line with Keith Hopkins' model (1980) and institutionalized competitive office-holding in the cities, drawing on Hopkins' conception of elite competition (1983). The latter involved an engagement by the provincial elite with *Romanitas* and, in consequence, Romanization was potentially 'entirely indigenous', or 'stimulated by passive encouragement', or failed when the 'Roman presence was socially disruptive' (Millett 1990a: 101). Importantly, the indigenous population actively engaged with Romanization in order 'to assert, project and maintain their social status' with emulation being 'a means of obtaining and retaining social dominance' and 'being used to express and define' that dominance (Millett 1990a: 212).

Crucial to all this are some key variables, set out by Millett (1990b), which include the temporal aspect of speed of conquest and demilitarization, speed of integration of the 'native elite', the nature of the existing society, including level of urbanization, the intensity and direction of trade and the speed of development of agriculture (presumably in relation to taxation). Ironically, Millett's attempt to create a more nuanced economically-focused account of Roman Britain, that would supplant the traditional accounts that had been seen as progressivist and written from the point of view of the successes of Roman conquest, became a new tradition to be critiqued and seen as exactly what the author had attempted to replace (for example, of critique Hingley 1997: 82–86; Webster 2003).

Rome as a world empire

Millett's picture of Romanization in Britain was rather different from another model that drew heavily on the observations of Roman historians. This was Richard Hingley's (1982) conception of Britannia as an administered economy, conceptualized within a framework drawn from Immanuel Wallerstein's world systems analysis of the modern world. At the heart of his argument was the idea that the tribes or *civitates* of the province and other infrastructure of the administration were an imposed system that lay over the top of the existing Iron Age societies. The administration exploited the resources of the province through taxation. However, the infrastructure of the province (I would add, including the road system) focused on London and the south-east, creating a new geography of exploitation or economic domination (Hingley 1982: 23). At a more local level, towns administered (collected) the tax from the countryside and controlled inter-regional trade. There is a considerable contrast to the model put forward by Millett/ Finley, in that the towns were the centres of import of agricultural goods and raw materials and, at the same time, exporters or at least places of exchange for luxury or manufactured goods. Trade was both unequal and monopolistic in the sense that it was centred in towns and the monetary economy was limited to the towns (Hingley 1982: 24–26). Although the countryside is seen in this model to be subsistence-based, money was needed for the conversion of produce into tax and for the purchase of luxuries (Hingley 1982: 26). What is suggested in this model is that the economy as such was an administered economy, in which the town holds sway over a large territory, unlike in, for example, central Italy, where towns were more closely spaced and competed with one another for produce in terms of market share from their rural hinterlands. The proposed system of administrative market exploitation drew not on models from Roman history but from modernization theory as applied to colonial Africa. It shares with Millett's conception of Romanization a need for the use of *Romanitas* to maintain social status, but allows for economic development within or close to or in relation to the major towns to which many migrated. Through the eyes of a historian working on Italy, this model has much in common with Hopkins' (1978) model of economic change that mapped onto the landscape of Roman Italy in the 2nd to 1st centuries BC, but significantly without the factors of recruitment into the Roman army, the development of slavery or capture of booty given consideration in the provincial situation from the mid- to late 1st century AD onwards.

Working independently of Hingley, Greg Woolf (1990) published a paper discussing the validity of using world systems analysis as a framework for the study of the Roman Empire. His article takes a wider view than that of Hingley's application of world systems to Britain, but the conclusions are quite similar. Woolf is adamant: it is possible to see the Roman Empire as a world empire, but not as a world economy, which deviates from Wallerstein's conception in that the centre and periphery in the Roman Empire included a large number of professional soldiers on the frontiers acting in the interests of the centre (see Revell 2009: 109 drawing on Barrett 1989). Importantly, the world-empire is 'cellular' and formed from 'independent mini-systems' that had been taken over and incorporated by the centre. Within the world empire of Rome, it is the elite that is unified and inte- grated, whereas the rest of the population continues to remain segregated and separated as prior to their conquest. Like Hingley's (1982) 'adminis- trative economy', Woolf views the political as having primacy over economic factors. Woolf (1990: 44, 47) observes that Finley's work on the economy underpins Wallerstein's conception of the Roman Empire that, as Woolf then points out, needs to be adjusted to include significant levels of long-distance trade, as exemplified in the archaeological record by studies of amphorae, but it does not follow that the existence of such a trade should not be seen as an indication of the development of a Roman world economy or 'an economy analogous to that of early-modern mercantilism' (1990: 53–53).

The positions arrived at by Hingley and Woolf are not so different from those of Millett (1990a), yet interestingly the Wallerstein model of a world empire has not taken hold in the archaeological literature in the same way as Millett's conception of Romanization. This may be due to a need for adjustment of the model of the world empire put forward by Wallerstein to include other factors, such as a conception of symbolic dominance and the use of luxuries to enable the maintenance of social/symbolic capital (Woolf 1990: 54–55). Another difficulty is that the study of Roman archaeology tends to be broken down into regional studies of a single province whereas more than one region needs to be studied for a world empire analysis, to include both core and periphery. What Hingley and Woolf demonstrate, however, is that there is a model into which the overall analysis of Roman imperialism can be set. Nonetheless, these two studies would seem to be invisible to the archaeological literature that comes later (for example, Mattingly 1997), and the views expressed by Hingley and Woolf have simply not entered the literature, whereas for example Woolf's 1992 review article with the word 'Romanization' in its title has been fully incorporated. Even in Richard Hingley's 2005 book, *Globalizing Roman Culture*, no mention is made of his own much earlier article (Hingley 1982) or that of Woolf (1990). There is an irony in that; Hingley (2005: 117) would seem to be arguing for the Roman Empire as a world empire in the manner of Woolf (1990).

Agency and power relations

The problem of the scale involved in the frame of analysis in the 1990s' conception of Romanization and that of Rome as a world empire (as outlined above) is that the role of individuals and the agency of the individual disappeared in the discussion of the macro-scale model. Such a problem was not unique to Roman archaeology: prehistorians were also grappling with the problem of agency and the theorization of a role for the individual. Eleanor Scott (1993) at the first meeting of TRAC suggested that Roman archaeology could make a positive contribution to the current debate on human agency conducted by prehistorians (citing Barrett 1990: 15). One of these prehistorians, John Barrett, was drawn into the debate over the nature of Roman imperialism and Romanization. His short pieces on Roman archaeology not only criticize the very presence of Romanization within the discipline of archaeology but also introduce Anthony Giddens' theory of structuration into the discipline (Barrett 1997a; 1997b; see Revell 2009: 10-). Giddens (1984) sets out a novel conception of society, in which all individuals are born into a structure – be that a city, a society or an empire – and within which individuals can make choices under the constraints of that structure.

structuration

The proposal for the re-focusing of Roman archaeology in this manner shifts the centre of the study of Roman culture away from that of imperialism and acculturation, which Barrett (1997a) saw as about domination and control of a sense of power at a national and/or personal level. This concept was seen to engage with an economic explanation as well as the political realms of the Roman Empire. The problem, put simply in models of acculturation, is that there is a necessity of having two cultures in opposition, but the key problem is that we do not know what 'Roman' is or was thought to be or how it changed (Barrett 1997b: 51; Wallace-Hadrill 2008). This can be made clear with reference to the villa site north of Rome discussed in the previous chapter. In its earliest plan form it does not look very Roman to us, but by a certain point the villa is transformed into an atrium-style house that all would recognize as Roman. The question is, how did the Romans living here become this Roman?

Within Barrett's suggested reformulation of Romanization is an attention to the temporalities of the human lifespan, public time and the long term or *longue durée* that can also be linked to memory of the past. In so doing, he is seeking a means of empowering the people of the past to have an active part to play in the formation of the material record, from which archaeologists deduct trends and generalized patterns. This process is seen to produce localized, or even cellular, to use a term from world systems analysis, patterns rather than a 'grand-narrative' or 'meta-narrative'. However, as Colin Forcy (1997) points out, the structure of empowerment is one in which, following Antonio Gramsci's conception of hegemony, the ruling class maintain their power at all costs, having obtained the consent of their social inferiors. The agency of empire is placed by Forcy (1997: 18–19, also Mattingly 1997) in the hands of the army and in the elite, who are integrated both socially and culturally into the structure of the empire through the action of town-building, dress, the use of Latin, etc. (quoting Tac. *Ann.* 21). These cultural traits are inserted or incorporated into the *habitus* (following Pierre Bourdieu) of the elite. This brings into sharp focus the 'repressive' nature of the Roman Empire. The application and response to the empire varies in time and place, of course, which causes this aspect of empire to be easily incorporated within a world empire approach set out by Woolf (1990).

More recent studies in archaeology, such as those by Louise Revell (2009) and John Creighton (2006), have directly incorporated agency into their work and are explicit on their position that seeks to understand the use of Roman material forms in different contexts. Underpinning this position is a realization that knowledge of practice or use of any aspect of material culture varied considerably according to context and space-time distancing from discussion of its usage found in texts, for example those of Cicero or Vitruvius. The veterans in Colchester or town-builders of Silchester were a long way from these authors in both time and space. Indeed, we need not imagine them seeing any convergence of outlook with these authors – yet there is something that identifies Roman material culture as culturally desirable and that was appropriated, used and manipulated in these settings.

Resistance and postcolonial discourse

A response to *The Romanization of Britain* (Millett 1990a) was an evaluation of the book in terms of its step away from the traditional narratives that had 'sided' with the Roman conqueror (Hingley 1991, 1993; Freeman 1991; Barrett 1997a). This led to a period of consideration of the British experience of empire in the past, and to an evaluation in terms of the historiography of the impact of British Imperialism on the study of the Roman Empire by British scholars in book-length studies (Hingley 2000; Freeman 2007). It is possible to make a similar comparison between the French experience of empire and Marcel Bénabou's (1976) discussion of resistance to Romanization in the North African provinces. The debate over Romanization parallels the debate over the nature of the Roman economy discussed by Peter Bang. His observations are relevant here – the debate should be understood in the context of the politics of the postcolonial age, in which academics are implicitly redefining their own European heritage as like or unlike the colonial Third World (Bang 1998, discussed in Saller 2002: 257). Moreover, located within our imperial heritage is a conception of 'our' resistance to Rome that is in need of some deconstruction (Jiménez 2008). The important difference in the case of Roman Britain is that archaeologists are conducting a debate in which the heritage of Britain is implicitly aligned with that of the colonized in the Third World and the heritage of modern Italy is implicitly aligned with that of the colonizer.

Perhaps we can see a reflection of the politics of the postcolonial age most clearly in an interest in cross-cultural comparisons with other colonial situations (see, for example, Hingley 1982), and within an explicit framework of study drawing on postcolonial discourse (Webster 1994). This approach juxtaposes the discussion of, for example, art in Roman Britain with the discussion of colonial art as resistance (Webster 2003). The work of Jane Webster focused initially on the texts of ancient historians with a view to evaluating the ancient authors' outlooks on such matters as Druids (Webster 1999), with a view to understanding resistance to Rome, or an elite that was incompatible with Rome. Whatever classicists and historians may think of the use of source material and the need for contextual critique of ancient writers and their *topoi* (see Mann 1985 for examples), Webster has a point: resistance to Rome had become a minor issue in the narrative histories of Roman imperialism. Hence, what is pointed out in drawing attention to the values of Roman culture regarding Druids and other inhabitants of the provinces needs highlighting to ensure that the violence associated with war and conquest is not removed. Interestingly, Creighton (2000: 217) would suggest that changes experienced by Druids of this nature could occur prior to incorporation within the empire. This is perhaps an extreme example of resistance and might be unrepresentative. Taking a wider view of material culture, Webster (2001, 2003) suggests that the process of cultural change was not straightforward acculturation but could produce a whole variety of forms. Some coincide with the iconic images found in books such as Diana Kleiner's *Roman Sculpture* (1992), but others do not (Webster 2003). The question is whether we should see the non-convergence of forms as 'resistance' or a form of 'negotiation' in the colonial context of Roman Britain, and how we conceptualize the issues of technology transfer and uptake (Greene 2000; Johns 2003). Perhaps, what is more significant is Webster's development of a conception of the creolization of material culture to match the use of this term in relation to linguistic change (Webster 2001 for clearest articulation, adopted by Mattingly 2004; note that Adams 2007 does not include creolization in his discussion of regional languages but provincial Latin was not the same as the Latin of Italians). The result is a position between 'acceptance' and 'resistance' of the dominant culture of the elite, and a less than straightforward reading of cultural traits within material culture (Webster 2003). Whatever the basis for 'creolization' as preferable to 'Romanization' (for example, Webster 2003: 50–51), many Roman historians might have some trouble in realizing the distinction for the study of material culture. Yet there is a point here: we need to recognize that 'pre-Roman' value systems could be expressed within the idiom of Roman material culture (Mattingly 2003, contrast to examples in Wells 2001: 124–28), and as a consequence the recognition of its presence does not necessarily denote acculturation *per se*.

Resistance of this type is a theme supported by others (notably Hingley 1997), to suggest that, far from the indigenous culture of Britain fitting into the Roman Empire, there was wholesale disruption to the lives, the geography and the power structures in the creation and maintenance of the new province. In line with Barrett's (1997) conceptions of empowerment of the people in the past, Hingley (1997) sought to place into the archaeological narrative of Roman Britain a number of voices. These could only be accessed through material remains. In so doing, he makes it clear that material culture did not project an abstract conception of identity or a sense of belonging to the Roman Empire. There are reactions to the newness of this material; in so doing Hingley (1997: 87) seeks to abandon the bipolar definition of 'Roman' and 'indigenous'. He views the grid plans of the 'civitas capitals' as a landscape of control, in contrast to the plans of the 'small towns'. These observations led towards David Mattingly's (1997, 2004) development of the concept of 'discrepant experience', in which, within colonial contexts, the discourse of the colonial writers (such as the classical authors on Druids) can be utterly different from the experience of those dominated by the colonialists. The problem for Roman Britain is the sources are stacked on the Graeco-Roman side with nothing to counteract them, and perhaps the use of resistance creates new continuities rather than inventions of traditions within the context of imperialism (see Wells 2001:124–28 for inventions of traditions via archaic styles). The important point is that the varied societies and varied groups within the hierarchical structures of those societies used material culture in quite different ways, and it would be a mistake to assume that cultural change simply trickled down from a provincial elite to the lowest levels of the hierarchy (Mattingly 1997: 16–17; substantiated by a paper by Mouritsen published later in 2005). The position is supported by some studies in *Dialogues in Roman Imperialism* that demonstrate quite different appropriations and use of Roman material culture (Mattingly 1997); others stress a more traditional position – perhaps encapsulating the situated experience of academics within a postcolonial context in the 1990s.

However, the debate is important and is influential in the study of archaeological material. In an extensive study of lighting in Roman Britain, Hella Eckardt (2002) finds that oil lamps tend to be associated with the military in forts and in the larger urban centres such as Colchester and London. She rejects this distribution pattern as evidence for 'resistance', a 'lack of Romanization' or 'failure to Romanize' (Eckardt 2002: 153–55). What her data led conclusions to show is that even where lamps were used this was for a very limited period from 43 AD to the end of the 1st century. This was not due to a lack of importation of olive oil that peaks in the 2nd century AD, but there is a need for a contextual study of the relevant types of amphorae (Eckardt 2002: 36). Hence, it would seem that lighting from oil lamps was simply not used in Britain even on military sites. This is not just true of lamps, but of other forms of what we regard as typically Roman cultural forms – for example, amphitheatres (Laurence et al 2011).

And what happened to the economy?

Michael Fulford (1989: 175) observed that: 'Our understanding of the economy of Roman Britain has surged so far ahead over the last ten to fifteen years.' Importantly, archaeological analysis of ceramics had adjusted the Finley model of the Roman economy to include the aspect of long-distance trade (Fulford 1989, 1991). It was a subject that underpinned Millett's (1990a) understanding of Romanization. Fifteen years on, Fulford (2004) surveyed the economic structures of Roman Britain more pessimistically. Little mention of the economy occurred in discussions of cultural change on the part of archaeologists concerned with resistance, agency and identity (discussed above), as the focus of discussion moved away from the structure of societies and towards the actions of individuals (for example, in Fincham 2002: 1–6). There was still plenty of evidence being accumulated (demonstrated by Fulford 2004), but what had happened? Greene (2005) analysed both the pages of *Britannia* and those of TRAC with a view to determining the position of the economy within the discipline. His study revealed that it was a subject that was marginal and mostly the concern of those working on ceramics – the subject of choice for doctoral theses in the 1970s (Greene 2005: 10–11), but not in the last decades of the 20th and first decade of the 21st centuries. This would suggest very little actual work has been conducted on the archaeology of the Roman economy. This creates the unhappy situation in which the structure of society in terms of the economy has not been investigated, evaluated and theorized to the same degree as agency or actions of individuals. Hence, although many might criticize or reject Millett's (1990a) conception of Romanization (for example, Fincham 2002: 6), implicitly the model of the structure of the economy (and thus also of society) continues to depend on this work derived from a Finley-based conception. The scale of re-evaluation of the economy by Roman historians in the first decade of the 21st century cannot be underestimated. Peregrine Horden's and Nicholas Purcell's *The Corrupting Sea* (2000) shifted the view of the entire Roman landscape towards a complex series of connected interlocking micro-regions. Re-assessment of the conceptions of Finley have been undertaken and set forth to include the incorporation of economic growth in the Roman empire (Scheidel and Von Reden 2002). Within the discipline of archaeology, Greene (2000) demonstrated Finley's total underestimation of the degree to which technological change was transferred across the empire. Importantly, for the discussion of cultural change, his view places a far greater emphasis on a second temporal phase of change after a first phase of incorporation (Greene 2000: 55). Assessments in Roman history have been made of new institutional economics and their appropriateness for application to the Roman Empire, alongside a whole debate over the ancient economy (papers in Bang et al 2006). Bang (2008) has recently developed a new conception of long-distance trade and intercity trade. To cap it all off, the publication of *The Cambridge Economic History of the Greco-Roman World* (Scheidel et al 2007) has quite simply re-configured how we think about the ancient economy. These histories tend to use archaeological evidence, but what they do not do is incorporate contemporary archaeological thought on the interpretation of cultural change – after all, the historians involved are in the business of writing economic history. It will be interesting to see what impact these new histories of the Roman economy might have in the interpretation of cultural change in Roman Britain (these developments in ancient history occurred after the publication of Mattingly 2006).

Approaches to the Romanization of Britain in the 21st century

Much of what has been discussed in the debates over the nature of the Roman impact on Britain focuses on the lives of the individuals situated in that experience. It is very much about their identities (see Gardner 2007). There is a sense that the debate has a life of its own, divorced from actual archaeological evidence that has caused avoidance of the topic or explicit rejection to draw out the 'ambiguities and complexities' of a particular site (Millett 2007b). There was more to inhabiting a place in the Roman Empire than 'how far the occupants of a settlement absorbed or rejected material symbols associated with those who held power in the Empire' (Millett 2007b). We might add here material symbols perceived by us to have been associated with those who held power. However, it is productive to discuss the impact on the landscape which includes a sense of the experience of living within a situation of cultural change. This subject has been pursued by John Wacher (2000) in his *A Portrait of Roman Britain* and by Garrick Fincham (2002) in his *Landscapes of Imperialism*. Both works emphasize the lived experience of being within the landscape, but the former is much more engaged with the impact of Rome, whereas the latter draws on postcolonial theory and writes resistance into the landscape. Fincham (2002: 6) can assert that 'acculturative Romanisation is no longer a useful concept', but we seem to be in the same place as before: the categories of 'native' and 'Roman' have not been abandoned (compare Fincham 2002 and

Millett 1990b). However, archaeologists would tell you things are now different. Looking over the decade of the 1990s, J. D. Hill (2001) saw the debate as exactly that: a debate without real substance in terms of support from studies of material remains (see Hill 2001 for references; Millett 2007b also; Laurence 2001). Hill pointed to how the study of the material culture of Britain might enrich the debate via a greater emphasis on the material culture of identities, whether based on religion, gender, age, sub-group or class, and a need to focus the debate on identity on the material culture of the body, foodways, settlement space and consumption (see discussion in Chapters 9 and 10 below).

At the end of the first decade of the 21st century, Romanization was alive and to be criticized. The opening chapter of Mattingly's *An Imperial Possession* (2006) includes a critique of Millett's 1990 conception of Romanization for the fact that emulation was a motivating force, focuses on the elite, and is a 'hang-over from the period of modern imperialism' (Mattingly 2006: 14–15). Yet there is, more than this, the conception of cultural change dependent on the local elites and their incorporation lessens the role of the Roman state in that process. What Mattingly seeks is to situate his discussion so that both parties have agency in the process of cultural change and the resultant variability, but we find in the text a duality between 'Roman and native dialogue' and landscapes of 'resistance' and of 'opportunity' (Mattingly 2006: 522). The book itself is in a historical series and stresses the concerns of the historian over those of the archaeologist; hence his conceptions of 'discrepant experience' and 'discrepant identities' within a conventional framework (Mattingly 2006: 17–18) that causes the book to feel detached from these concerns and instead we can see in the book a masterful synthesis of archaeological work on Roman Britain (Freeman 2007: 603–5 for discussion of frameworks for archaeologies of Roman Britain).

The entire subject of Roman culture as a 'global' phenomenon was discussed in a book-length study by Hingley (2005). The end result is a full review of the literature and a recognition that the empire was a world that was fragmented, in which responses to Roman culture could be and were quite different. The focus is wider than Britain and hence the variation is greater, as we shift from the lower Rhine to north-west Iberia (Hingley 2005: 102). What needs some clarification is how the cellular nature of the Roman Empire was connected together: was it just the elite who appropriated Roman culture? If so, the model of a world empire put forward by Woolf (1990) seems of some utility – particularly for ideas of the development of underdevelopment (Hingley 2005: 115–16). The connectivity of cultures leads us in a different direction from the Roman native dichotomies (that exist in the literature even if denied). Network analysis is also relevant and it should be seen as a way of establishing meaning within the patterns of material culture, as it has done for the study of the Antonine Itineraries (Graham 2005; compare approaches in S. Graham 2006; and Ruffini 2008). Hingley (2005) suggests numerous ways forward for the future, but these will need close contextual studies for them to be pursued effectively, something that Eckardt (2002: 153–55) and Hill (2001) also stress. Yet, re-reading the debate and viewing its outcome in Hingley (2005), it is striking that 1990s-style Romanization seems to survive – due to a need to rehearse its conceptions in establishing how an author is distancing their own work from it. Perhaps it is impossible to create a distance when using the term 'Romanization' at all. Even avoiding the word as Creighton does only causes him to return to it at the end of the book and to define its meaning not as a question of passive acceptance or assimilation on the part of the Iron Age elite, but as an active creation of a new society (Creighton 2000: 217, drawing on Woolf 1997). Obviously, in any change of this kind there will be winners and losers, and even those who resist change and seek to maintain continuities, real, re-invented or imagined (Wells 2001: 124–26 for examples). However, it would seem it is fundamental for Roman archaeology that in a situation of change there are multiple voices, in a way that seems strange for historians whose focus tends to be on surviving texts that speak for so few from antiquity, yet whose voices we turn into the evidence from which we might construct our historical syntheses. At the end of nearly two decades of scrutiny, it has to be concluded that Roman archaeology slips back towards a narrative of Roman and native, even if the rhetoric changes as our own modern *habitus* changes, and perhaps we should agree with Creighton (2006: 10–12) who points to the intrinsic conservatism of Roman archaeology. However, what the debate has produced is a greater awareness of this that has resulted in a re-evaluation of the conception of cultural change – some of these revisionist arguments will be found in subsequent chapters, for example Creighton's (2006) and Revell's (2009) approaches to urbanism in the next chapter. Meanwhile, for Roman historians looking into the discipline of archaeology, the message is clear: do not be deceived by the rhetoric; deep down the author is probably still relating a Roman invader to a conception of an indigenous Iron Age society.

The debate is far from over and varies currently according to whether an author is focusing on the identity and agency of the individual or the macro-structure of a world empire (Faulkner 2008). However, what has been exposed by the debate of some 20 years or more is that the issue of cultural change, when seeing agency of individuals, is not black and white but a series of grey shades that vary according to context that affects both sides of the rejected categories of Roman and indigenous (see Webster 2001 for development of this position). There is a role in all this for the Roman historian still because to create a decolonial analysis we need to shift the focus away from the analysis of two cultures and analyse 'the creation of a new imperial culture that supplanted earlier Roman cultures just as much as it did the earlier cultures of indigenous peoples' (Woolf 1997: 341) and focus much more on the structure of imperialism. More importantly, as Walter Scheidel (2004: 22–24) observes, Romanization can now be redefined by those outside the discipline of archaeology, to include both Millett's and Webster's positions (as can be seen in Scheidel 2004: 23) as a form of 'transnational extension' that forms one of the 'most important pre-conditions for successful empire building'. In so doing, Scheidel shifts away from the focus on individual groups acting differently under Rome, and returns the debate to the structure of imperialism. There will be more to come on Romanization over the years (in the meantime Faulkner 2008 or Revell 2009 are the most recent critiques). What perhaps is shifting this debate, currently, is a greater understanding of mobility and migration that is discussed further in Chapter 8 below.

Chapter 6

The Archaeologists' Roman Towns

The Roman town or city is taken for granted when we look at the Roman Empire. At the beginning of the 21st century, the place of the Romans in the formation of modern urbanism exists in the minds of most architects. Some would even say that every urban form that they see today is shaped by their knowledge of the Roman city (Rem Koolhaas et al 2001). A century ago in Britain, the Town Planning Act (1910) was passed to establish a new era of the city as distinct from the experience of the city under industrialization in the 19th century. It was also in the same year that Town Planning conferences were held in both Berlin and London. At the latter, Francis Haverfield presented a lecture on Town Planning under Roman rule (Haverfield 1911b; Freeman 2007: 334–42). The lecture became a book that was illustrated with numerous plans of cities, mostly defined by their walled circuits of defences (Haverfield 1913), a format that was to be expanded with the advent of aerial photography (Ward-Perkins 1974) and for which there is still a market (Owens 1991). It was possible to read the expansion of Roman urbanism from these studies as a key feature of 'Romanization'. However, those working later in the 20th century on pre-Roman archaeology in Gaul and Britain realized that the hill forts might have displayed features of what could be described as urbanism or proto-urbanism (Cunliffe and Rowley 1976; Collis 1984; Wells, 1984; Audouze and Buchenschutz 1991). Underpinning this discussion was an assertion that there were towns north of the Alps prior to the appearance of Rome. However, there was also a recognition that these settlements displayed considerable diversity. Sites vary from two hectares to 350 or even 650 hectares, so whether or not to define a site as urban is problematic (see Woolf 1993 for full critique). Interestingly, the literature on these Iron Age forms of urbanism places a different emphasis from that found in the literature on the Roman city. It is profoundly different from the Moses Finley economic model of urbanism (discussed in Chapter 5) and emphasizes instead a link between urbanism and commerce, political centralization, industrial growth, occupational specialization and zoning. Towns and Romanization were demonstrated to fit together, whereas outside the boundaries of the Roman Empire in the west lay a region of barbarians without towns, supported by reference to Tacitus' account of his father-in-law promoting and encouraging the Britons to build towns (Tac. *Agr.* 21). Ideas from the past do not simply go away but instead creep back in through footnotes and references (or can be re-invented through the absence of reference even). John Creighton (2006: 71–78) shows how within the discipline of archaeology, the treatment of towns in Roman Britain shifts over the course of the last decades of the 20th century from a position whereby the governor and/or the military promoted towns, to a situation in which the native elite adopted the town as a format for the expression of their power (for example, in Millett 1990a). Yet, the structure of discussion divides the evidence for towns via legal definitions of *coloniae*, *municipia* and *civitates*, mapping onto modern concepts of regional centres (*civitas capitals*) and small towns. These definitions come from much earlier scholarship, but are maintained in the 21st century (for example, Revell 2009), as is an emphasis on the legal structuring of power in the larger towns that is seen to have conformed to the town charters found in the Roman province of Baetica in southern Spain (Revell 2009: 50–54). It has to be said though that Baetica has a far higher density of towns than found in Britain and also a much higher density of inscriptions. In the past, individual types of towns could be studied, for example *coloniae* (see papers in Hurst 1999) or the smaller towns or *vici* of an individual province (Burnham and Wacher 1990; Whittaker 1990), to produce an overview of a group of settlements with similar characteristics. What we are now seeing in the 21st century is a move away from these types of studies towards a detailed discussion of a number of towns and juxtaposing these with each other. For example, Creighton (2006) picked out contrasting examples from Britain, whereas Louise Revell (2009) chose sites from Spain and Britain with high incidences of excavated public spaces and survival of inscriptions. These studies tend to draw out the variety of forms in terms of urban ideology, urban experience or urban ways of living found in quite diverse settlements. What we will look at in this chapter is the interpretation of a number of Roman towns and their associated public spaces, and examine approaches to this material that focus on the actions of individuals (or their agency) within a local context (or structure). It is an approach that can be applied to other archaeological sites that are open to interpretation.

The violence of monuments

Looking at the towns of Roman Britain, both Tacitus (*Agr.* 21) and modern scholars concur that the Britons were willing to spend money building forms that were familiar within the Mediterranean core of the Roman Empire. There is a sense in all cases that what they were building was not quite what Tacitus thought urbanism should be, but also a realization that the town was the locale in which cultural change was most visible – familiar to the visiting governor and his entourage while being alien, strange and novel to distant farmers visiting the same town to attend an annual religious festival. Drawing on recent approaches to agency, Creighton (2006: 83–86) suggests that what we see in the construction of towns in Britain during the Flavian period is the use of knowledge of what a town could be. Creighton makes a comparison with my own interpretation of the archaeology of the town of Pompeii (Laurence 1994), from which he can establish that the feature that made a town Roman was 'a series of arenas in which individuals repeatedly recalled and reaffirmed their position within the local social structure and their place in the empire' (Creighton 2006: 86). This might be described as a Mediterranean model of urbanism, the direct knowledge of which was experienced by very few residents in Britain apart from the regular migration of the governor and his staff. In addition to this group of migrants, Creighton (2006: 86–92) draws in the regular discharge of veterans (400–800 legionaries per annum) whose experience of communal living for 20 years of their adult life had been within Roman forts and a similar spatial format to that of Pompeii, but with a quite different social structure, even if both situations were hierarchical (Figure 6.1). Yet it is necessary, perhaps, to add an experience of urbanism to Creighton's veterans' understanding of urbanism. All would have had memories of their past prior to recruitment into the legions and these would have included an idea of urban living, an experience of living in a city or in contact with a city, all of which had been learnt in childhood. These memories of experience would not have been standard for any group of veterans, whose communal living for their adult lives was focused on the Roman fortress. The after-life of Roman forts that were transformed into colonies (for example, at Wroxeter or Colchester, discussed by Creighton 2006: 108–22) has an order to it that creates centres of amenity, in ways that are dissimilar to the pattern of public buildings found at Pompeii, where the new amenities, including an amphitheatre, were fitted around what were recognizable features of urbanism under the gaze of the new inhabitants whose experience of military life had been but a few years, in contrast to the veterans of the empire who served for 20 years (Figure 6.2). Yet, there are similarities between the two colonial contexts: in Pompeii a new temple dominated the skyline, while the amphitheatre provided an arena for punishing criminals by definition that could have included the opponents of Sulla (i.e. most of

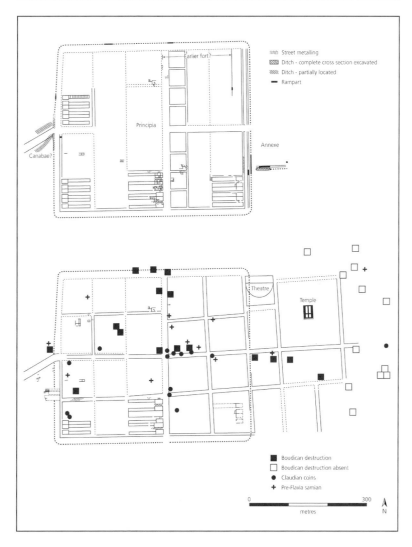

Street metalling
Ditch - complete cross section excavated
Ditch - partially located
Rampart

Earlier fort?

Principia

Annexe

Canabae?

Theatre

Temple

Boudican destruction
Boudican destruction absent
Claudian coins
Pre-Flavia samian

0   300
metres   N

Figure 6.1 Colchester: plans showing the transformation from military base to Roman city

the population of Pompeii who had opposed Sulla and Rome in the Social War); whereas at Colchester, a temple to the emperor was constructed that became the focus of the Boudiccan revolt against Rome in 60 AD. The monuments found at both locations, but at different times, point to a domination and subjection of a segment of the local population by

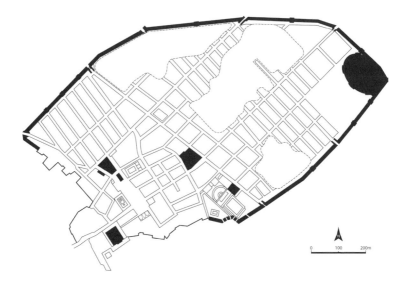

Figure 6.2 Pompeii: monuments built at time of the settlement of Sullan verterans shown in black

Figure 6.3 Pompeii: the Sullan Amphitheatre encapsulates the dominance and violence of monumental building

another (Figure 6.3). It should be stressed that at Pompeii, the veterans did not use a different material culture or architecture from the inhabitants; they were of the same culture and, within 70 years, we can see the disappearance of the Oscan language at Pompeii in favour of Latin. Amphitheatres were built in other colonies of veterans founded by Sulla and are a monument seen as being linked to this phenomenon (Welch 2007).

However, Katherine Welch (2007: 88–90) suggests that the pattern is more complicated than this and that we should include consideration of not just colonies but also of older Latin and Roman colonies and some *municipia*. She suggests that these structures when they appear in Cales or Capua or Teanum in Campania could be seen as signs of 'self-Romanization' and signs of allegiance to Rome on the part of these independent communities (Welch 2007: 90). This explanation has been applied to the spread of the basilica in the 2nd century BC in Italian towns. However, underpinning the argument is a duality between Rome and, let us say, Cales or Capua or the Roman veterans settled in Pompeii and the town's inhabitants that in the light of the debate over Romanization (see Chapter 5) should be resisted. Instead, we need to view the context of the turmoil of the 1st century BC in Italy. Italy was composed of a series of cities allied to Rome. Within any city we can assume there was a debate over the acceptance of the rule of Rome in the context of the social war and the civil wars. There were towns that opposed Sulla and the Roman state, such as Norba or Palestrina, and there were towns that did not. Regardless of their opposition or acquiescence to Rome, there were plenty of enemies of Rome and her allied states. Punishment of enemies could have taken place in the forum, of course, but increasingly stone amphitheatres were built for this purpose through the 1st century BC and the 1st century AD (Jouffroy 1986: 321). The correlation between phases of political instability or perceptions of instability and amphitheatre construction at an empirical level is impossible, since the former is a permanent feature of the historical record (including that of the age of Augustus). The civil wars in the aftermath of Caesar's death resulted in the mass settlement of veterans in colonies and these colonies included, in many cases, amphitheatres – for example in places as distant as Mérida and Aosta. In Rome itself, the first stone amphitheatre was constructed in 30 BC (Welch 2007: 102–27). The new order emerging from the terror of the civil wars also created purpose-built venues to view the destruction of enemies of the state. Another period of civil war in 69 AD produce the Colosseum – the canonical form for the Roman amphitheatre (Welch 2007: 128–62). This monument is written into a change of government from the oppression of Nero into the oppression of the Flavians, and an ideological transition from the rule of Nero to that of a new regime (Welch 2007: 158–61). Spectacles in the amphitheatre needed a regular supply of criminals and enemies of the state, whether they were those captured in war or enemies from within the Roman state.

The discussion above on the violence of monuments shifted from Roman Britain under the Flavians to Pompeii more than 150 years earlier and ended with discussion of Flavian Rome. What it allowed for was a discussion of how we talk about monuments and the violent association of these types of buildings with veteran soldiers. It was about the comparison of two quite different types of monument associated with a specific group of inhabitants. Yet, what it demonstrated was that it was not just veterans in colonies that were associated with amphitheatres in the Republic, but another group of allies to Rome who had enemies to punish and wished to do so with their fellow citizens present in amphitheatres. These monuments delineated communities into citizens and criminals/traitors. In Colchester, it was not an amphitheatre that was the monument at the centre of this delineation of Roman and other but a temple. This, to my mind, need not matter – monuments are *foci* for identity; the Roman amphitheatre provides an extreme example because it allows for the viewing of the destructive power of the state and the humiliation and annihilation of enemies. Monuments become the sites of cultural memory and can accumulate meaning; they can be symbols of conquest, metaphors for oppression and sites of revolt. In terms of Roman urbanism, the monument was the site or place at which identity was performed and articulated. These architecturally prominent places are also sites of continuity over time and become associated with the routines of the city. Not every Roman city has an amphitheatre, but every Roman city has at least one monument that was the site at which identity, memory and history were conceptualized.

The urban experience

The opening pages from a recent book by Louise Revell highlights a problem for anyone looking at the many excavated remains of Roman towns: they look similar but turn out on closer inspection to be quite different. This causes Revell (2009) to identify a paradoxical discourse that causes the global and local situations to intersect and to produce a variety of outcomes. This is also a conclusion of a group of students on Harvard University's Masters in Architecture programme mentored by Rem Koolhaas: for them the Roman city is 100 per cent local and 100 per cent global (Koolhaas et al 2001). Embracing this conception allows archaeologists to choose examples and juxtapose them to ensure that the urban history being produced ensures that the context of the examples under discussion is kept in mind, but is constantly eroded via the citation of contrasting examples to it. This is a modern discourse on the city that actively resists a grand-narrative of the urbanization of the Roman West. Yet within these studies patterns can emerge. Revell's (2009) focus is upon the architecture and associated inscriptions that place the figure of the emperor, not seen in actuality, and the gods at the centre of urban living. What is shared between cities is a similar range of imagery that was experienced through seeing, from which a conception of the global figures of gods and emperors could be conceptualized. The intersection of the local community with these imagined figures was encapsulated via the magistrates, who also had a religious role in the community, the various priesthoods and individual actions of a religious nature that can be identified in inscriptions (Revell 2009). Manifestations of the conceptualization of these figures structure the form of urbanism and include the building of temples, calendars listing festivals and theatres for staging dramatizations of mythology. However, what they all share is a discursive practice that focuses on a global conception of these unseen figures that shapes the form of each individual town or city.

The relationship of the individuals within a community to the physical form of the city needs some discussion in this context. In antiquity, cities were not simply seen as 'places', but were also sacred sites that had a mythology, a history and an expectation of continuity in the future (Laurence 1996; Revell 2009: 100–1). The cities were sacred sites that shared a similar language in the form of the architecture of theatres, fora, amphitheatres, statues and so on that articulated the relationship between the inhabitants and the metaphysical beings in the form of gods, the emperor and the individual cities. For those born into these environments, they learnt the city as they grew up and became citizens of that place. Their agency was structured by the environment they were born into, and they became active agents in the maintenance and survival of the city into the future (Laurence 2007; Laurence et al 2011). As adults, these individuals (or a selection of them as magistrates), had the agency to incorporate the present situation into the fabric of the city through the process of euergetism (gift-giving in return for status enhancement) and thus altering the fabric of the city for the future generation and the structure of society into which their grandchildren would be born. The survival of these actions in the archaeological record is incomplete – both in terms of the survival of monuments and inscriptions, and in terms of the ephemeral nature of endowed banquets (see Patterson 2006: 169–76). The dominant idiom for this incorporation that is recognizable in the archaeological record is the architecture, the statues and the inscriptions – it is a global phenomenon. However, the meanings associated with these features of a city might be quite different according to the understanding of these items at the local level. Before leaving this subject, it has to be said that the addition of a religious structure, let's say a temple, to the fabric of the city was also an alteration to the spatial structure of the city. If it was located on a new site, away from the existing concentrations of religious buildings, processions might pass between these two points. The route of the procession might later be enhanced with statues and inscriptions and incorporated into the physical shape of space within the city as a prominent route. Nevertheless, religious space, in this context, should not be isolated to the temples themselves but spills over into the other parts of the city as Guy Rogers (1991) shows in connection with Ephesus, and Revell (2009: 137–42) demonstrates with reference to Italica. Whatever the conception of meaning to the rituals enacted (and they certainly varied from city to city), these actions shaped the city and their alteration in form re-shaped the city.

The concept of urban change

Archaeologists, like historians, can get very involved in cataloguing changes to cities from their origins through to late antiquity. In setting out these changes in a chronological framework or narrative of an individual city, there is a tendency to lose sight of urban change as a phenomenon. This is partly due to a need within the literature to discuss urban change in relation to other major debates, not least that of cultural change and identity formation discussed in the previous chapter. What is clear though is that the experience of urbanism in the Roman Empire included the experience of urban change and that change – for example, in the characterization of Pompeii (Laurence 2007), of St Bertrand-de-Comminges (Esmonde Cleary 2008) or of Colchester (Creighton 2006: 110–19) – was a fundamental part of what made a city. Archaeologists recover changes when excavating remains or studying standing buildings, but they do not necessarily see change as a phenomenon or characteristic that defines urbanism. The speed of urban change at individual sites can be impressive. Just think of Pompeii in 70 BC: the entire fabric of the city was remodelled via the building of new monuments – an amphitheatre, a covered theatre, a set of baths, a new temple of Venus – and the town's name had also changed. The population had also incorporated a few thousand new inhabitants – Sulla's veterans – and the Latin language was becoming dominant. Looking at things over a longer time frame, we can see at Pompeii by 79 AD the transformation of the forum, the development of baths with large panes of window glass and the introduction of the figure of the emperor into the urban landscape. We could add to this viewpoint of change a whole range of new products for consumption (see Laurence 2009a for discussion). Not everything was new though: in the 1st century AD, descendants of the pre-Sullan inhabitants could re-invent the usage of Oscan inscriptions to highlight their claim to a longer cultural heritage (Adams 2007: 67–68; 441–43). These changes can be identified within the archaeological record and create a vision of novelty that can be found not just in the cities of remote provinces, but also at the very heart of the empire. The speed of change is particularly difficult to measure, but varied from that found at Ostia during the city's expansion in the 2nd century AD (Meiggs 1973: 64–65; for publications in English on the stratigraphy at Ostia see Martin 1999; DeLaine and Wilkinson 1999; Jansen 1999) and that found in cities of Italy over the 3rd century AD. What is perhaps clearer is that, regardless of the speed of change and its variation from city to city, all inhabitants within the Roman Empire experienced some form of urban change and were conscious via collective memory of changes in the past, particularly if reminded by inscriptions associated with buildings and/or the statues of those involved.

Turning to an example from the Eastern Mediterranean, it is possible to see how urban change can be initiated within an already existing urban environment. The city of Perge in Pamphylia (modern Turkey) lies 12 miles inland on the river Kestros. Unlike the examples from Colchester, or to a lesser extent Pompeii, the new monuments in Perge are associated with inscriptions detailing who constructed the monuments. What we find when looking at these developments is that it was a very narrow group of families that rebuilt Perge under the emperors. Excavations from the 1950s onwards have revealed the extent of the city and have caused Perge to become a place in which monuments, their associated inscriptions and sculpture can be studied in context. The sculpture from the site is remarkable and can be seen on display in Antalya's archaeological museum. Nearly all of it dates from the 2nd century AD, when Perge began a programme of city reconstruction using imported marble for the first time (Boatwright 1993: 197).

Within the south gateway was a u-shaped courtyard that formed a monumental framework for niches on which sculpture was placed in the manner of the *scaenae frons* of the theatre, upon which were displayed gods and local heroes (Boatwright 1991, 1993 provides detailed analysis, much of which is followed here – Figure 6.4). Among which can be found reference to 'city founders' of the 2nd century AD: M. Plancius Varus and C. Plancius Varus; the former is also mentioned as the father of Plancia Magna and the latter is her brother. The u-shaped courtyard was delineated at its open end by a triumphal arch dedicated by Plancia Magna to her *patria* with a range of the imperial family included: the contemporary – Hadrian and Sabina Augusta dated to 121 AD; and those of the past – Nerva and Trajan, alongside Trajan's wife Plotina, his sister Marciana and his niece

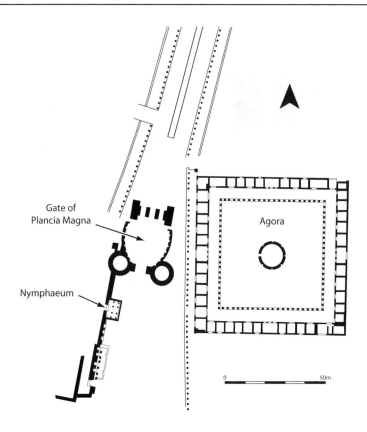

Figure 6.4 Perge: plan of the location of Plancia Magna's gate adjacent to the Agora

Matidia, who was also Hadrian's mother-in-law. The monument does not follow conventions; it is dedicated to the local city/*patria* rather than the emperors in the inscription, but the visual imagery conforms to the expectation of the decoration of arches – the new rulers of the Roman Empire. More remarkably, maybe, is that she dedicated the arch in her own name alone, rather than with a male relative. Interestingly, Mary Boatwright (1993: 200) notes that the city's *ordo* or council set up statues of her and commemorated her in one as daughter of M. Plancius Varus and in another as daughter of her *patria* of Perge. She was also a priestess in the imperial cult and of Artemis Pergaia. The connection between her local city and the empire is made real through a realization that she was married to C. Iulius Cornutus Tertullus and the mother of C. Iulius Plancius Varus Cornutus: both were senators (Van Bremen 1996: 105).

Figure 6.5 Aspendos: the *scaenae frons* of the theatre, contemporary with that at Perge, with space for the placement of sculpture

However, evidence for this does not appear to come from the monumental rebuilding of the southern entrance to the city – Plancia acts alone. She is a reminder, just like Eumachia in Augustan Pompeii, that women had agency in antiquity and, if they were priestesses, had considerable status and even resources that could be spent on the redevelopment of the city. Looking at the surviving sculpture, of which there is a lot, among the gods, goddesses, emperors and their female relatives there are quite a number of dressed women, including Plancia, but few men of a similar status (Özgür 1996 for catalogue and plan locating sculptures).

Beyond this monumental gateway lay a monumental street that bisects the lower part of the city. It was begun under the Emperor Tiberius, when a monumental street was constructed leading down to the city's southern gate (Abbasoğlu 2001 for fuller description). This was no ordinary street: in its final form, it included colonnades and a large water channel running down its centre that terminated in fountains (nymphaea) at the entrance to the city (Figure 6.6), close to the baths dedicated to the emperor Vespasian by the Roman citizens, the *ordo* of decurions (town councillors) and the republic of Perge or the *Ci(ves) R(omani) et ordo et res publica Pergesium*. What is unclear is whether the Roman citizens were immigrants or locals who were citizens. However, whatever their origin,

Figure 6.6 Perge: monumental street at Perge with water channel in its centre

these were a separate group higher in the pecking order than the local town councillors on the *ordo*. The final form of this street was only fully realized in the 2nd century. There is a sense of renewal to the city that can also be located in the renewal of the *scaenae frons* of the theatre, originally built by senator Marcus Plancius Rutilius Varus in Nero's reign. The scale of this project can be seen today in Antalya's archaeological museum, where nearly every piece of sculpture is from Perge and a near complete *scaenae frons* can be reconstructed (Öztürk 2009). In the 3rd century, we find inscriptions from Perge that refer to the city as the greatest of Pamphylia, and look back to the establishment of the imperial cult centre there from the time of Vespasian, a place where the governor held assizes, a metropolis (Roueché 1989; Abbasoğlu 2001: 173–75). It has to be noted that it is in the 2nd century that there is a notion of cities being categorized as 'greatest', 'greater' and 'others' (Roueché 1989: 217 on basis of *Dig.* 27.1.6.2). A city, such as Perge, wished to be the greatest and its inhabitants wished to be from one of the greatest cities – especially if they were senators. This notion that had developed by the 2nd century AD was a motor for urban renewal, and is confirmed within Pausanias' discussion of cities in his 2nd century guide to Greece (10.4) by an expectation of seeing in the greater and greatest cities sufficient numbers of public buildings. This has some relevance, since many pilgrims came to the temple of Artemis and they entered the city through an entranceway funded by the priestess of Artemis, Plancia Magna, and saw an honorific arch that was dedicated to the city they were visiting – Perge paid for by 'a daughter' of the city, Plancia Magna (for sources for pilgrims to Perge, see Rigsby 1996: 449–52; Jones 1999: 13–17; see papers in Elsner and

Figure 6.7 Perge: statue of a 2nd century AD woman (193cm tall) from the monumental nymphaeum north of Plancia's gate (see Figure 6.4 for location)

Rutherford 2005). Agency of the individual is bound together with their *habitus* in a place made famous as a place of worship, and their role in the worship of Artemis. This factor explains perhaps the absence of statuary representing human males (apart from emperors) from the entrance to the city and the presence of females in the reshaping of Perge.

Spatial archaeology and the Roman city

Roman towns and cities come in a variety of forms. Some have walls around the inhabited space (such as Falerii Novi), others have no walls (such as Jublains), and some expanded beyond the original walled area (for example, Timgad). The straight streets and right-angles at which the streets appear to meet might suggest there is a common design to Roman cities. Yet, over the course of the last two decades, archaeologists have developed new ways to analyse the layout of a Roman city with its grid. The impetus for this work came from William MacDonald's (1986) observation that the most fully preserved Roman cities of North Africa in particular did not produce an even distribution of monuments across the grid of streets. Instead, he suggested that key routes accumulated functions and caused such streets to become central routes or what he called armatures. These routes accumulated not just functions, but became preferred routes on which to build new monuments, thus further enhancing their importance in terms of cityscape. This phenomenon found in the ancient world has, subsequently, been established in modern cities – for example, the route of the annual London Marathon has become a corridor of redevelopment and is now associated with prestigious architectural development. These observations shifted attention from the monuments studied as individual items of architecture to a study of streets and the arrangement of monuments and activities within space.

Spatial organization can be interrogated in a number of ways. The first is to look at the actual layout of the streets and to consider how the layout of the city affects the use of space. The underlying natural topography can cause any part of it to become more prominent than others. Hence, a contour map allows us as viewers to understand the nature of the cityscape – something to be seen from afar that could influence a visitor's or traveller's conception of the city prior to arrival. The number of gates and their position in the walls of a city are fundamental factors in the organization of space within the city because the flow of traffic into and out of the city was channelled through roads leading to gates. If the city was constructed on a major road, it is worth looking at the role of this long-distance route in the layout of the grid. For example, we might expect to see forms of ribbon development along a major road and it is worth looking to see if

Figure 6.8 Minturnae: The Via Appia forms an armature through the city on which statues were erected and monuments placed

these appear in the archaeological record. The city of Minturnae on the Via Appia expanded via the construction of a Forum outside the walls of the *castrum* with ribbon development along the road running through the city to the wooden bridge across the river Liris (Figures 6.8 and 6.9). Other small nucleated settlements in the form of *castra* expanded in a similar fashion – as can be seen from an examination of the plan of Ostia.

Nowhere has space been studied with a greater impetus than at Pompeii. A key problem, of course, is that Pompeii was destroyed by the eruption of Vesuvius, during which pyroclastic surges moved objects, destroyed the upper floors of houses and disrupted the pattern of the archaeological record. However, what that process also reveals is that there is more information available on where thresholds to doors were found, the nature of road surfaces, and the overall spatial organization of a single city (Laurence 2007). The subject has been developed to new levels of sophistication with whole volumes devoted to the subject matter (Laurence and Newsome 2011). Underpinning this work lies a whole series of detailed analyses of the streets of the city. There is much fascination in bringing to life the streets of the city – through, for example, a study of wheel-ruts to develop our understanding of traffic flow or even now the prevention of traffic flow (Poehler 2006). The wheel-ruts can be seen and measured (Figure 6.10), but it is a conceptual leap to move from reporting your survey of these to discussing how we should interpret the

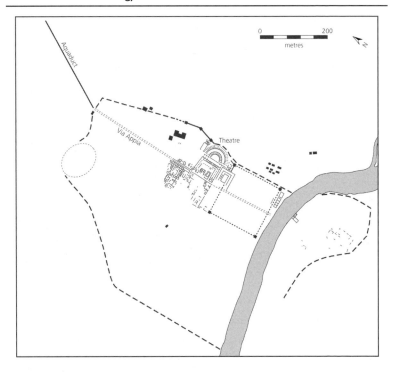

Figure 6.9 Minturnae: plan of the development of the city that is focused on the linear route (the Via Appia) through the city

pattern and to make statements about how traffic flowed through the city. Indeed, there is an ongoing debate that has shifted in the past five years from seeking a means to understand how traffic was facilitated by local government (Poehler 2006; van Tilburg 2007: 127–70; Beard 2008: 65–72 for a light-hearted discussion; interestingly, the question of why ruts should be studied has been used in University of Oxford entrance interviews) to seeing vehicle traffic in the street as an undesirable element within the urban environment (see papers in Laurence and Newsome 2011). However, an important element of the city is identified here – movement and the flow of people that requires study and is an aspect of ancient urbanism of as much interest as the building of amphitheatres.

Underpinning studies of urban space in Pompeii and, to an extent, Ostia lies a powerful body of theory developed in the late 1970s and 1980s by the Bartlett School of Architecture at University College London under the direction of Bill Hillier (Hillier and Hanson 1986 is the best known work). It is known in the literature by the umbrella term 'space syntax' which has made an impact across archaeology, but it is at sites of

Figure 6.10 Pompeii: wheel-ruts and crossing stones in Via degli Augustali

exceptional recovery, particularly of thresholds of buildings and plans (that at least for their ground floor level are virtually complete), that we find the largest number of applications. The underpinning technique involved in this form of analysis is to focus on the connections between spaces, rather than focusing on rooms within a building. This can result in counterintuitive discoveries and others that would seem obvious with reference to rooms in atrium houses (Grahame 2000), but can allow us also to ascertain how the salvage and rebuilding of houses was undertaken to facilitate continuity of usage (Anderson 2011). Underpinning such studies is mathematical analysis that allows for comparison between structures that appear different in plan but in terms of the connections between spaces may actually be quite similar, as Janet DeLaine (2004) discovered in her study of the apartments of Ostia which should relate to domestic structures in Pompeii (Figures 6.11 and 6.12). These structures appear to be perceptually different in plan and in the experience of visiting them on site, yet spatially they are very similar. This allows us to see less of a disconnection between the architecture of 1st century Pompeii and that of 2nd century Ostia.

Figure 6.11 Pompeii: looking out to the street from the *atrium*, note the *lararium* or shrine of the household gods on the right of the entrance. Spatially the *atrium* house has much in common with the apartments of Ostia, compare Figure 6.12. These similarities are only revealed through the mathematical calculation of their space syntax

Figure 6.12 Ostia: insula blocks may appear distinct from the low-rise accommodation in Pompeii, but spatially the apartments of Ostia have much in common with the houses of Pompeii – compare Figure 6.11. These similarities are only revealed through the mathematical calculation of their space syntax

Figure 6.13 Pompeii: a water fountain narrows the street and draws attention to the house behind

The techniques of space syntax also allow us to study the city plan in greater depth, particularly in the evaluation of urban change over time. David Newsome (2009) examined the closure of streets leading into the forum of Pompeii in the Augustan period with a view to explaining how this would have affected traffic flow. The closure of streets had an effect on traffic not just in the street that was closed but on all other streets in the city (Figure 6.13), thus causing those who owned property to adjust the focus of activities in response to the alteration of space. This shifts the analysis onto a new level that encapsulates a comparison between the two situations to evaluate how the alteration of the configuration of the grid of streets would have altered traffic flow in all its parts. It should be noted also that the alteration of the forum disrupted the flow of drainage as well as that of traffic (Poehler 2011). The strength of the space syntax approach can be seen in two books devoted to streets and their interpretation in 2011 (Kaiser 2011b; Weilguni 2011). The whole subject of the streets and their definition in relation to traffic continues to be revised (Kaiser 2011a and papers in Laurence and Newsome 2011).

Roman urbanism

The discussion in this chapter has set out some lines of research into the Roman city that show a progression from description towards analysis of patterns of behaviour. Inevitably, there is much to write about the material culture found within the urban context that could include colour, lighting, production, animals, gender, foodways and a host of other subjects – since the city/town is the most complex human artefact and was the place with the greatest materiality in the Roman Empire. Hence, the city continues to provide archaeology with an endless range of opportunities to contribute to the history of the city. The bibliography that has developed over the last 30 years or so demonstrates a strength of this developing area that in the 1980s had been characterized by city-country relationships (but see Millett 2011 for reconfiguration). The analysis, today, of Roman urbanism has shifted to include a far wider remit and this is most clearly seen in the study of Pompeii. The fact that other sites may have been neglected (including Ostia) in favour of further work on Pompeii points up the need for the diffusion of techniques and researchers across the cities of the Roman Empire to create a fuller bibliography that might truly go 'beyond Pompeii' (see papers in Corsi and Vermeulen 2011; Laurence and Newsome 2011).

Chapter 7

Military and Civilian

Re-interpreting the Roman Fort at Vindolanda

The archaeology of the Roman military, unlike in some other areas, integrates the written record, whether in literary texts, epigraphy or on papyri and writing tablets, with the archaeological evidence from surveys and excavations. The scale of the enterprise should not be under-estimated, since there is an abundance of documentary material that reveals the everyday experience in the military (see Campbell 1996; Fink 1971; Bowman and Thomas 1983, 1994; Bowman 1994; Salway 1965 is still fundamental for the study of epigraphy). This evidence provides a more informed textual context to approach archaeological material, yet there is no certainty regarding, for example, the dating of the writing tablets from Vindolanda and relating these to the archaeological evidence from the site itself. This should not diminish the value of this evidence from Vindolanda for the elucidation of the social system within the fort that included evidence for married officers, their families and slaves. However, the editors of the tablets took care to place women and children not connected to officers outside of the fortress in the *vicus* or nearby civilian settlement (Bowman and Thomas 1994). More importantly, the existence of these letters leads to the realization of the social and cultural changes (and also of that to the landscape) that were felt in the north of the province of Britannia at the end of the 1st and beginning of the 2nd century AD (Haynes 2002). The engagement with these changes was total for the soldier, as can be seen in the writing tablets from Vindolanda, but for the natives or civilians of the region, their conception of these changes may have been quite different resulting at best in a partial engagement with the cultural landscape that was dominated by the soldiers on the frontiers and their needs. Roman social historians tend not to focus on the history of the military, and leave such matters alone or to persons who might be described as military historians interested in the logistics, strategy and tactics of fighting for the empire. However, we need to accept that there is a social history to be written and the archaeological evidence from Roman forts can provide a means to opening up the Roman fort as a milieu for sociological analysis. The first step to doing so is to alter our preconceptions of these forts and to accept that these form archaeological locales for the exploration of all the issues that might be evaluated in the study of civilian sites from the Mediterranean – for example, at Pompeii.

Historians are very familiar with the concept of a division in Roman society between those in the army and those who may be classified as civilian. The military was a different situation or different form of *habitus* from that experienced by the civilians in the Roman empire, symbolized and exemplified perhaps by the soldier wearing a sword and sword belt (Haynes 1999a). Soldiers, particularly in the empire, have been conceptualized as existing or *being* in a different *habitus*, that of being a soldier. Their difference is also encountered in Roman law, and a provision from the time of Augustus that soldiers could not enter into marriage in the same way that civilians did (see Scheidel 2007 for discussion). This distinction on marriage has in the past been interpreted within Roman archaeology as a simple ban on not just marriage but any form of cohabitation, and has caused interpretations of military archaeology to become focused on the male gender of the soldiers, their equipment and the organizational structure of the army as a whole. Underpinning the conceptual difference is not just this, but also a tradition of study that need not fully engage with the premises of social history and social archaeology. The separation of the archaeology of the Roman military from the history and archaeology of Roman civilians is unhelpful and is challenged by the evidence produced at military sites and through analysis that links explanations of the archaeology of the military to the civilian sphere. Some of these are discussed in this chapter in connection with the interpretation of the early 2nd century Roman fort at Vindolanda (Figure 7.1). Other material is easy to locate, but what I wish to set out here, quite briefly, is the scale of re-interpretation that is required to enable the re-engagement of the archaeological evidence for the military with current preoccupations in Roman social history and social archaeology.

Gender and space

The first preconception that needs to be challenged is that the area of land bounded by the ditches of the fort was in some way exclusive to the military. Dick Whittaker (2002: 210) discussed the supply of materials to forts and pointed out that in the Vindolanda writing tablets there was evidence for civilians and soldiers working together, but no evidence for civilians within the fort itself. This causes him to view the space within the fort as exclusive to the military, whereas the *vici* or civilian settlements that

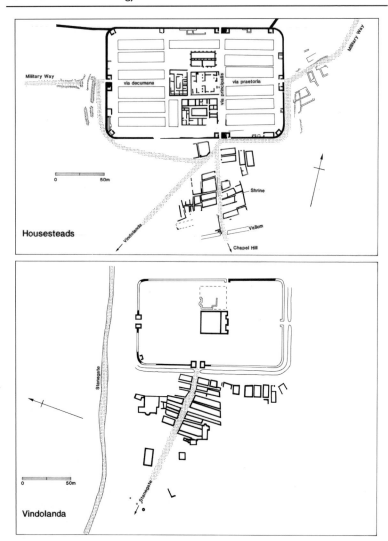

Figure 7.1 A comparison of the fort and *vicus* at Vindolanda and Housesteads
(figure provided by Jim Crow)

grew up outside the forts were the *locale* in which soldiers and civilians
interacted. For him, these were places that provided supplementary goods,
homes and employment for veterans, and the locations 'for communications
with the local population (especially with women)' (Whittaker 2002: 217).
Such a view can be found across the literature on forts, but it flies in the

face of evidence from Vindolanda that was published in the 1990s. Carroll van Driel-Murray (1993, 1998, 2001) studied the abundant deposit of leather from water-logged archaeological contexts from the fort at Vindolanda and provided the analysis that has fundamentally altered our conception of the population of forts and of the Roman military as a whole. The material astonished scholars. There was evidence for the nature of army tents, alongside a large assemblage of shoes from stratified contexts from which a chronological investigation of the body of material could be developed. What she found was that there were not just shoes that were of an appropriate size for male adult soldiers, but there were also shoes in styles and sizes for women, and for children (for methodology see Groeneman-Van Waateringe 1978). In the short period from the fort's construction from about 80 AD or shortly after to 120 AD, there was a change in the composition of the material that pointed to an increase in the number of women and children in the fort over time. Van Driel-Murray (1993: 31) regarded this as an increasing inclusion of civilians within the fort, in a process that could be described as the civilianization of what was initially an installation built by the military. A more recent study of jewellery from the fort and external settlement (*vicus*) at Vindolanda (Birley and Greene 2006, compare Henig 1975) confirmed this pattern derived from the study of shoe sizes. Women and children lived in the fort. For UK-based historians and archaeologists, this was difficult to accept, but as van Driel-Murray (1998) pointed out in a subsequent paper, this refusal to accept the archaeological evidence for children and women in the fort derived from modern conceptions of the military forts as spaces in which men should exclusively interact with other men. In doing so, she presented numerous parallels from both Dutch and British military practices to demonstrate how modern preconceptions of gender and military space created a Roman military in an image of the modern British practices of the mid-20th century.

The combination of palaeodemography derived from the study of footwear and the tablets found at Vindolanda allows us to consider the nature of family structure within an auxiliary fort. At the top of the hierarchy of command that coincided with status and with wealth was Flavius Cerealis and his wife Sulpicia Lepidina in the early 2nd century AD (Allason-Jones 1999: 41–43 for further examples of Roman commanders and wives in Britannia). The footwear associated with this time period establishes that they had children living with them at the following ages: two, four or five, five and between seven and ten years old (van Driel-Murray 1993: 44–45). Whether the children were their own or belonged to slaves living in the household cannot be known (Bowman 1994: 5–8 for discussion of house-hold structure). However, the combination of 60 texts relating to this *familia* found at Vindolanda (Bowman and Thomas 1994: texts 225–94) presents us with knowledge of their household structure and the physical layout of the building in which they lived, and provides us with one of the fullest accounts of domestic setting of a Roman equestrian *familia* from the whole Roman Empire (Holder 1982: 64–65). However, the excavated remains of the Praetorium from Vindolanda are not contemporary with this time and date from after 300 AD (Birley et al 1999), but they can be linked to the occupation of the fragmentary plan of the *principia* of stone fort 1 built with stucco decoration, Corinthian capitals from columns and associated with the find of a statue base (Bidwell 1985).

For those living in the barracks, living conditions varied. The officer's or centurion's quarters took up about a third of the barrack block in a space about eight metres by ten to 12 metres, and was designed with a view to making provision for the housing of a wife and children, who moved with the officer as he changed postings (Allason-Jones 1999: 43–44). Building XIII at the fort of Housesteads provides one of the best excavated bodies of material for the understanding of the dynamics of a barrack block (Rushworth 2009). The centurion's quarters – nine metres by ten metres – was constructed to include a hearth in its earliest Hadrianic phase, but the space was always subject to alteration through the use of internal partition walls (Rushworth 2009: 272). It is interesting to note that the accommodation for centurions at Housesteads to command auxiliaries was about three times smaller than the accommodation for legionary centurions (Hoffmann 1995). The soldiers in the barracks may have been accompanied by their families, who may have migrated with them (Haynes 1999b: 167). Certainly, the palaedemographic structure presented by van Driel-Murray (1998) points to women and children living alongside the soldiers – perhaps in a situation quite different from that associated with families in Roman towns, and unlike the socio-spatial situation of the commander and his centurions that recreated a Roman domestic setting (see Allison 2006 for further study of gender and forts).

Are forts cities? Seasonality and demography at Vindolanda

Forts in phases of the conquest of territory provide an effective and logistically efficient means of protecting the resource of soldiers in hostile territory, but, following the establishment of a period of service of 25 years and the normalization of non-expansion, the fort became 'home' for soldiers for a considerable period of time (see Dobson 2009 for full discussion of this topic). They are, in short, permanent settlements, even if they are seen to be occupied primarily in winter and Vindolanda is referred to by

Flavius Ceralis as his *hiberna* or winter quarters (*Tab. Vindol.* II: 225; Birley 2002). In summer, as Brian Dobson (2009) forcefully argues, the soldiers were expected to be undertaking the business of warfare, returning to the forts for the winter – a period associated with *otium* or leisure. This causes the fort to become a different category of settlement – a refuge or a place of repose. It is also a place to be occupied by a varying number of people, as indicated in the Vindolanda writing tablets in a report from June stating that 296 of 752 Tungrian soldiers were in residence (Bowman and Thomas 1991, 1994: 90–98, dating varies but can be pinned down to between 90 and 121 AD). The others were at a number of locations in Britain with 337 of the 456 absentees stationed at Corbridge. Of those in residence, 31 were sick and unfit, whereas the others with one centurion were described as healthy. Presumably, the fort's population of soldiers was at a maximum in winter and a minimum in summer, when the soldiers were expected to be elsewhere. Thus, the fort is quite unlike a city for the very fact that its military population in residence varies so dramatically over the course of a year, if the soldiers were mostly elsewhere in the summer months.

The fluctuation in the number of soldiers raises a further question in relation to the population of Vindolanda. What did the dependents – as defined through the study of footwear by van Driel-Murray (1993) and present in the writing tablets (Bowman 1994: 67–68) – do when these male soldiers were absent? Did they go with them or did they remain in the fort? Both literary evidence and the gravestones of soldiers point to soldiers having male slaves or servants who went with them on campaign (Speidel 1989). However, it seems likely that women and children of the soldiers did not actually campaign with the soldiers and remained in the forts. Hence, rather than viewing the population of Vindolanda in June as just composed of 296 Tungrian soldiers with their centurion, we should add in a population of slaves and the soldiers' dependents in the fort itself on a permanent basis. This adjusts the view that such persons were resident only in the *vicus* outside of the fort – see Figure 7.1 (Somner 1984: 30–31). However, it leads to another question – why did people live in the *vicus*? The answer has to lie with the fact that they were not permitted to, or did not want to, live in the fort itself, and that those 'civilians' living in the fort needed direct connection to the soldiers – were part of their *familia* or quasi-*familia* based on a Tungrian or Battavian model of family structure. Veterans, if present at Vindolanda, were inhabitants of the *vicus* rather than the fort itself. Thus, in the *vicus* (for the most part) were a population of individuals who were not part of the *familiae* of the soldiers in the fort. As we have seen in the study of jewellery and of footwear, the material culture of the two parts of the settlement at Vindolanda has much by way of convergence rather than structural differentiation. However, what it also demonstrates is that the fort and *vicus* spatially made clear the differentiation of who was and who was not directly associated with a serving soldier in the army. In these terms, it is a form of urbanism that emphasizes the distinctions of soldier with dependents and those who were not direct dependents of the soldiers, and importantly was established with the construction of the fort in stone (Bidwell 1985: 88–89; Birley and Blake 2005). In consequence, the *vicus* should be seen as an integral part of any fort, rather than being seen as a separate settlement form. Yet, within the *vicus* were key facilities that included religious sites and 'the military bath-house' (Birley and Blake 2007: 12–13).

If we are to accept that forts were a form of Roman urbanism, we should expect to find some of the features of public buildings that are so prominent in the cities of Italy or the developing cities of the provinces. The ability to bathe and to cleanse the body of dirt would seem to be essential in both contexts, but provides a means also to see the distinctions between settlement forms. Louise Revell (2007) examined the nature of military bath-houses in Roman Britain and, in a short note, established a fundamental dichotomy between those in legionary fortresses and those in auxiliary forts. The former (such as Chesters) had much in common with the bath-buildings found in cities across the empire, for example the Stabian Baths at Pompeii, whereas the latter were quite different with far less emphasis placed on public space for display and social interaction. The spaces for bathing for legionaries (i.e. Roman citizens) were similar to those found in Roman cities, whereas those provided for auxiliaries (non-citizens) tended towards the functional need for cleanliness in a Roman manner without the spaces for social interaction that were prominent in baths in cities in Roman Italy. This leads to the conclusion that the auxiliary bath-houses are derived from a different building tradition from those provided for legionaries (Revell 2007; Bidwell 2009). This is a good clear explanation. However, the earliest bath-buildings built at auxiliary fortresses in the Flavian period (Bidwell 2009 for examples) are architecturally congruent with private bath-buildings preserved by the eruption of Mount Vesuvius in 79 AD in Campania – see Figure 7.2 (Fabbricotti 1976 for a survey of examples with plans). These private bath-buildings found at villas in Campania were designed for use by not just the owner and his family, but also by others such as guests and visitors. The congruence between these structures in Campania and the bath-buildings found in auxiliary forts were not designed as public buildings for all residents in the fort, but for a more exclusive group: the commander and his family, who needed the facility since they, unlike the auxiliary soldiers they commanded, were Roman citizens and of high status and wealth.

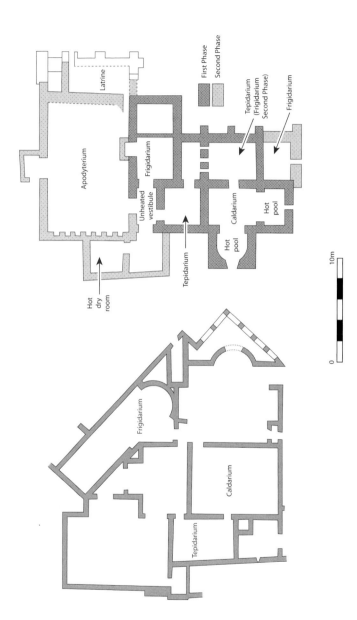

Figure 7.2 A comparison of the bath-houses at the Villa of San Marco (Stabiae) and the auxiliary fort of Chesters on Hadrian's Wall

Moreover, these were facilities for entertainment of visitors of a similar status in both Campania and on the frontiers, who may have travelled over some distance (*Tab. Vindol.* II. 292–93 for visits to Vindolanda by an equestrian woman to the commander's wife; Allason-Jones 1999: 41–42), and hence needed, immediately, the baths for their use at the end of a journey of more than half a day. The bath-houses at auxiliary fortresses need not have been available for all, but were for a small group or the elite who utilized a similar architecture in their civilian sphere. Hence, the presence of a bath-house reinforced the social differentiation between citizens and non-citizens, or Romans and non Romans – the fundamental basis of organization within the Roman military from the point of recruitment (Haynes 1999b: 165–66), and the facility should not be seen as a feature provided for the mass bathing of the soldiers at the fort, but for its elite – the commander's family. The fact that considerable resources were expended on the construction of these types of buildings, as can be seen from the Vindolanda tablets and physical remains (Birley 2001), should not cause us to assume that this was a facility for the entire population at the fort. Importantly, bath-house construction is associated with the earliest phase of the fort at Vindolanda (Birley 2001: 11–12). Another bath-house was developed, at an early date, adjacent to a timber building in the *vicus* for the provision of bathing to those who were excluded from the more substantial bath-house built by the soldiers from the fort (Bidwell 1985: 91). This proposed division between the lives of the commander with his family and the lives of soldiers in barracks is confirmed by a study of the range of meat available to a commander and that available to his men (Stokes 2000). That study identified the commander eating better cuts of cattle, more birds, deer and hare.

What the evidence from Vindolanda allows us to see is that, although the auxiliary fortress has some features that are shared with towns, there is much that is quite different. There is a hierarchy of status that is formalized through the organization of space. The membership of the families of soldiers (however defined) was the basis for the organization of who should and should not live within the fort. The building of a bath-house and *vicus* coincided with the earliest phase of the settlement within the fort. The former should be seen as a feature that has a parallel not with an urban context (unlike the baths of legionary fortresses), but with the private bathing facilities found in villas of the wealthy elite in Italy. This feature points to a structure that is quite different from that of Roman urbanism and from which we might conceptualize the community of auxiliary soldiers as commanded by an equestrian, just as there were families of slaves living in the villas of the elite in Italy.

Soldiers, Latin and Romanization

In discussion of Vindolanda, we encountered evidence for a Batavian unit. This was formed from individuals recruited in the area of the Rhine delta (in the modern Netherlands). One or two members from each Batavian family were recruited into the Roman Army (Derks and Roynams 2002: 87–88). This fact would suggest that the region was well connected to the Roman state and we might expect the people in the area to utilize the features that we often associate with Roman culture: Latin inscriptions, villas and towns. However, it is very clear from extensive studies of the region that this is simply not the case. Even though Batavian auxiliaries from discharge returned home, once in their homeland they did not utilize the features that we today associate with Roman material culture. This poses a major question: how did auxiliary soldiers engage with living in forts such as Vindolanda? Ton Derks and Nico Roynams (2002, 2006) added a further dimension to our understanding of the relation between the families of Batavians and recruits in the army stationed in forts by an examination of the evidence for seal boxes in the Netherlands on rural sites and in military forts. These seal boxes were the remains of Latin documents and were suggested by Derks and Roynams (2002) to have been evidence for letters sent from soldiers serving on the frontier to their families. This would suggest that the Batavians had a greater understanding and linguistic command of Latin than previously thought, and that there were clear advantages for them to know and use Latin. Not least of these advantages was that of communication between family members separated by huge temporal distances. This causes Latin to be seen as part of an apparatus of engagement with a state that deployed its members over a wide geographical area. It is a chicken and egg scenario to determine whether knowledge of Latin enabled the recruitment of Batavians into the Roman army or that the use of Latin was a result of their recruitment into the Roman army. This might be less important than the realization that knowledge of Latin was associated with recruits into the auxiliaries prior to enlistment (see Haynes 1999b: 169–72). Interestingly, it does not follow that the use of Latin of necessity results in monumental or commemorative inscriptions or in the development of monument types. Stone inscriptions need not be seen as an indicator of the use of Latin per se, but as the adoption of a particular usage of Latin – inscribing on stone for the purpose of display in the present with a view to the survival of those letters cut in stone in the future.

The soldiers' use of Latin was not simply functional to communicate across distance. At Vindolanda, Derks and Roynams (2002: 103; *Vindol Tab* II no 118) point out that there is evidence for a line from Virgil's

Aeneid. This might be said to belong to the world of the commander, but Jim Adams (1999), in an examination of poems cut as inscriptions on stone at Bu Njem in Tripolitania, evaluated the poetic use of Latin by centurions. The attempt by the centurion Iasucthan to write Latin poetry can be seen to result in error-strewn hexameters, but there is also a degree of success and indication of understanding and correct spelling (Adams 1999: 113–19). Moreover, this poem articulates the activity of restoring a gate of the fort. The implications of this evidence points to clear knowledge and use of sophisticated Latin on the part of the commanders in the army, but also the deployment of the sophisticated form of poetry as a source of legitimacy of their power over others (compare Phang 2007). There is a contrast here with the *ostraca* (pottery with writing on it) from the site that demonstrate not a pidgin or creole form of Latin, but that of those not proficient in Latin; in other words those who are learning Latin within the army, or perhaps those who have learnt some Latin but ceased to progress further (Adams 1994 for full study). This is exemplified by a predominant use of the nominative case, rather than usage of accusative and other cases (Adams 2007: 563). What we see at Bu Njem is differing competence in the usage of Latin in the fort. This has a parallel in the hypothesis that the small villa-style bath-houses associated with auxiliary forts were not provided for use by all, but for use by the commander and his family. There is another feature worth commenting on with reference to the use of Latin at Bu Njem: the usage of local (perhaps Punic or Libyan) terms for measurements that were derived from the place of service pointing to the intersection of the military with civilians (Adams 2007: 563). It needs to be stated also that the terminology used by soldiers in Latin crossed over into the civilian context (Haynes 1999b: 170).

Returning to Batavians and the carving of Latin on stone, it is significant that for the most part inscriptions that include reference to Batavians tend to do so with reference to actions of their commanders, such as the setting up of altars at Carrawburgh on Hadrian's Wall (*RIB* 1.1534–36, 1544–45). Tombstones for the most part commemorate the exceptional soldiers – trumpeters and standard-bearers, as seen again at Carrawburgh (*RIB* 1.1559–60; compare *CIL* 3.13760; *AE* 1982: 842, 1997: 1307). The commanders and centurions were also commemorated by tombstones for example at Romita in Dalmatia (*CIL* 3.839, 3.10329). Veterans with an origin in the Batavian homeland appear at Wiesbaden (*CIL* 13.7577), Lyon (*CIL* 13.1847), Adonis (*AE* 2003: 1454) and Kosteneuberg (*RHP* 254, 255). There are finds of tombstones from Rome dedicated to Batavian soldiers, but this points more to the presence of a funerary *collegium/collegia* in Rome than to a direct usage of Latin (*CIL* 2548, 3289, 3547, 8802–6, 31162, 32834,

32839a, 37255; see Haynes 1999b: 167 commenting on *Dig.* 47.22.1 and role of *collegia* for the military). There is also a concentration of commemoration of Batavians in Concordia in northern Italy. Interestingly the precise ages of the Batavians are not known and others display considerable age rounding with a range of ages from 25 to 60 years (*CIL* 5.8743, 8752, 8759, 8761, 8773, 8776; *ILCV* 498, 544). Intriguingly, a centurion of Legio II Parthica commemorated his dead son, aged 8 months, 11 days and 4 hours, as an *eques Romanus* of the Batavian nation in 244 AD in distant Knidos in Asia Minor (*CIL* 3.14403a). Finally, in Parma, a find of a grave stele to a Batavian *retiarius* provides evidence of their recruitment as gladiators (*CIL* 11.1070). Overall, the Batavian epigraphic habit points to the role of officers and the commemoration of those that commanded Batavians, rather than the routine usage of inscribed stones by Batavians. Combined with the evidence of seal boxes, this would suggest that inscriptions need not give us the full picture for the usage of Latin. These examples of monumental writing or commemorative epigraphy were written in the language of command and power over others, whereas more ephemeral forms of writing were universal phenomena available to all and subject to the linguistic knowledge of the participants. However, it needs to be noted that the incidence of graffiti found on pottery vessels in Roman Britain is most prominent in those areas in which inscriptions on stone were more prominent (including Hadrian's Wall, Evans 1987). The vast majority of graffiti found on pottery were personal names, regardless of the location of the finds and tended to be upon fine ware pottery rather than coarse wares (Evans 1987: Figures 7 and 8). This is a response to the need to mark an item as owned or associated with an individual, a need that may have been of greater importance in communal settings such as forts, large households, etc. The inscribing of letters onto either stone or pottery artefacts also has a visual or symbolic meaning. It is argued with reference to inscriptions on stone that this aspect is probably as important as what the words themselves actually say (Lomas 2007: 16–17). It should also be noted that the process of stone-cutting, inscribing and erection of a monumental stone was a process or performance to be observed and participated in.

The deployment of inscriptions alongside the basic writing of names and labels on pottery vessels would seem to be part of a single phenomenon: a focus on the individual and articulation of the identity of that individual via writing in Latin, which in turn articulates a position for that person within an imagined community of a Roman Empire – stretching from 'home' (whether Rome or Batavia) to that person's current location. It needs to be stressed that this use of writing for symbolic rather than functional purposes does not create a uniform epigraphic assemblage for the empire (Häussler and Pearce 2007). Instead, there is considerable variation that can be related to local interactions that vary from not just city to city, but even from fort to fort. Latin inscriptions allowed for the articulation of aspects of social hierarchy and were a means to underpin power relations. As a consequence, the use of Latin tells us more about those relations than about the overall pattern of dissemination and adoption of Latin, or the cultural changes we may wish to read into the evidence in a search for elusive evidence for Romanization. In short, although Latin was part of the colonial structure of the Roman Empire, how it was used was subject to the agency of individuals (see papers in Draper 2004). This causes Latin to be ubiquitous but used differently by Roman soldiers in different contexts. It was a feature of their inclusion in the empire. Like the shoes and other material items that they wore and used, Latin would be familiar to others from other parts of the empire (on shoes and Roman culture see van Driel-Murray 1999). It was part of the apparatus of empire, just as a soldiers' dress was distinctive (Wild 2002: 25 on language of dress at Vindolanda).

The demographic and economic impact of the Roman army

In the first two centuries AD, it can be demonstrated that there were about 30,000 Roman soldiers in Britain, of whom about half were Roman citizens serving in the three legions. In addition, we would also expect a population of discharged soldiers (or veterans) living in Britain to the tune of 10,800 (Verboven 2007: 303–4 for figures; Tac. *Ann.* 14.27 for settlement of veterans), as well as the servants of soldiers – probably more than a further 8,000 persons (Roth 1999: 113–14). An allowance should also be made for other dependents, identified in our discussion of the evidence from shoes and the presence of women and children in Roman auxiliary forts. The capacity of this military population in terms of manpower is adequately demonstrated by a consideration of the construction of Hadrian's Wall over a period of ten years (Birley 2007). Koenraad Verboven (2007: 305–8) points out that although the army had the capacity to produce goods for its own consumption (such as basic pottery, bricks, tiles, etc.), it also purchased a variety of goods including fine ware pottery, wine, olives, *fibulae*, weapons and other imports of food. This situation or need to supply the army with its non-subsistence needs, so Verboven argues, created a new class of *negotiatores* (or a business class) to whom the soldiers of Britain may have handed over some of the 34–45 million sesterces paid or lent to them (Verboven 2007: 309–10). There is also the possibility that the 5,000 men in the fleet also supplied the army in Britain with these materials (Breeze

2000: 62–63). The discussion above outlines the macro-economic picture, but given the now accepted rejection of Moses Finley's economic model (that we saw also underpinned Martin Millett's conception of Romanization in the previous chapter), what sort of economy are we looking at?

Elio Lo Cascio (2007) is critical of the evidence-based formulation of David Breeze (2000), in which it is suggested that there was a two-tier model of supply – one conducted primarily on the basis of taxation and another that depended on market forces but was parasitic on the transport of supplies by the state. The use of the word 'parasitic' should lead to alarm bells ringing and a suspicion that Finley's primitivist model of the ancient economy continues to persist, and is exposed by Lo Cascio (2007: 201) as based on Karl Polanyi's thinking. The key problem for interpreting the impact of the army is that the primitivist model is persistent and has not been challenged by more recent work on the role of the state in the Roman economy. Lo Cascio (2006) presents the case for a different economic model drawing on the new institutional economics of Douglas North. The theory is in some ways seductively simple: market forces continue to determine matters but there is a greater emphasis on transaction costs and an emphasis on the role of institutions. Thus, the Roman army as an institution might promote transactions due to the institution containing information and ameliorating costs (not least through paying its soldiers). The presence of the army can thus be seen as an 'economic accelerator' (Lo Cascio 2006: 222). The role of the state in the promotion of measured distance, use of written Latin and other features that may be associated with the loose notion of 'Romanization' were part of the state's or institution's attempt to facilitate and promote transactions by increasing the certainty of communications – a sense of certainty that was needed most in the supply of the army, when it was going to fight (see Roth 1999 for discussion). Certainty of supply was achieved through an infrastructure of empire or colonialism that also facilitated economic opportunities for others (see Lo Cascio 2007 for interpretation).

The whole question of supply can be evaluated with reference to the animal bones found on military sites. The analytical framework for the analysis has been pioneered by Anthony King (1999a for overview and bibliography; 1984 for study of Britannia). His work illuminates quite different patterns of consumption of meat on military and civilian sites in the province of Britannia. The military consumption was focused on cattle with the important distinction that legionary fortresses were consumers of considerably more pork than any other type of site, whereas civilian sites were associated with a greater consumption of goats and sheep. This observation made from the animal bone assemblages can be mapped onto the identities of the inhabitants – legionaries were Roman citizens and

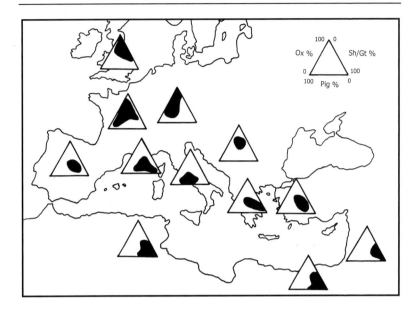

Figure 7.3 Animal bones and consumption. The triangles plot the percentage of pig, cattle and sheep/goat bones found at sites in each region. It is notable that these show that pig consumption has a far greater prominence in Italy. Sheep/goats predominate in the diet of the rest of the Mediterranean, whereas cattle are more prominent in the diet of those living in the Northern Provinces (reproduced with permission of Tony King)

tended to consume more pork. This coincides with their status as the most Romanized, whereas the civilians in the countryside had quite a different diet that did not feature this Roman element. The data as represented in Figure 7.3 demonstrate the differentiation of the pattern of consumption, which allows us to see how the military had the greatest access to the supply of cattle and pigs, whereas all had access to sheep and goats. Importantly, Sue Stallibrass (2009a is fundamental for what follows) has observed that the absence of neonatal bones of animals at military sites points to an expectation from this evidence that the military did not raise cattle, sheep/goats or pigs. Moreover, analysis of the various bone types found at military sites in northern Britain suggests that the animals were not butchered prior to transportation to the forts (Stallibrass 2009a: 104). Hence, we should expect animals to have been driven to the forts over quite long distances from the upland zones of northern England and southern Scotland. The use of the whole animal would have been essential for the production of tents from the hides (Stallibrass 2009b: 144). On the subject of animal bones and transportation, it is worth noting that statistical studies of horses and mules from across the north-west provinces can establish that the Roman period saw the production of larger transport animals (Johnstone 2008 for figures and analysis). Importantly, the reliance on mules for transportation resulted in the breeding of mules across the region displaying a remarkable similarity of size (compared to regional variation in size of horses). This causes us to realize that the mule was both a commodity and a critical element in the logistics or the connectivity of the Roman Empire, thus contributing to the infrastructure of the state as an improved breed – perhaps more important even than the action of road-building (Laurence 1999b: 123–35). Looking at all types of domesticated hoofed animals, it would seem that the supply of animals to the state and the army was fundamental to the military on Hadrian's Wall. Animal bones reveal some of the dynamics of supplying a large group of soldiers in the province of Britannia.

Communities of soldiers and civilians

The studies by archaeologists of the military have re-shaped our conception of the army to include not just the soldiers but to recognize the presence of others in the forts and the relationships between soldiers and civilians (James 2001). This shifts the focus from the soldiers to the community of soldiers and civilians based in a particular place. Interestingly, the research agenda developed for Hadrian's Wall continues to place an emphasis on the division between those within the fort and those outside the fort, or between Roman and 'native' (Symonds and Mason 2009: 15, 24), whereas Rob Collins (2008) has advocated comparison between these and rural sites located further afield to define the fort community comprised of both the fort and its *vicus*. The material culture of these communities can be described as very different from other communities – rural or urban. There is (or certainly was in the past) a tendency to view the identities of the military sites through the lens of an understanding of the modern army as a state institution – the Roman army was conceptualized monolithically as a war machine or similar (James 2001: 77–78). What we see emerging in Roman archaeology is a conception of frontier communities rather than placement of a stress on separated identities of members of those communities (Collins 2008). What has been stressed in this chapter is an overview that places an emphasis on how archaeological and textual evidence allows us to see these frontier communities connected to other parts of the province and of the empire. In seeing the connectivity of the frontier derived from materials excavated and studied by archaeologists, Roman historians are able to begin to understand how the infrastructure of the state ensured that these communities were supplied and integrated as communities into a more distant and never-seen Rome with its changing emperors. Such concerns engage directly with the development in ancient history of an entirely different conception of the Roman economy from that prevalent 20 years or more ago and located in Millett's *Romanization of Britain* (1990a). Given the evidence of the scale of consumption, the new economic model that involves the state as a key institution should be seen as a factor in the explanation of landscape and settlement patterns of regions associated with the frontier communities of the Roman Empire, and perhaps also in the distribution of 'Roman' artefacts (see Hingley 2009).

Chapter 8

Peopling the Roman Past
Do the Dead Tell Tales?

In Roman history, there has been an upsurge of interest in collaboration with archaeology and its practitioners on the part of those studying social history over the past three decades. This can be seen most clearly in the study of the Roman family that has so clearly embraced the study of houses and households (Wallace-Hadrill 1994 opened the way, but see papers in Rawson 2011 for full development of approaches to the household). Of course, there are tensions in relating archaeological and textual evidence (Allison 2001), but the detail perhaps distracts us from what has been achieved: an engagement of the two disciplines with a view to establishing people inhabiting the archaeological remains. This can be done from artefacts alone (an approach that is met with some scepticism by ancient historians), texts alone (an approach that ignores archaeology) and a combination of texts, plans of structures and artefacts (that is attempted in part only). What has happened is that the study of the household has been fully incorporated into mainstream Roman social history and is a topic recognized as of interest to ancient historians. In part, this has involved ancient historians 'colonizing' a section of the discipline of archaeology and making it their own through a thorough consideration of archaeological material. Interestingly, it is not possible to identify the reverse of this intellectual trend in which archaeologists explore the textual sources to develop an interface between archaeology and material culture in text.

Having made these observations, I wish to consider some material explored in archaeology of relevance to the study of societies across the Roman Empire and to suggest where Roman historians might become a little more attentive to some of the key developments that could help us have a more informed view of the Roman past.

Skeletons and childhood

Cities in the Roman Empire, even new ones such as London, developed large cemeteries relatively quickly (Melikian and Sayer 2007), from which skeletons have been recovered in large numbers. However both Walter Scheidel (2001) and Tim Parkin (1992: 41–58), as demographers, have taken the view that skeletal evidence is a bit of a dead-end for the study of ancient history and in particular that of ancient demography. The problem of the evidence is a crucial one: for a vast period of Roman history (from the time of Sulla into the 2nd century AD) cremation was the standard burial rite with relatively few skeletons recovered with the exception of those from Herculaneum and Pompeii (Laurence 2005). Interestingly, the concerns of those who study skeletons or osteoarchaeologists are quite different from those of demographers hoping to reconstruct the macro-population history of the Roman Empire – although sample cemeteries do suggest patterns of death in childhood (Pearce 2010: 89–93). The field of osteoarchaeology is developing rapidly, as can be seen from review articles of the state of the discipline with respect to classical archaeology (Mackinnon 2007a; 2007b) and more recent work that can be readily identified in the *Journal of Archaeological Science* or the *American Journal of Physical Anthropology*. The potential of skeletons as a historical source is at last being realized in the development of archaeological discussions of childhood and age, migration, and health.

Historians have written whole books on childhood (Rawson 2003; Laes 2011), but for the most part these books are derived from the study of ancient texts with some recognition that osteoarchaeology can make a contribution. There is a realization in the subject that osteologists produce data about age according to the physiology that can be categorized by chronological age, but needs also to take into account cultural age (Lewis 2007: 5–8). Human development in childhood involves calorific consumption for human growth that in early childhood (often said to be the point at which permanent teeth emerge) is today seen to take place between the chronological ages of three and seven (Gowland 2006: 143–44; see Lewis 2007: 4–8 for discussion and references), and is associated with dependence on others for food and feeding. This is followed by a period of juvenility to the onset of puberty (about the age of 10 in females and 12 in males, compared with minimum marriage ages in Roman law of 12 and 14), associated with greater independence. For those familiar with ancient etymologies of infant or age of adulthood in Rome, a certain amusement can occur in reading that osteologists can be adamant that the term 'infant' should refer to a child less than one year of age, whereas many would see an infant as up to five years; or that one osteoarchaeologist can categorize a 15-year-old as an adult, whereas another would not do so unless the skeleton was over 25 years old. Looking back to how the data was derived is an essential feature of understanding osteoarchaeology's conclusions, but clearly chronological age is still accepted as an objective fact for many with little problematization or discussion of alternatives (as Gowland 2006: 144 argues).

It is tempting to see in the study of skeletons absolute data, since the conclusions are derived from bones that were the skeleton of an individual from antiquity, and their study is characterized by both the methods and the language of science. However, Sofaer (2006) makes an important point: skeletons are proxies rather than data, because we derive from the skeleton information about the flesh, the age and the gender of the person from the past. The growth of social analysis based on the skeletons found in cemeteries has increased over the past two decades, and can be seen to be allied to the development of a focus on gender in archaeology. Jo Sofaer (2006) places a greater emphasis on reading the body as a social object alongside artefacts associated with it. This causes the skeleton to become less an object to be categorized by sex as male or female, and more an object to be categorized by age and development, including the development of the characteristics of male and female gender. The intersection of age and gender allows for the development of a bi-archaeological approach that characterizes childhood as a phase of the life span that is associated with physical change and changes in the interaction of the body with the human environment (see Sofaer 2006 for discussion).

There is another factor that we should recognize in approaching children via the skeletal remains found in cemeteries or, in the case of infants and foetuses, burial places within or close to houses (see Waldron et al 1999). What we are looking at is the child deposited after death, in all likelihood, by the agency of adults. This shifts the subject of study away from the child, who being dead is as inanimate as an artefact, and onto the actions of the adults and children that survive the child. This allows the funerary practices associated with children of different ages to inform us about how adults viewed children of different ages (Gowland 2001). Infanticide has been a subject of much discussion (Gowland and Chamberlain 2002), but what these studies actually identified was that foetuses from 24 weeks and infants up to the age of six months were not buried in cemeteries but were found in domestic settlements. Osteoarchaeology persists in attempting to identify 'infanticide' (see Smith and Kahlia 1992 for the article that initiated the debate; Gowland and Chamberlain 2002; see Mays 2003 for critique and discussion of methods). However, what is being identified is a set of burials that is archaeologically distinct and is associated with foetuses at full term (Mays and Eyers 2011). In the osteoarchaeological literature, the normative death of foetuses at birth is disregarded in favour of theories of deliberate killing based on textual accounts of child exposure (see Harris 1994 for discussion of the less than conclusive textual evidence). Veronique Dasen (2009) provides alternatives to infanticide that combine textual and skeletal evidence more effectively and suggest that infants had a liminal status, due to breast-feeding and absence of teeth, and that the liminal period extended to at least six months. Perhaps infanticide is a distraction, since most societies included some form of infanticide (think today of abortion of a foetus). Instead, more interesting is Rebecca Gowland's suggestion that dead children prior to and after birth were treated as similar categories of human being, occluding our own modern distinction of the foetus as yet to be born and a baby as having been born (Gowland 2001; Dasen 2009). Yet, there does seem to be a quite different pattern to the distribution of age at death of foetuses in Roman Britain, when compared to patterns discovered at Kellis in Egypt (Tocheri et al 2005), that requires further investigation and reminds us that cultural practice need not be the same across the Roman Empire.

Looking at Ostia's and Portus' cemetery population

The excavation of Isola Sacra's cemetery located between Ostia and Portus at the mouth of the river Tiber produced in the 1920s and 1930s one of the best preserved cemetery samples in terms of tombs and inscriptions (see Hope 1997; Helttula et al 2007), but further excavation of the ground around these tombs in the late 1980s produced a large number of skeletons from inhumations (accounting for 90 per cent of the burials, Angelucci et al 1990; Baldassarre 1990; see E. J. Graham 2006: 85–97 for account in English). This contrasts with the mixing of crema-tions and inhumations within the house tombs with some converted for use as places of inhumation (Taglietti 2002; note the prohibition of inhu-mation from tomb 87). Some 2,000 skeletons have been excavated from the site and form a key sample of individuals from the Roman period (Cho and Stout 2005: 217). However, due to mixing up of bones from the early excavations only 800 skeletons can be identified with a full set of bones. Of these 800, researchers have identified 334 as sub-adult (adolescents, chil-dren and infants) and 66 as children under the age of one year (FitzGerald et al 2006). It is an important sample not just for Roman archaeologists but also for the longer history of paleobiology of the human population of the Earth.

Much has been said by demographers of ancient populations on the subject of hypotheses of the living conditions of urban populations (Scobie 1986; Scheidel 2003), but actual data remains rather elusive. The adult popu-lation in terms of stature (estimated from length of femurs) would have males growing to a height of 1.63 metres and females to a height of 1.52 metres, which is completely in line with stature found at other Roman sites (Gowland and Garnsey 2010: 150–52). Intriguingly, these figures for stature are on average about two centimetres shorter than those derived from the study of skeletons from the preceding Iron Age period and from that follow-ing it – the Middle Ages. Explanations are difficult to locate, but we might be seeing Roman culture as reducing the growth in height of its population –

Figure 8.1 Ostia: Isola Sacra cemetery – showing house tombs with burials in spaces between the tombs

perhaps by diet, distribution of economic resource or other factors (Gowland and Garnsey 2010). The study of skeletons themselves though (Gowland and Garnsey 2010 for all figures that follow) identifies via marks on the skull (*cribra orbitalia*, or cranial lesions) that there was a presence of anaemia and a basic deficiency in vitamins B_9 and B_{12}, and through a decrease in the thickness of the enamel of teeth, *hypoplasia*, that are indicators of periods of sustained ill-health and an inability of the body in childhood to form calcium. The presence of *cribia orbitalia* was found in skulls of children at Isola Sacra in the majority of cases – 70 per cent of all skeletons. This high figure is also found in studies of Rome, but elsewhere in Italy is found to have been rather lower (56 per cent or less) and in Roman Britain to have been far lower (19 per cent or less). *Hypoplasia* was identified in an equally high incidence in skeletons studied from Isola Sacra, in line with data collected from cemeteries in Rome, whereas elsewhere in the Roman Empire, figures are much lower (Gowland and Garnsey 2010: 143–44). The variation observed by Rebecca Gowland and Peter Garnsey (2010) is discussed in relation to a presence of malaria and its impact on health in the first three years of life that has been shown to lead to anaemia. They also consider the possibility that the variation may also reflect differences in the cultural practices associated with weaning, but reject this and assume a similar Roman diet in Ostia/Portus and in Roman Britain. Such an assumption may be unfounded, since there is clear evidence that in terms of diet, admittedly

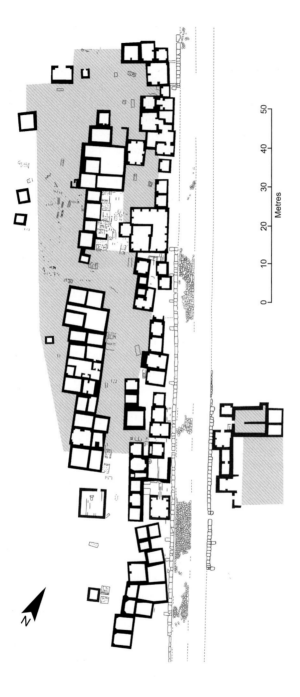

Figure 8.2 Ostia: plan of the Isola Sacra cemetery – shading shows area from which the skeletons were excavated that form the basis for the study of migration

in relation to meat consumption, cultural practices were quite distinct (King 1999b).

In terms of diet, studies of the geo-chemistry of the bones pointed to high levels of cereal and marine animals in the diet of those buried at Isola Sacra (Prowse et al 2004; 2005). However, there is an important age-differentiation: those who died as children had a diet that we might associate today with vegetarians and, in comparison to those that died in adulthood, did not contain as much fish or meat (Prowse et al 2005). This highlights the problem of making general statements from skeletal evidence: those who died young, in this case associated with a low fish/meat diet, need not be representative of their contemporaries who survived to adulthood. A similar note of caution should be voiced when looking at the weaning age of children from Isola Sacra as between one and two years of age (Prowse et al 2004). It should be noted though that from a study of milk teeth (deciduous teeth) it is possible to identify periods of early life associated with poor health causing the human body to be unable to produce calcium for the growth of teeth. The research team discovered that in the first month, about 20 per cent of children suffered such a problem, but subsequently this rose to between 50 and 80 per cent over the course of the next eight months (FitzGerald et al 2006).

The skeletons from Isola Sacra can begin to provide us with actual data for the establishment of a number of variables associated with ageing and health in general. Helen Cho and Sam Stout (2005) sampled rib bones from the Isola Sacra skeletal archive housed in the Museo Nazionale Preistorico Etnografico 'L. Pigorini' in Rome and found that, unlike modern European American population samples, the bones from Isola Sacra displayed denser bone mass and a lower likelihood of fractures and maintained bone mass into mid-life (40s to 50s in terms of chronological age). A study of the skulls of the males from Isola Sacra pointed to a high proportion (30 per cent of adult males, 21 per cent of population) of what is often called today surfer's ear or auditory exostosis, when compared to a similar sample from Lucus Feroniae north of Rome (Manzi et al 1991). However, this was much lower than that found at Velia (Crowe et al 2010) and perhaps reflects a greater diversity of land-based employment in the Portus-Ostia region than found in the small coastal town of Velia in southern Italy. Strikingly, the incidence or likelihood of suffering from auditory exostosis increased over the life span (Crowe et al 2010).

The skeletal sample from Isola Sacra formed the basis for the first ever data-led study of migration to Italy, published in 2007 (Prowse et al 2007; see Bruun 2010 for an ancient historian's critique; Killgrove 2010). Fundamental to this study is the recent realization that isotope analysis of teeth (grown by definition in childhood or early youth) remains stable over the course of the human life span, whereas isotopes associated with bones are subject to change (Killgrove 2010 for an account of the academic development of this work). This allows for a comparison between the diet and rainwater drunk in childhood and that drunk in adulthood or other associations of the body with variations in the chemical intake to the body that are later a constituent part of bone or dental formation (Prowse et al 2007; Bruun 2010 provides further explanation for historians). The majority of the population (67–72 per cent) were raised in the locality of Ostia-Portus or Rome, whereas the rest of the population (28–33 per cent) had migrated to Italy during or after childhood. This has important implications for the study of migration and implies that families or children associated with other adults or children on their own should be included in the current discussion by ancient historians of human mobility (for example, Scheidel 2004). However, Christer Bruun (2010: 124–26) is critical in that the study based on isotope analysis (Prowse et al 2007) does not cross-reference its results to the 350 inscriptions for the most part associated with tombs excavated in the 1920s and 1930s with some 20 additions from more recent excavations (Helttula et al 2007). Olli Salomies (2002) conducted a study of the names of the Ostians to pro-duce a study of another form of proxy data that might inform us about migration. Bruun would suggest that the two data-sets, inscriptions and skeletons at Isola Sacra should be directly related. This should be done, but we should be aware that the majority of skeletons studied were those from recent excavations (because the bones of skeletons from the excavations of the early 20th century had been muddled together) and from burials in the ground outside of the tombs associated with the inscriptions – for locations see Figures 8.1 and 8.2 (mostly discovered in the excavations of the early 20th century). Hence, the bodies of data come from two quite different archaeological or social contexts and need not be related, since those commemorated with a tomb and an inscription might not be the same class as those interred in the ground with no or limited epigraphic com-memoration. However, to date, the publication of analysis of the skeletons and that of the inscriptions has often ignored the point of deposition or place of commemoration in the cemetery at Isola Sacra.

The study of migration can also be enhanced through the analysis of DNA from skeletons (Prowse et al 2010). Skeletons from the site of Vag-nari close to the Via Appia in southern Italy have been analysed and it has been shown that, while most of the skeletons have DNA that was associated with haplogroups with origins in western Eurasia, there were two individuals in this small sample of ten skeletons associated with hap-logroups from both sub-Saharan Africa and eastern Asia (Prowse et al 2010: 186). This data, combined with stable isotope analysis for teeth of skeletons from the site, points to a degree of migration that in the case of one skeleton occurred in early childhood (less than three years of age). As a whole, the study of this rural site near to the migration route to Rome along the Via Appia had a population that contained a number of migrants (Prowse et al 2010). This has an importance for Roman historians – migration was very much part of the dynamic of the Roman Empire and we should expect migration and build this factor into the experience of communities, whether close to Rome or at a distance from Rome, in places such as Vagnari. Moreover, we should see migration as occurring over far longer distances and at a whole variety of ages from early childhood onwards.

Cultural diversity and migration to the towns of Roman Britain

Recent work led by Hella Eckardt has sought to understand patterns of migration to Roman Britain through the study of stable isotopes (oxygen and strontium) of teeth (Eckardt et al 2010 for overview). The project seeks to create a scientific basis for ethnicity and migration to the towns of Roman Britain. It found that 21 of the 45 individuals studied in Winchester were likely to have grown up in the region, eight were identified as from Britain but outside the locality, five were from Wales or the south-west of Britain and 11 were from outside of Britain (Eckardt et al 2009). Interestingly, these parameters based on stable isotopes do not map neatly onto patterns of burial or grave goods, pointing to a far greater cultural variation that does not map back onto a point of migration in childhood. What this does show is veracity to the assumption by ancient historians that the towns of the Roman Empire were sustained by considerable migration, even when the size of the town contained a relatively small population.

The same team chose to study a mass burial from the city of Gloucester dated to the 2nd century AD (Chenery et al 2010). The rarity of such burials has been noted and they tend to be associated with an epidemic or other catastrophe, hence mass burials tend to contain people living at a similar point in time, perhaps relating to the phases of the Antonine Plague from 165 AD. Twenty-one sample teeth were taken to be studied – ten from the main cemetery and 11 from the mass grave – to allow for comparison between these two quite different archaeological contexts and to demonstrate a consistency of overall data, which proves that those buried in the mass grave were not of a different ethnicity. Hence, we should assume that an epidemic resulted in this burial. The study identified Wales and/or the south-west of Britain as a point of migration and an element within the population of Gloucester who grew up outside of the province of Britannia. Placing any preciseness on their point of origin remains uncertain at present, due to the limited numbers of studies of isotopes in human populations from the rest of the Roman Empire undertaken to date, but the indicators show that North Africa could be a point of origin.

Moving to a military context, the team looked at the variation in the stable isotopes in teeth of those associated with the fort at Catterick and those associated with the small town or *vicus* lying outside the fort with comparison to earlier studies of the population of York (Chenery et al 2011). This established that the teeth analysed for the study pointed to an absence of long-distance migration and that at least 48 per cent of the population grew up in the locality. The authors (Chenery et al 2011) point to changes in recruitment into the Roman army in the 3rd and 4th centuries as an explanation of the deviation from the patterns of migration associated with the nearby town of York that displays considerable diversity found in both isotope analysis and the physical structure of crania (Leach et al 2009).

What has become very clear from the innovative studies looking at particular isotopes in teeth is that we are seeing evidence for migration. This is something that has been identified from the study of inscriptions – as can be seen from a perusal of *The Roman Inscriptions of Britain* – but what isotope analysis adds is some certainty over the percentage of persons who may have migrated, whereas a single inscription or even five inscriptions (or ten or even 50) are subject to cultural practices associated with the setting up of inscribed stones that mention a point of origin. Ancestry assessment of skeletons allows us for the first time to critically evaluate how modern conceptions of migration have shaped our understanding of the appearance of black females in the Romano-British archaeological record, for example the status of the 'ivory bangled lady of York' (Leach et al 2010) and to suggest affirmatively that black migrants were not only present in Roman Britain but also displayed a social identity associated with a far from low status (Leach et al 2010). This opens a way to view a history of mobility as part of what some continue to see as a 'process' of cultural change still known simply as Romanization (discussed in Chapter 5).

Images of people: people and images

So far the discussion in this chapter has focused on work on skeletons to highlight the diversity of the population that inhabited and moved around the Roman Empire. A key question is how these various populations represented the human form. We are well aware of the icons of classical art found mostly in Italy and studied from the Renaissance to the present day (see Kleiner 1992). Most of the images found in the museums in

Rome today remain out of context or can only be placed back into a topographical context, rather than precise position – an exception would be the statue of Augustus found in Livia's villa at Prima Porta (although perhaps this statue today has become an icon of Augustan 'propaganda' in the public sphere; see Chapter 4). There are other images though, many associated with archaeological contexts (see papers in Scott and Webster 2003). To this end, there is a move in the literature to assert a value to objects found in a provincial context that need to be understood in more complex ways than simple imitation (Scott 2003). Equally, we may disagree with the polarity that images produced an opportunity for resistance (Webster 2003) – since in this reversal of Romanization, we are at a loss to define the 'what' that is being resisted beyond an absence of imitation located in Romanization and this leads us towards negotiation between cultures – but again, negotiation of what? An imagined Roman set of symbols that is not attested in an archaeological context amalgamated from the museum collections of the Renaissance (see Chapter 5 for discussion)? These arguments tend to get rather messy because the art of Rome is decontextualized and remains decontextualized in many of the debates regarding imagery, revolving around the invented terminology of *Romanitas* (occurs once in Tertullian *De Pallio* 4.1) and its invented opposite *Gallitas* (Aldhouse-Green 2003). These polar visions of Roman imagery as having defined semiotics of representation and a pre-Roman set of images fail to incorporate explanations of a whole new set of images produced during the half millennium of the Roman Empire (Aldhouse-Green 2003: 102–6).

David Mattingly (2003), in his study of tombs at Ghirza, escapes from the polarities and search for signs in a semiotically embedded code from Rome or the Iron Age. He does this effectively by arguing that the capacity to produce or reproduce elements of imagery was about much more than the reproduction of a semiotic code and, instead, presents a case for what might be suggested to be a larger than previous image bank that could be deployed in the representation of symbolic scenes, daily life and religious scenes (Mattingly 2003: 159–61) that are ultimately interpreted through our understanding of these symbols in ancient texts or through parallels (see references in the notes of Brogan and Smith 1984: 224–26). Yet it needs to be remembered that there was a time-depth to what Jennifer Moore has described a 'mausoleum culture' in North Africa that includes a Punic epigraphic tradition in the region (Moore 2007).

Strikingly, the deployment of these symbols is directed towards funerary monuments rather than to houses or everyday contexts. Some key examples can shape the way we discuss the use of symbols in the context of multicultural identities and migration (Eckardt 2010: 8). A case in point is the tombstone of a freed slave, Regina, found at South Shields (England).

The inscription gives her name and her legal status as a freed slave (i.e. formerly not a citizen); she was of Catevellaunian origin but was married to a Palmyrene. There is an implicit mobility on the part of the couple: neither grew up in South Shields. She died at the age of 30 (*RIB* 1065; Noy 2010: 18–23). The imagery that goes with the inscription includes Regina as a seated figure on a wicker chair with dress to indicate her status alongside her jewellery and wool-working equipment. In his analysis, Mattingly (2004: 11; compare Pearce 2010: 87–88) underplays wool-working that could be seen as a symbol of modesty or reference to the simple epitaph found elsewhere (Larsson Lovén 2002 for discussion of Italian and Gallic 'textile' imagery in epitaphs; Noy 2010: 23 sees the presence of wool-working equipment as a Palmyrene influence). The text is worth quoting:

> This tomb, which is not fair, is for a fair woman. Her parents gave her the name Claudia. She loved her husband in her heart. She bore two sons, one of whom she left on earth, the other beneath it. She was pleasant to talk with, and she walked with grace. She kept the house and worked in wool. That is all. You may go. (*CIL* 6.15346: Hic est sepulcrum hau pulcrum pulcrai feminae Nomen parentes nominarunt claudiam. Suom mareitum corde deilexit socio Gnatos duos creavit, horunc alterum in terra linquit, alium sub terra locat Sermone lepido, tum autem incessu commodo Domum servavit, lanam fecit. Dixi. Abei).

However, wool-working was an essential element of the identity of Regina – as is the presence of writing in three languages: Latin, British and Palmyrene (Adams 2003: 32). It has to be said, of course, this is a male vision set up by Barates, identified as having the role of husband, that asserts via the hand of a sculptor his vision of his wife – who is constructed to have an identity that depends on her being seated rather than standing. This in itself creates a sense of activity that is contained within her seat, her body enveloped by clothing, her status signified by the presence of her jewellery and the only signifier of any activity being one of the instruments of wool-working, a distaff. The image of female identity is thus mediated and contained within an androcentric prism of representation (see Rodgers 2003 for discussion) that can be elucidated via writing to provide additional information of name, origin, age, status, the name of her husband and his origins. It should be noted that the age of 30 is the most represented female age at death in inscriptions from the Latin west. What we see at South Shields is an ideal of a provincial freedwoman that includes information very deliberately chosen (Noy 2010: 14), whose mobility both spatial and social is made apparent through the inscription but whose status as a citizen (a freed slave was a citizen, contra Mattingly 2004: 11) is made apparent through an idealization of her aspirations or those of her husband, that could incorporate three languages and distil their cultural backgrounds and their related lives into this compressed commemoration of a person's identity at death.

The discussion so far points to the difficulty of interpreting images and the problem of generalizing from the specificity of inscriptions (Allason-Jones 1999: 50; Eckardt 2010: 8). However, perhaps we need to ask a different question: how did this set of codes for representing Regina, a freed slave born in Britain, find its way to South Shields and come to have meaning? John Creighton (2000) has argued that the Iron Age societies of pre-43 AD Britain adopted and adapted images from Roman coins, most notably the imagery that can found in Paul Zanker's (1988) discussion of the *Power of Images in the Age of Augustus*. His work has shown how classical imagery was adapted into the context of kingship in the pre-Roman period. Images of seated figures on these coins are plentiful, even if the dress is rather different from that found on Roman coinage. We might point also to a dominance of male over female imagery (see Creighton 2000 for examples). Hence, the place of Regina's origin was infused with a culture of Roman imagery prior to 43 AD. Subsequent to Claudius' annexation of Britain, we can find examples of Roman coins that provide images of ideals as stray finds and in hoards (Reece 2002), which can include figures such as Concordia, Fortuna and other female deities (see Bland and Orna-Ornstein 1997 for specific examples). These images on coins, like the coins themselves, circulated across the Roman Empire and, even if coinage was only used to pay tax, were objects with images that were encountered every year (Reece 2002: 98). The taxation of a province needed to be paid in money and the soldiers had to be paid in money, two factors that combined to produce a need for the circulation of a distinctly Roman coinage with a set of images that identified those coins as Roman. What we see is a flood of new images into Britain that could be picked up on, appropriated and re-combined to produce what is loosely referred to as 'provincial art'. However, that imagery associated with art in the provinces has a relationship to other images found in the provinces on coins that were the images of the state. The crossover of state image on coins to the private sphere in other media is a question yet to be discussed by archaeologists of the provinces.

Mobility and cultural change

The examples of new archaeological work on skeletons has pointed to evidence for a greater degree of migration in the Roman Empire than previously assumed by both archaeologists and ancient historians. This has a fundamental implication for forms of cultural change, such as the assumed forms associated with 'Romanization'. Not only did people circulate, taking with them ideas, but also their imagined ideals of how things should work. The images of ideal Roman anthropomorphic identities (gods, goddesses, men and women) circulated via what we might today describe as monetary union and a coinage that was minted in a few locations (such as Lyons or Rome), but was supplied to most parts of the empire. The focus on stable isotope analysis of skeletons has led scholars of Roman Britain to reappraise their archaeological data and their archaeological narrative. Michael Fulford (2010) re-writes the narrative of Roman Britain to focus on 'immigration'. Underpinning his focus on migration lies the epigraphic evidence for veterans staying and leaving; roughly half of these veterans set up inscriptions in Britain (Fulford 2010: 67). Following the annexation of Britain in 43 AD, he argues for a migration of 100,000 soldiers and others to Britain. How we assess the effect of these multi-ethnic migrants is difficult to see. Fulford (2010: 77) argues for the quantification of the popularity of pottery vessel forms as a means to understanding not so much economic trade, but consumption preferences leading to a better understanding of what changes might have occurred. Yet, most archaeologists, including Fulford (2010: 77), reject a direct link between a particular ethnic group and certain shapes or styles of pottery. However, there is another dimension to migration. Often it results in an epitaph asserting a point of origin (Noy 2000 for listing for such persons from Rome) including those from Britain (Noy 2010). Importantly, Johan Nicolay (2007) posits a life-cycle model for understanding the archaeological deposition of the weaponry of Batavians, in which veterans serving outside Batavia returned 'home' with their weapons and ritually disposed of them, with the next generation inheriting most items, and some items being buried with the soldier. What this points to is the objects associated with service in a military context migrating with the discharged veteran.

The situation of mobility and migration creates the opportunity to represent difference and conformity via a variety of concepts that are familiar within the study of epigraphy (and particularly epitaphs): name, language, origin in nation or city, as well as visual and verbal formulae (see Noy 2010 for discussion). How such modes of representation may be mapped back onto the living is open to questioning, since within the domestic spheres such issues associated with identity are less apparent and it is at the moment of death that ideas about identity, origins, and what material objects to inter with the dead come to the fore (Pearce 2010). Commemoration is a moment in which identity of the deceased was articulated and an identity was fixed for others in the present and future to see, and can include a named point of origin (Eckardt et al 2010: 105–6). However, artefacts found in burials and cremations cannot be read-off to identify migrants and non-migrants, as has been shown in the studies based on stable isotope analysis. Even in the context of commemoration, patterns of interaction between migrants and the communities in which they lived become apparent (Eckardt et al 2010). This observation points up the obvious demographic fact, that for towns or even settlements to flourish over the long term, migration contributed to their continuing existence and growth.

Chapter 9

Plants, Animals and Diet

The landscape and/or seascape as an artefact in its own right has proven an object of interest for both historians and archaeologists (for example, Horden and Purcell 2000). In this chapter, the subject of discussion turns away from these approaches to the landscape with a view to an examination of how archaeological evidence can be drawn together to present a better understanding for the historian of the variety of approaches to landscape exploitation. It has to be admitted that, although archaeologists collect masses of material through their activities, often synthesis of the material simply do not appear in print. This is particularly true of reports on plant, molluscs and animal remains. There is a whole volume documenting the *Natural History of Pompeii* (Jashemski and Meyer 2002) with each species carefully identified and documented. However, this takes us little further than a list of where items were identified from recent and past excavations. There is a danger that the evidence from this type of material is simply consigned to the back pages of a report and seldom found by even the most determined student of Roman history. Yet, there is an importance to these studies that needs to be discussed in the context of understanding how Roman society functioned. Embedded within the archaeological record are attitudes to plants and animals as well as straightforward questions associated with economic production and functionalism. In this chapter, some examples are set out to illustrate the range of approaches to the varied foodways within the cultural matrix of urbanism and landscape exploitation found within the Roman Empire.

The gardens and small holdings of Pompeii

There is a remarkable amount of space in the city of Pompeii given over to gardens (8 per cent of land use) or productive small holdings (9.7 per cent of land use). These are apparent to visitors to this remarkable site, where the Soprintendenza has replanted the gardens based on the archaeo-botanical evidence. Much of the information derived for the study of gardens can be found today in Wilhelmina Jashemski's two volumes on *The Gardens of Pompeii* (1979, 1993). The second of these volumes provides a description of every garden in the city with plan, description and bibliography. The work behind these volumes took some three decades from the 1950s through to the 1980s. This period saw the development of the means to excavate soil levels buried in 79 AD, and to reconstruct the planting patterns and species of plants in the gardens with a view to establishing a full understanding of orchards, vineyards and gardens attached to houses. It is surprising the work is not more fully recognized in the development of archaeological techniques – including the use of plaster casts of voids left by organic material that when filled revealed the size and type of tree planted in a garden.

The work by Jashemski recognized that outside space was as much a part of the domestic environment as the actual architecture of the house. It perhaps needs to be remembered that prior to the 1990s, the study of the archaeology of Pompeii was dominated by art and architectural historians, who had little interest in the everyday or social archaeology of the town. What Jashemski achieved was a series of groundbreaking publications that showed there was much more to Pompeii than just art historical description. She quite literally discovered orchards and market-gardens (Jashemski 1979: 232–50; 251–65), and proved that the assumed Forum Boarium or cattle-market was in fact a vineyard (Jashemski 1979: 201–18). As she points out, not everyone encouraged this new activity of garden archaeology. However, as with most things in archaeology, persistence paid off. We can now look on Pompeii as a place where the archaeology of gardens was pioneered, and where we came to realize that there were productive gardens as well as houses, shops, temples and streets. The distribution of the gardens across the city of Pompeii is quite haphazard with no clearly defined market-gardening zone and, instead, even insulae close to the forum contained productive gardens or small holdings.

Animal bones, meat consumption and improved breeds

Animal bones are found in large numbers on most archaeological sites with the result that specialist reports are commissioned by excavators. Zooarchaeology has become a specialized field that need not be fully integrated with the agendas of social archaeologists (Dobney 2001, Mackinnon 2004: 31–32). Animals were of course not just eaten, but also used for ritual purposes. The overall pattern of consumption of sheep/goats, pigs and oxen/cows in the Roman Empire has been recognized thanks to the work of Anthony King (1999a; 1999b) – also see Figure 7.3. There is considerable variation in the consumption of these three species across the Roman Empire. Broadly speaking, the northern provinces consumed oxen/cows in greater numbers than in Italy or within the Mediterranean. In southern France and within the Mediterranean, a greater emphasis was placed on the consumption of sheep and goats with one notable exception – Italy, a region in which pig consumption, uniquely, held a prominence in the diet of the population. These broad differences can be explained by cultural factors, but the uniqueness of Italy needs a little more explanation. We may speculate a connection with the fact that the greatest densities of urbanism were experienced in Italy and we might be tempted to see pigs as ideally suited to the urban situation because they do not need large territories on which to graze.

Animal bones in Italy was the subject of Michael Mackinnon's PhD thesis that formed the basis of his book that actively sought to integrate the evidence of animal bones with the evidence for animal husbandry found in texts (Mackinnon 2004). There are two abbreviations that prevail in such studies: NISP (number of identified species) and MNI (minimum number of individuals) that account for the members of all species found at a site and then correlates those with the minimum number of individual animals identified. For Italy, there is a remarkable convergence in the relative percentages of cattle, pigs, and sheep/goats found in clearly identified urban sites with the known status of a *municipium* or *colonia* (urban 1 in Mackinnon 2004) and rural sites: cattle, less than 20 per cent; sheep/goats, 30–40 per cent; and pigs, 40–45 per cent. What is intriguing is that there is a fundamental dichotomy between these rural and urban sites and the animal bones found at lesser urban sites, at which a far higher percentage of cattle bones were identified (more than 30 per cent) and a much lower percentage of pig bones (just over 20 per cent).

Animal bones provide a mass of data that can be used to characterize production in Roman Italy. Just like with human skeletons, the teeth of animals provide evidence for age at death: in Italy, most pigs were slaughtered at an age of less than two years (Mackinnon 2004: 142); sheep between one and four years (Mackinnon 2004: 106–7); whereas most cattle were kept to at least three years of age prior to slaughter (Mackinnon 2004: 80). More significantly, the measure of withers or height of cattle shows a rise in size from the period of the Republic (114cm) with an increase of roughly seven centimetres by the Imperial period (122cm) and maintenance of this increase into the period of Late Antiquity (Mackinnon 2004: 84). A pattern of increase replicated for sheep/goats (66cm in Republic to 69cm in the Empire and Late Antiquity, Mackinnon 2004: 111), but that is less apparent in the sample for pigs – perhaps due to a mixing of two different species of pig (Mackinnon 2001 identifies wither size variation 57–86cm), pointing to a presence of wild boars. What is more apparent is that the size of animals found at urban sites tended to be within a standard range of about 70 centimetres in terms of withers height (Mackinnon 2001: 657–58). However, overall through time, we do see an increase in height of pigs from the Republic into the Empire. Overall, it is apparent that animal husbandry improved to create larger animals. This occurred, as we saw in Chapter 4, in the period in which the number of sites identified by field survey is known to have increased in parts of Roman Italy.

The pattern of changes in size of animals can also be identified within the provinces, for example in the Rhine delta. Evidence for larger 'Roman' animals replacing smaller Iron Age cattle has been documented, but has led to a discussion of how we should not just interpret the evidence but also question our preconceptions (Groot 2008: 22). What is at stake here is a question of whether we place the stress on larger animals as more efficient within a modern ideology of animal husbandry at the expense of recognizing the merit of earlier Iron Age practices of husbandry. However, there is evidence that larger animals were introduced in the Roman period either with respect to a perceived need for more traction animals or in connection with the marketing of meat (Groot 2008: 91–92). Yet, when looking at the provincial context, we need to reflect back on changes occurring in Italy over the course of the same period, for the reason that it is far too easy to view every change in the provinces as a result of 'Roman' dominance.

The games, town foundation and ritual deposition of animals

Exotic animals, as every ancient historian knows, were viewed at the games. However, the archaeological recovery of bones of these exotic beasts imported into Rome or Carthage for such a purpose is rare (Mackinnon 2006). Even at Carthage, the bones of gazelle, wild boar, deer, camels, bear, ostrich and heartebeast were found dating from the 4th to 7th centuries, demonstrating a profound absence of lions and other 'big cats' (Mackinnon 2006: 151–52). The 5th to 7th century fill of a drain 50 metres south-west of the Colosseum did reveal a mixture of bones: horses, bears, leopards, ostrich, deer, fox and wild boar (Mackinnon 2006: 155). Mackinnon (2006: 156) suggests that exotic animals killed in the arena may have been eaten – Apicius refers to recipes for ostrich, and bear was eaten at Trimalchio's feast (Petr. *Sat.* 66). The exotic animals – big cats – seen by many may have been very few in number and were eaten by the very few granted access to this source of food. This takes us to theories beyond the archaeological evidence but it does open up some possibilities for further investigation. We should note that there was an expansion in the rearing of fallow deer that is now attested archaeologically, for example, on the Isle of Thanet as well as at the villa of Fishbourne in Britain (Sykes et al 2011). It needs to be noted that previously fallow deer were assumed to have been a Norman introduction to Britain (Sykes et al 2011). The degree which animals were introduced to new areas has yet to be fully appreciated and there may be numerous examples of animals in the archaeological record that were in many ways exotic.

It has been recognized by ancient historians and archaeologists working in Italy that *fora* of towns were associated with pits connected with ritual, but explanation of these has been hindered by a focus on texts rather than examination of the actual contents of the pits themselves (see Mouritsen 2004 with robust response from Coarelli 2005). Such pits are also found in the towns of Roman Britain, where excavators have revisited earlier interpretations of the pits and identified from their contents that these were pits with a selection of items in them that were deliberately deposited. These pits contain chosen items including whole pottery vessels, animal bones and fully articulate skeletons – particularly those of dogs. There has become an awareness that pits are located near to the centre of these new towns (Fulford and Timby 2000). Evidence from a pit in Dorchester contained the skeleton of a frog that might suggest the pits remained open and certainly were re-opened for the placement of additional items into them (Woodward and Woodward 2004; Maltby 2010b). Pits associated with ritual deposition have also been identified at the military site of Newstead and were a regular form of deposition in the Antonine period (Clarke and Jones 1996; Clarke 1999). The interpretation of these forms of ritual deposition tends to be automatically linked to a pre-Roman past in the minds of most commentators on Roman Britain (Fulford 2001 for example), whereas others (Woodward and Woodward 2004) connect such ritual deposition with Roman rituals associated with town foundation and planning. What is clear from work in Britain is that the contents of pits needs further discussion; after all most historians working in Italy will be aware of the sanctuary site at Terracina (Coarelli 1987: 113–40), although far fewer will be aware of the miniature objects recovered from the pits associated with the temple (see *Notizie degli Scavi* 1894: 96–111). Animal bones seldom are reported in detail in reports from Italy (Mackinnon 2004 for examples of detailed bone reports). However, this does raise new options for producing an interpretation of pits in both Roman Italy and elsewhere in the Roman Empire. As Simon Clarke (1999, see also Groot 2008) argues, we must connect these Roman deposits to forms of interpretation that prehistorians have specialized in – ritual and the symbolic, rather than the pure logic of arguments based on texts that ancient historians have to date specialized in – with little or no reference to the actual contents of the pits (Mouritsen 2004; Coarelli 2005). We should not blame any scholar for this; after all most discussion of animal bones in archaeological reports and syntheses tends to discuss the utilitarian production of meat for the table (King 1984; Mackinnon 2004). It should also be recognized that there is a far greater emphasis on the inclusion of zooarchaeology in the study of sites from Roman Britain than those published in Roman Italy (see King 1999b).

However, a recent book-length study of the subject has been completed by Maaike Groot (2008), in which the subject of ritual deposition of animals and parts of animals is discussed at length in the context of two rural sites in the Netherlands. The rituals at these rural sites are seen by the author to mirror those found at nearby temple sites such as Empel and Elst (Groot 2008: 31). The study arises from an intuitive feeling by excavators at these sites that there was 'something odd' about the animal bones recovered that led to the development of a protocol for excavating these animal bone deposits that included the possibilities of them being ritual deposits that had been very deliberately made (Groot 2008: 97). The presence of the protocol allowed for a higher recovery rate of data likely to shed light on ritual activity and prevented a loss of data. Equally, ritual is not independent from other routinely studied areas such as the economy, since ritual practices cross over into what we today regard as quintessentially secular realms – in the cemetery of Tiel-Passewaaij, a chicken with osteoporosis was sacrificed as a grave gift. Equally, practices associated with ritual can be quite different to general animal husbandry – for example at a temple in Nijmegen very young cattle were sacrificed (Groot 2008: 109–10), a pattern also identified at temple sites in Britain (Harlow and Great Chesterford, Legge et al 2000). A study of animal bones found at Roman period temples in southern Britain demonstrated that animals were deliberately selected (King 2005). However, ritual was not limited to public spaces and was performed in rural settlements as Groot argues persuasively (2008: 113), and deposits need to be identified with a view to identifying formalized behaviour that communicates with the supernatural (Groot 2008: 118–20 discusses the criteria in detail): fully articulated skeletons, articulated limbs, whole skulls and large concentrations of bones are all signs of ritual deposition that would seem to increase within the Roman period (Groot 2008: 120–40). What has proven particularly diagnostic in the study of ritual deposits has been the presence of bones of dogs, whose bodies were discarded whole, as were horses in some cases (Stallibrass 2000). The fact that few of the bones were gnawed by animals would suggest that there was more than likely some special form of deposition that protected the body of the horse or dog from interference after death. Indeed, the deposition of whole or part skeletons of animals (or what are called Associated Animal Bone Groups) can provide an indicator of change over time from the Iron Age to the Roman period in Britain; for instance there was a very marked increase in the deposition of dogs with a decrease in deposition of parts or whole bodies of sheep. Interestingly, in the early Medieval period, there is an absolute and total decline of deposits of cattle, pig and sheep in this format – the three animals most associated with Roman sacrifice. It is not beyond reason to suggest that this can be associated with changes in ritual associated with early Christianity. It is clear that interpretation of animal bone deposits, particularly those of whole or partial skeletons, needs to account for the possibility of ritual underlying the depositional processes in the Roman as well as the earlier Iron Age periods.

Meat for townies: Winchester

Although the ritual and symbolic deposition of animal remains needs to be considered, the study of animals bones allows us to have a greater insight into the economic provision of meat in rural and urban contexts. A recently-published volume that explores this type of evidence is entitled *Feeding a Roman Town* (Maltby 2010a). The book sets out to establish a full picture of the material and its implications. Animal bones do appear in graves, but also in the context of early butchery waste that included dogs, pigs, and sheep/goats, alongside horses and cattle (Maltby 2010a: 31–41). For the later period from the mid-2nd century through to the 4th/5th centuries, observations were made with regard to 2,000 butchery marks on the cattle bone assemblages (Maltby 2010a: 126–42). What is made clear by this analysis is that there were professional butchers in Winchester, who processed the carcasses of animals in similar ways to those found at military sites and in other towns in Roman Britain. Interestingly, although horse bones do display butchery marks, the incidence of these is much lower than for cattle bones (Maltby 2010a: 208–9). Most cattle were mature at the point of slaughter in Winchester, in contrast to finds from Dorchester that were considered to represent calves sold to individual householders for butchery or rearing, and it is also worth noting that cattle in Winchester were larger than those of Dorchester by approximately four centimetres (Maltby 2010a: 143–46). The cattle and sheep slaughtered at Winchester were larger (117cm for cattle, 59cm for sheep) than the mean wither height found elsewhere in Roman Britain, but were much smaller than cattle and sheep found in Roman imperial Italy (Maltby 2010a: 292–95, see above for figures from Roman Italy). Although cattle constitute the main assemblage, reference needs also to be made to birds – including ducks and geese (Maltby 2010a: 225–27). The value of the Winchester study of animal bones is that it can be compared to other similar assemblages in towns and also to that of the nearby rural settlement at Owslebury (Maltby 2010a: 253–54). The major conclusion from this study points to the advantage the urban dweller had in that they were provided with meat at the optimum age for consumption and that meat was skilfully butchered by professionals. This thorough investigation points to a major difference in the supply of meat to a town in Roman Britain, when compared to the overall pattern of meat consumption in the countryside of Britain or with the evidence for animal bones and meat consumption in Roman Italy. For Roman historians, it identifies the advantages of town life that was differentiated not just by architecture and population density, but also by the availability of quality produce skilfully slaughtered. However, in the history of cattle, the Roman period marks a shift in perception of cows as primarily a source of meat, rather than a multi-purpose animal also associated with ploughing and dairy production. In the urban context, cattle become seen as a commodity in the Roman period (Seetah 2005).

Roman impact on the paleo-landscapes

The study of environmental data – pollens, seeds, insects, beetles and so on – has allowed for a more rigorous analysis of landscape change in the long term. Studies of this kind have been limited by the number of academics capable of undertaking such work, the fact that not all of this material has been routinely collected by excavators and that very few syntheses of the evidence have been undertaken (Dark 1997: 1–18). Britain provides some solid examples of how this evidence can be used to highlight changes and to reconstruct the environment (Dark 1997; 2000). There has to be an initial recognition though that prehistoric Britain contained a farmed landscape. The biggest innovation in terms of landscape transformation in the four centuries of the Roman period was in drainage associated with an expansion of agriculture into the fens, and the development of what may be defined as a 'villa landscape' characterized by a particular architectural form that included window glass, tessellated floors, mosaics and other features of Roman material culture (Dark 1997: 43–47). However, there is a need to define far more than the physical structure of the villa building and to include the landscape around the villa as part of the definition of what a villa is (Dark 1997: 47). This takes the villa out of the cultural realm of aesthetics and towards a discussion of economic power that enabled the economic exploitation of the landscape, including by those of lesser social status and less economic wealth. However, there are parts of Britain, such as the south-west, that show an absence of change in the Roman period (see Fyfe et al 2004).

The pollen record provides a means to understand what changes may have occurred in the Roman period. Pollen is the most specific evidence of what was growing in Roman Britain, rather than what may have been grown or imported (Dark 1997: 106–7). Overall there was a shift from finding cereal pollen at 50 per cent of Iron Age sites to 75 per cent in the Roman period (Dark 1997: 106). This demonstrates an expansion of the growth of cereals that is confirmed by the analysis of charred grain that suggests that, although spelt and barley continued to be grown, these crops were supplemented by bread wheat that is particularly well-suited to clay or silty soils in areas of agricultural expansion in the Roman period (Dark 1997: 110–11). This alteration of the landscape may also be relevant to the introduction of larger cattle for ploughing such heavy soils (Dark 1997: 101–3).

However, there is a more dramatic level of landscape transformation at work in the northern part of the province of Britannia. The settlement of troops in forts on Hadrian's Wall presented a logistical problem of the supply of water to any settlement. The latter was provided at Housesteads fort by harvesting the rainwater run-off from the roofs of the fort buildings. In fact, Peter Beaumont (2008) demonstrates that, in a climatic region with rain at least once in every 15 days, there was little need for aqueducts to supply water to the fort (which was impractical in any case, but compare complexity of supply of water to Ephesos: Ortloff and Crouch 2001). Water harvesting was a fundamental feature of, for example, the 'atrium house' of Italy and would seem to be a design feature of other forms of Roman architecture. Indeed, in Britain with its very different climate from the Mediterranean, water harvesting need not have been as efficient as the inward-facing courtyard villas and houses – hence climate and ease of water harvesting may provide a key to understanding the variation between villa architecture across the Roman Empire.

The alteration of the landscape did not cease at Hadrian's Wall itself and pollen sequences from a three-metre core with radiocarbon dates from Fozy Moss close to the Roman fort of Carrawburgh and only 200 metres to the north of the wall (Dumayne 1994) provides new guidance on the changes associated with the presence of the military. The evidence points to a long period down to the 2nd century AD during which the vegetation was associated with woodland. That was followed by a period of clearance of this woodland and its replacement with grassland in the period from about 129 to 370 AD – probably due to the need to use timber in the construction of Hadrian's Wall (Dumayne 1994). Once cleared in the period of construction, the ongoing demand for wood for charcoal or for heating and cooking maintained a cleared landscape.

Diet: did it change with Roman annexation?

So far our discussion has pointed to evidence from animal bones providing answers to questions regarding consumption. However, when turning to human diet, we need to be very clear that it differed markedly from any modern European diet – for example, the consumption by the average Dutch citizen today, over the course of one year, of 43 kilograms of pork, 22 kilograms of chicken, almost 18 kilograms of beef and less than two kilograms of mutton; the evidence from Nijmegen points to an almost total absence of chicken being consumed (Lauwerier 2009: 158–59). Looking across the Roman Empire, we can see that the meat eaten within diets found in Rome and Italy (as evidenced by animal bones) was unique in the inclusion of a large amount of pork, and that this emphasis was not found in the provinces, whether the sheep/goat-dominated diets of provinces of the Mediterranean or the cattle-dominated diet of the northern provinces (King 1999b: 188–90). The cultural changes associated with Romanization did not produce a change in the animals produced and consumed in terms of diet. However, Anthony King (1999a) argues that the pork-rich diet of Italy was a byproduct of the economic exploitation of the empire.

A more direct method for assessing diet is to examine skeletal evidence in areas of the Roman Empire that practised inhumation before and after the annexation of a territory by Rome. One region that has a skeletal record of this nature is Dorset in southern England. Rebecca Redfern and Sharon DeWitte (2010) examined 518 skeletons (203 Iron Age, 315 Roman) excavated in Dorset with a view to identifying how changes associated with the Roman period – such as urbanization, changes in diet and increased heterogeneity of the population – impacted on the health of males and females. The increase in diversity of population was not regarded as a factor, since migrants from the northern Mediterranean display little genetic dissimilarity, in contrast to say the early modern population change associated with the European arrival in North America (Redfern and DeWitte 2010). Certainly, there was an increase in the consumption of marine animals, but also an increase in dental disease, as well as metabolic and infectious diseases, alongside a decrease in trauma – perhaps caused by violence in the pre-Roman period (Redfern and DeWitte 2010). The key diseases that were found to be far higher in the Roman period were rickets and tuberculosis (Redfern and DeWitte 2010). Hence, although changes in material culture and production can be found within the archaeological record, the Roman period in Dorset was characterized as a time of increased risk of death for children and the elderly (Redfern and DeWitte 2010). There was also a change in the gendered risk of death: in the Iron Age sample of skeletons, men and women faced a very similar level of risk of death, whereas in the Roman period, the male risk becomes much higher. This is at odds with a perception that cultural factors would have provided men with greater advantage in the Roman period and causes historians to pause in their general assumption that patriarchy favoured males over females. What Redfern and DeWitte (2010) also reveal is that there was some variation in their data according to whether it was located in Dorchester or in nearby Poundbury. Interestingly, it would seem that the greater risk to male health in the Roman period was also accompanied with a wider application of healing practices (Redfern 2010).

Chapter 10

Looking in Museums
Discovering Artefacts

There is a challenge in the study of the Roman past which can be put quite simply – who used the various artefacts that have been found? Our textual sources produced by a male elite provide some guidance, but there is a fundamental problem – their writing often intellectualizes the meaning of words and the study of how material culture is represented by this elite is hardly a subject of literary analysis (unlike for example, objects of artistic merit). More importantly, as can be seen from a survey of the modern literature, to contemplate the use of material objects by, for example, slaves in Britain leads to the conclusion that there is a scholarly lacuna waiting to be filled. When there are specific studies of slavery and material culture, there is a tendency to focus on the use of space in houses and villas in Italy to look for slave quarters but then to shift attention to the representation of slaves in art (see George 2011, especially the bibliographic essay). The absence of written documentation is regarded as a hindrance to the development of an artefact-based approach to the subject, that is further hindered by an absence of a defined 'material culture' of slavery – possibly because material culture was less available to slaves, just as it was less available to peasants and the poor. This exemplifies a problem that affects the study of artefacts – how do we identify who may have used an object? This is especially true of uses that need not conform to the function of the item – for example, children use a variety of items today which serve a quite different function for adults. Once we begin to question the use of an object in this way, it moves on to a discussion of which objects should be associated with a particular gender or age-group, and how do we prevent the mapping of our own preconceptions of gender and age onto the Roman past?

However, objects themselves are coming to be seen to have a life course starting with their production or their formation, often via craft activity, that then leads to a moment of economic transaction and then usage (Hurcombe 2007: 38–43). The life course of the object to this point is well attested in the archaeological record through the study of the production

Figure 10.1 Pompeii: amphorae found in the House of the Menander

of, for example, Samian pottery that has a long tradition in the study of production sites and of its distribution (for example, Willis 2005). An amphora that was designed to transport a particular liquid was produced in, say, Spain and then disposed of in Italy establishes a trading connection (Pena 2007: 47–56). The primary function of transportation could be followed by subsequent or secondary usage – many amphorae are found empty in the *impluvium* or in other parts of houses in Pompeii (Figure 10.1, see Pena 2007: 299–300, see also 119–92 on other uses). Their function had been changed and could be changed again if broken and utilized as a building material or disposed of in the massive pile of amphorae in Rome known as Monte Testaccio (Pena 2007: 300–306). It is notable that deliberate breakage and organized disposal characterizes this deposit. More complex items, such as furniture, were purchased for longer-term usage and pleasure – examples of wooden furniture found in Herculaneum include a *lararium*, basically a cupboard with doors for the storage or deliberate placement of figurines of gods relevant to the household members (Mols 1999). The container and its objects had a quite different life-course from a pottery vessel or an amphora; these objects were acquired with the intention of preservation and their relevance to the daily existence of the inhabitants of the household was maintained across time (a concept also found in literary texts, see Foss 1997).

Into the museum: a visual experience

Museums are full of artefacts, it is what museums generally do – but the other thing museums do is to prevent you from touching (or taking) the

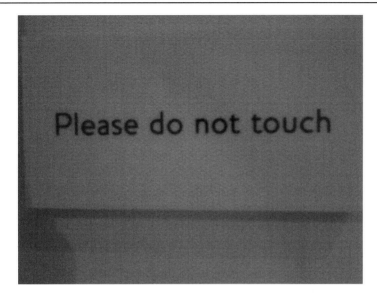

Figure 10.2 The caption describes the approach to museum display – touch is not a sensory perception that is allowed. Instead, objects are imagined through vision (from the Wellcome Institute)

objects (Figure 10.2). They have collections, some put together many years ago, others based on recent excavations. Some of these artefacts or objects are placed in display cases in association with other objects – these may be grouped by type of material (such as glass) or a theme (such as religion), or in association with other artefacts found together. Visitors may look at these objects and it is via looking that artefacts are mostly experienced in museums. What is missing is the sense of touch and feel of an object that is so important for the sense of living in a material world. There are options to create a sense of touch – a handling collection in a museum (such as found in the Canterbury Roman Museum) or a box of objects provided to a school (as the Canterbury Archaeological Trust does). However, for most objects, especially jewellery, coins, glass and even large pottery vessels, only academics, the museum staff or select volunteers can touch the collection. For the majority, there is a need to work from their visual perception to judge weight (often incorrect), size (fairly accurate) and texture (hard to imagine).

What was it like to be Roman and use these artefacts? There are numerous schemes to enable the visitor to better imagine or empathize with those in the past. The Canterbury Roman Museum (developed in the 1980s on the site of the earlier Roman Pavement Museum – formed

Figure 10.3 Canterbury Roman Museum (2011): mannequins recreate modern gender roles?

after the discovery of *in situ* mosaics) addresses this problem through the use of mannequins dressed as Romans – a hairdresser, a soldier, a crafts-men, a cook and so on, with carefully researched fabric for clothing (Figure 10.3). There are also scenes staged around the mannequins – a Roman dining room with couches and tableware, and a cooking range with cooking ware. These three-dimensional reconstructions are intended to reveal how material culture was used and allow the visitor to relate objects in cabinets to human usage. Yet, empathy depends on sight rather than touch and is directed by what and who is reconstructed. The 'what' ranges across status groups, but the 'who' is intriguing – because as historians we are aware that, in all probability, about 50 per cent of the population would have been aged less than 18 and 50 per cent of the population would have been female. In the Canterbury Roman Museum, there are three women – one is cooking, one is a hairdresser and another is seated having her hair done in a Flavian style (Figure 10.3). The men, in contrast, are running shops, one is a soldier with a horse, other mannequins are male archaeologists discovering the past. What we have reflected here is a world in which the mannequins and the use of the objects reflect adult gendered roles from a point in our own past (see Kokinidou and Nikolaidou 2000; Allison 2006 with responses). It is also surprising that there are no children. After all, the museum is popular with children and there is a real need to explain how children (50 per cent of the population) led their lives. It has to be stressed at this point that Canterbury City Council plan to re-develop the museum to be more inclusive in the future, and the current opportunity to at least dress as a Roman provides a guide for children to experience the texture of textiles and the feel of a metal helmet (Figure 10.4).

Objects and communication

The museum experience provides us with a key to understanding objects: there are those that are regularly touched (such as cutlery) and those that are not (such as figurines). Yet in museums, you can neither touch these nor imagine their use – the objects are staged to be visually pleasing (Figure 10.5). There are other distinctions too: tools tend to be associated with particular functions and to present a set of rules of interpretation, when for example found in a Pompeian house *in situ* ready for use in 79 AD (Allison 2004). Penelope Allison (2004) found in her study of arte-fact assemblages from 30 houses that rooms could not be defined by function of the objects that they contained. Her study places an emphasis on the fundamentals of urban existence: food preparation, food storage and food consumption alongside sleeping and ablutions, before moving on to luxury, religious activity and household productivity. The distribu-tion patterns identified within these categories, she argues, are as much a result of the categories themselves that do not map neatly onto our own mentalities of the use of objects in the Roman household (Allison 2004: 157). Her study is proof, if it was needed, that the recording of objects even found *in situ* does not automatically lead to conclusions and explanations about the past. For example, scales for weighing are an item of kitchen equipment today, but weights for scales are seldom found in kitchens in Pompeii

Figure 10.4 Canterbury Roman Museum (2011): the ability to dress up makes children Roman and perhaps able to view adult mannequins as real figures

(Allison 2004: 149–50). This work allows us to question the categories we use when approaching such evidence and to conclude that the primary function of an object only partially accounts for its position or placement within a house. Moreover, the association between certain objects and room-types – whether described via Latin terminology such as *atrium* or discussed as courtyards – seems to show the adaptability of spaces to the presence of a variety of objects.

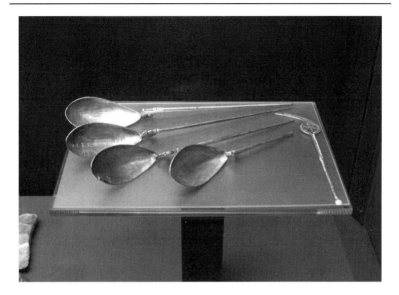

Figure 10.5 Canterbury Roman Museum (2011): to be seen but not used – an
example of the museological aesthetic of the visual

It has to be said that most objects found by archaeologists tend to be
neither displayed nor published; they effectively remain secret and only
available to specialists (Hurcombe 2007: 24). There is a danger that
artefacts become secret and remain unstudied, or even simply lost (for
example, the objects found at Ostia in the late 1930s). In the UK, with 90
per cent of all archaeology in the last two decades undertaken by commercial units in the face of property development, we have come to see
an absence of publication of these discoveries. A recent report by the
British Academy noted that, of the excavations undertaken between 1990
and 1994, less than 6 per cent had been published (Fulford 2011). The
figures alone are damning, but for anyone who has seen an archaeological
or museum store, the reality in three dimensions by volume of material is
striking. This is where students can make a difference and there is a need
for human labour to publish in digital form at least the excavations from
the past. With the recession, the slowing in the pace of redevelopment
contributes further to the problem of publication – let alone synthesis of
past excavations by commercial units. This situation is far different from the
regular books published on the archaeology of say Roman Canterbury in the
first half of the 20th century (for example, Frere 1947 reprinted through to
1965). Michael Fulford (2011) argues for a fusion of endeavour between

universities and commercial units to address the problem that archaeology in the UK is becoming more like that of Italy, in which recent excavations remain unpublished and basically secret. I would argue that the problems associated with commercial archaeology in the UK are also pervasive in museums, where objects are stored and their existence only known to museum staff. There is much debate about the de-acquisition of collections, basically the disposal of collections that are not displayed (papers in Davies 2011). Many museums face funding problems or even closure, yet their vital asset – the collection – needs to be displayed and visitors need to have it explained to them (see MLA 2010). Museums often simply do not explain what an object meant in the past – see Figure 10.6. Importantly, the label informs us of the type of object, where it was found and its catalogue number. This is where the digital age could benefit museums with images of the objects and further text (subject to re-interpretation) being presented to a wider public over the internet or via a smartphone. This is where universities with their small army of students in ancient history, classics and archaeology can develop and disseminate knowledge, via the simple action of building websites or creating a discussion forum – it could simply be 'my top ten objects in x museum', but even that would disseminate knowledge of a collection (as advocated by Hill 2001: 17–18). More importantly, it would allow visitors to come with ideas and to search out particular

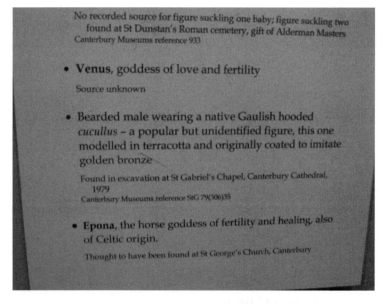

No recorded source for figure suckling one baby; figure suckling two found at St Dunstan's Roman cemetery, gift of Alderman Masters Canterbury Museums reference 933

- **Venus**, goddess of love and fertility

  Source unknown

- Bearded male wearing a native Gaulish hooded *cucullus* – a popular but unidentified figure, this one modelled in terracotta and originally coated to imitate golden bronze

  Found in excavation at St Gabriel's Chapel, Canterbury Cathedral, 1979
  Canterbury Museums reference StG 79(306)35

- **Epona**, the horse goddess of fertility and healing, also of Celtic origin.

  Thought to have been found at St George's Church, Canterbury

Figure 10.6 Canterbury Roman Museum (2011): labels and objects

objects rather than being distracted by mannequins on entry or being involved in an exploration of what the museum contains or a simple walk around the layout of exhibits.

Over the last two years, I have frequently visited the Canterbury Roman Museum with its former curator, with groups of students, visiting academics or on my own. Return visits have caused me to see the collection differently – I have discovered one of the best collections of Roman glass in the UK, but at other times focused on a single glass bracelet, and then there are the figurines that struck a resonance for the writing of this chapter. There is no way of really knowing what objects are on display prior to a visit. The phenomenon of needing to know in advance what is in a museum to see what is actually there causes all visits to museums to take on an aspect of urban-exploration of the building, rather than an activity directed at finding an explanation of how objects can be utilized to communicate ideas in the past and about the past in the present. Some museums give little away on their website (www.canterbury.co.uk/Canterbury-Museums. aspx), whereas others provide information for the visitor to gauge their level of interest (www.doverdc.co.uk/museum.aspx). As we have seen, the experience of the museum is delivered through the sight and movement of the visitor with the stopping and looking (including reading) being structured around cabinets of objects or displays – while groups might gather in key rooms for presentations and then disperse to move and to look.

The discussion of objects in the rest of this chapter will mainly focus on an investigation of a single object from the Canterbury Roman Museum to evaluate how the archaeological literature presents this object and how alternative viewpoints could be presented to create new meanings for a single object. In so doing, the discussion is founded on an investigation of publications relating to that object. All museum objects can be investigated through the development of a bibliography on that object and the harvesting of knowledge far greater than what is displayed on the label in the museum itself. However, few visitors have the skills or time to create a bibliography and their own interpretative framework. Yet, these are needed to allow for the development of a multiplicity of interpretations and even to encounter some rather unusual interpretations. A single object can develop a multiplicity of narratives that can be presented prior to arrival at a museum or via smartphone technology.

Objects and goddesses: goddesses as objects

A close examination of the Canterbury Roman Museum display cases reveals two figurines of goddesses with breast-feeding infants (one of

Figure 10.7 Canterbury Roman Museum (2011): a Dea Nutrix – deposited with head broken off in a grave, but displayed in its repaired state with no indication of how it was found or why it was broken and deposited in a grave

which is pictured in Figure 10.7). The goddess is breast-feeding, hence her modern name Dea Nutrix, but there needs to be greater explanation of this goddess and her form in Britain, whether found in a civilian or military context, and seen as a 'Celticization' of a Venus figure (Aldhouse-Green 1976: 20–21, 231, 1978: 17, 86; see also papers in Häussler and King 2007–8). This type of figurine also appears in Gaul and Germany, where it has been found in graves, houses and shrines and is associated with children of a variety of ages from infants to much older children (Aldhouse-Green 1989: 30–32). The Dea Nutrix as a deity seems in many senses less Roman than say the mother goddess figure on the Ara Pacis in Rome, with the consequence that scholars (for example, Aldhouse-Green 1989: 9–10) see the Dea Nutrix type and other female seated deities as linked to a Celtic maternalism. There is an unwritten statement that the Romans did not share in this sense of maternalism; after all Tacitus (*Germania* 19) pointed to the fact that barbarian women breast-fed their own children, in contrast to the Roman practice of wet-nursing, and brought up all their children. This is a topic discussed and published on in ancient history with reference to literary and epigraphy sources (such as Bradley 1991: 13–36). Yet, the relative abundance of the find of a mass-produced image of a seated female breast-feeding figure has a relevance to the study of the histories of breast-feeding, wet-nursing and childhood in antiquity.

The female seated figures either with breast-feeding infants or with fruit or produce in their laps can be seen to have much in common with the female figure on the Ara Pacis in Rome that includes both of these attributes (Figure 10.8). Within the north-west provinces, the seated female figures tend to be associated with a single theme (child/twins or other object/s), whereas the Ara Pacis imagery draws in multiple objects to multiply meanings. To draw together additional themes, the goddesses or *Deae Matronae* were multiplied to two or three and themed objects added. For example, at Cirencester, the central female figure holds a swaddled baby, while the flanking figures carry trays of differentiated fruit (Aldhouse-Green 1989: 200, figure 87; also found in epigraphy of northern Italy – Mennella and Lastrico 2008). At Vertillim (Burgundy) an example

Figure 10.8 Rome: the Ara Pacis (Rome) – the so-called Tellus Relief features three goddesses. Is this a model for the finds of triple goddesses in Gaul, Britain and Germany?

has been found with one goddess with a swaddled baby and the others with a piece of cloth and a sponge (Aldhouse-Green 1989: 191, figure 84). Triads are seen by Aldhouse-Green (1989: 204–5) to triple the power in Celtic thought, but she also observes that Roman practices produced three gods: Jupiter, Juno and Minerva – or we might add the all-male combination of household gods: Genius and Lares. Looking back at the above discussion, it becomes intriguing to notice that modern commentators on the Ara Pacis image focus on the identity of the central figure and explain away the other two female figures as personifications of the winds. However, this is an image that has three female deities in view. Like those from the northern provinces, their breasts and objects associated with fertility are emphasized (Laurence 2000). The multiplier effect found in the images of goddesses might be seen to map onto the multiplicity of deities that could be identified as associated with child birth (Augustine *Dei civitate dei* 4.11). The various names in the texts discussed here provide the means to identify a goddess with a particular part of childbirth, within visual imagery, for example on Roman coins, and we use the objects associated with a seated female figure to identify her as Ceres (corn) or *Alimenta* (children) that correspond to textual names written on some of the coins (Laurence 2011 for discussion). What becomes difficult is when we step from the realm of one figure equals one goddess and view three female figures together as in Figure 10.8 with a multiplicity of objects as signifiers with the result that the goddesses become polyvalent embodiments of fertility through their dress (and our viewing of parts of their body) and association with symbolic objects. Alternatively, we do find the three 'Celtic' goddesses holding a baby and bathing equipment to symbolize the ritual of the first bath (Dasen 2009, figure 9). Simone Deyts (1992) sees all seated figures as related to prosperity that included the nurturing of children.

The life course of objects and the interpretation of objects

Looking at objects in museums raises questions and curiosity about the objects that are often simply not answered by the label in the museum. To return to the Dea Nutrix in the Canterbury Roman Museum that was found in St Dunstan's Roman Cemetery (Figure 10.7), museum visitors will find another one in another case but will not necessarily know that other examples have been found in Canterbury and other parts of the south-east of England. To look further or find out more, visitors have to find references to these figures, often in less than recent publications. In the case of the Dea Nutrix, they need to go back to the publications of

Frank Jenkins on figurines found in Canterbury (Jenkins 1953, 1956, 1957, 1958). His article on the Dea Nutrix figurines (Jenkins 1957) includes reference further back to a 19th century publication of a kiln site near Toulon-sur-Allier in France (1860). Interestingly, the Dea Nutrix figurines are relatively commonly found in Gaul, but are relatively rare in Britain. Some of these figurines were signed by a modeller Pistillus, and are of a similar form to those found in Canterbury that have no name on them. Pistillus is a name that also occurs on Samian ware in the 2nd century AD at Lezoux (*CIL* 13.10015, 84; Jenkins 1957: 38). This discussion by Jenkins takes us to a possible point of production or at least a place at which similar figurines were created. The connection with the kiln sites though was not an original contribution of the 20th century, but came a year after the lavish publication of that site in 1861 in a discussion of the cemeteries of Roman Canterbury by John Brent and the recent find of the Dea Nutrix statue from the cemetery of St Dunstan's churchyard now on display 150 years later in the Canterbury Roman Museum (Brent 1861: 33).

What is perhaps disconcerting for students investigating the literature on such objects is that their searches of the scholarship take them back to a time when the conception of Romanization was very different from the one that they have been taught based on Martin Millett's 1990 book or the work of David Mattingly (2006), and is also a contrast to the observations of Tom Blagg (1995) on the self-Romanization of the population of Canterbury. Equally, gender archaeology was not in existence in the late 1950s, so alien forms of thought are there in the literature and assumptions that need to be questioned by students in the 21st century – not least changes in the technologies of grooming the body that could influence forms of representation of deities (see Eckardt 2008). There is a basic association of a female deity with children at her breast and female worshippers: 'They were offerings made to the deity to invoke her aid in childbirth and to ward off the various disorders and disasters peculiar to the female sex' (Jenkins 1957: 40). This leads towards an association with a Gallic mother goddess, but could equally connect the figure to a 6th century BC figurine found at Megara Hyblaea in Sicily (Jenkins 1957: 41). However, we should not be too swift to judge the practitioner from the past. He raises an important issue in his discussion of deliberate breakage and deposition of such figurines in graves, including the one found today in the Canterbury Roman Museum that was excavated from a grave (Jenkins 1957: 41). What we are missing though is an understanding of the actual archaeological context that is at best vague (Brent 1861).

The absence of a context is a common problem for many objects found in museum collections formed in the 19th century, at a time when towns such as Canterbury were experiencing rapid expansion in terms of road-building, drainage projects, railway construction and the rebuilding of the built environment (see Brent 1861). The scale of redevelopment of the urban and rural landscape in the 19th century quite literally created the body of knowledge on which to begin to create interpretations of the past and also the material that formed the basis for museum collections of objects (Brent 1861 is a good account of the process). At the same time, archaeologists were connecting the de-contextualized finds, such as the Dea Nutrix from St Dunstan's, with sites of production found on the continent. These sites included moulds for the manufacture of the figurines and the actual kilns that produced the objects, alongside the names of persons producing the images (Tudot 1860). This remarkable kiln site benefitted from its dissemination to a European public in an excellent publication with a profusion of illustrations. The forms found at the kiln site are dominated by female divinities, especially those with children – like the Dea Nutrix from Canterbury – and also included numerous children. The publication (Tudot 1860) available via Google Books provides a starting point for the interpretation of these images, as well as the re-configuration of their interpretation with a greater focus on the representation of gender, age and style.

The presence of numerous female representations tends to be linked back to the writings of classical authors on pre-Roman Gaul and a stress upon matriarchy (Jenkins 1957). What gets lost in the discussion is an earlier 19th century connection between these figurines and 2nd century AD coins inscribed with the legend *Fecunditas* or *Fecunditas Augusta* that were observed in the 19th century (Dowker 1887). The coins were primarily associated with a range of images on the coinage associated with the older and younger empresses Faustina. These two empresses were associated with a variety of deities connected with fertility. Going back to the 19th century systems of thought aligns the figures with Mediterranean-based religion rather than an insistence of a linkage to a form of Gaulish or Celtic religion that need not have persisted into the 2nd century AD. Other finds of figurines such as that of the pseudo-Venus present scholars with the task of attempting to associate this clearly classical figure with concepts of Celtic religion that need not have prevailed at the time of deposition (see Jenkins 1958: 70 for intellectual gymnastics). What this discussion illustrates is that objects are written about within the context of interpretation of the author and their time of writing. Hence, critical awareness is needed by students of the time at which an object is described (in itself an act of interpretation) and, equally, there needs to be an awareness that observations made in the 19th century may well be repeated in the 20th century and then repeated again in the 21st century.

Adjustment in the 21st century: from Baldock to the internet

Excavations of a cemetery in Baldock (Hertfordshire) in 1988 in the face of development discovered a series of graves that included the burial of a child with a clay figurine in the form of a Dea Nutrix (Burleigh et al 2006 for factual account of the excavation – details given here derive from this account). This was a unique find of an infant with a figurine and two boxes laid across the body (1,800 graves have been excavated around Baldock without such grave goods) and was dated to the 4th century AD. The coffin was just over a metre in length, but the remains of the skeleton were much smaller – precision is not possible due to the acid soil that destroyed many of the bones. The figurine shares characteristics of that discussed above from Canterbury, apart from the fact that it was not deliberately broken at deposition in the grave. The excavators observe similarities between this figurine and that of those from the excavated kiln site in France discussed above and published on in the 19th century. This factor allows for the attribution of the figurine as produced in Gaul and imported into Britain. The connection is made, here, between a known point of deposition and a known point of production in a dated context of the 2nd century AD – although it should be remembered that the discovery of kiln sites is rare and that there were many more places of production than those that we know of. The conclusion is based on observations of style that make connections in the same way that the 19th and 20th century commentators on these figurines did. In short, this is a classic humanities-based methodology that leaves one wondering about whether the assertions could be verified by a greater use of scientific analysis (for techniques see Hurcombe 2007: 70–90). The interpretation of the find by the team depends on recent thinking about the biography of objects and social memory. Accepting a 2nd century date for the manufacture of the object, the excavators suggest that the figurine had a long life course of being preserved and becoming a focus of memory. The uniqueness of the burial of the object suggests that the grave was of a higher status than others in the cemetery. The positioning of the object mirrors that found in connection with the burial of female children with dolls from the Mediterranean (for references to excavated examples see Rinaldi 1956). This allows us to consider the dolls of the Mediterranean as much more than toys of the Barbie variety and to consider their role as similar to that of the Dea Nutrix figurine. This causes dolls to shift from category of toy to that of a symbol of childhood and an object via which childhood could be remembered. The question of what purpose the Dea Nutrix from Baldock served prior to deposition remains unanswered. We can imagine the figurine having a location, like others of this type, in a shrine – but it may be seen as emblematic of a phase of the life course, in a similar way to which the recently discovered Romano-British goddess Senuna might symbolize a later phase of the life course (for references to Senuna, see Burleigh et al 2006).

While searching the internet for finds of Dea Nutrix figurines, I came across a whole host of modern interpretations of the Dea Nutrix. Most were related to a set of spiritual beliefs or wiki religion, by which people share thoughts about their beliefs in the existence of a *numen* or form of life force. A form of *numenism* was seen to have emerged as long ago as the 1940s in an attempt to make sense of the Second World War and the atom bomb. For this form of religious belief, the Dea Nutrix is seen to reside within everything in the manner of a classical interpretation of *numina* (http://talon.dreamwidth.org/1215.html). However, the group American Neopaganism presents an alternative of the Dea Nutrix based around the imagery of breast-feeding with links textually to the goddess Isis and illustrated with the statuary associated with Cybele (www.american-neopaganism.com/deanutrix.htm). Equally, there is also a strand that focuses on her-story and emphasizes ideas of matriarchy and the various names for a female goddess, including that of Dea Nutrix (www.kathy-jones.co.uk/books/british_goddess1.html). The ability of the modern medium to provide, via a set of images and thoughts, a set of religious values demonstrates how the human mind can re-associate objects, names and images to create a new system of personal beliefs. This, of itself, allows us to appreciate how interpretation or the mapping of meaning onto objects is creative and may disregard systematic thinking associated with these subjects in formal academic writing on ancient religion. What we might conclude from these brief observations is that human beings do not necessarily know the rules of the game and may decide to use objects (or knowledge) for very different purposes and very creatively.

Raw materials, the landscape and sensory perception

Most of the discussion to this point has been addressed to the finished object, its study, its display and its significance. Yet, there is another side to objects. All are made from raw materials extracted in some way from the landscape. The effects of metal extraction in terms of pollution and landscape alteration in the Roman period are considerable (De Callataÿ 2005). Yet few studies of artefacts link the object back to the working of the raw material into that form (see Hurcombe 2007 for discussion and techniques of analysis). There are questions of why a particular material is used or preferred or utilized alongside another material. For example, lighting in Pompeii included both ceramic and bronze lamps. The former would seem to have been made of a less valuable material, but if dropped would break, whereas the latter were sturdy but involved metal resources. Interestingly, the conversion of the raw material involved the use of heat and the consumption of wood probably in the form of charcoal – presenting us with another raw material, wood, that needed to be converted into a low bulk, higher heat material. There is a whole series of human tasks involved in the production of artefacts that allows us to consider both the action of production and the making of the object. The latter lends itself to analysis, since for example, how an object was made or where a material was extracted from can be reconstructed, in some cases from geo-chemical analysis. This type of work has mainly been focused on sculpture, such as the Herculaneum bronzes or in the establishment of points of origin for marble exported across the Mediterranean (Mattusch 2005: 125–40). Increasingly, the equipment to provide the basic geo-chemistry of an object (not subject to corrosion or other forms of alteration) has become both cheaper and more portable.

Such studies are for the future. What has been established to date is a focus on the understanding of the extraction of raw materials from the hinterland of Rome for the building industry in the city. The mass-manufacturing of hand-sized rectilinear travertine or tufa blocks for utilization by the building trade, in preference over irregular fragments, shows the level of alteration of stone into a standardized commodity for building (Adam 1994; DeLaine 1995, 1996; Evans et al 2003). This, in many ways, anticipates the widespread adoption of fired brick by the building industry of Ostia and other places in the early 2nd century. Manufacture according to size for end-use created an object that would have been handled and transported prior to use in construction. The tactile nature of the object is often forgotten in the discussion of the point of origin and point of consumption – in between these two locales were a series of individuals who interacted with the object and whose lives were shaped by the dimensions, weight and size of the object being moved from a point of extraction/manufacture to point of final usage.

There is also a degree to which weight or combined weight of a series of objects creates a social *milieu* in which several persons are required to cooperate in the movement of goods: whether in the sailing of a vessel, the off-loading at a dock, or physically placing the goods onto a cart. The weight of the object transported would also have had an effect on the shape (if not size) and strength of the person whose labour power was consumed in the movement of the object across space. The use of pack-animals and carts for transportation involves a whole series of objects and materials that were not just made from metal or leather, but were associated with specific smells and forms of touch or human utilization. This shifts us into a new realm of analysis that involves far more than vision and allows us to understand the relationship of humans with objects as involving a variety of senses and forms of cognition (Classen 1993, 2005; Classen et al 1994; Bull and Black 2003; Drobnick 2006). Devising a means to analyse objects in this way may seem hard to pin down, but that might be a function of how we are used to only looking at objects in museums, rather than touching and feeling the textures associated with objects that are fundamental for their comprehension.

Chapter 11

End Piece

A Post-Archaeology Age?

This final chapter of the book considers the wider role of archaeology in society in the second decade of the 21st century. In so doing, I refer in this section to websites that will also update the text in the future. In the UK at present there is a sense that archaeology is besieged and the subject's values of conservation, collecting and recording are under threat. For decades, the *Time Team* programmes have presented archaeological material via television, but that does not seem to have resulted in a greater interest in the subject matter for the recruitment of students to university, in contrast to films such as *Gladiator* (2000) or more recently *Immortals* (2011), that have contributed to a growth of interest in classical studies and ancient history. This contrast is as much about the presentation of subject matter as the subject matter itself: one has engaged with popular culture and the other has sought to present the values of fieldwork and discovery as popular culture. However, there is a sense where *Time Team* sets out to create archaeologists as not like ourselves – they are different, are experts – whereas the movie creations are tangible and play with familiar plot lines presented alongside spectacle. The contrast is also between knowledge confirmation and knowledge that challenges people. It is the latter that is more often written into mission statements of museums than the former.

Re-animation

The first decade of the 21st century saw an explosion of archaeology programmes made for TV. The impetus behind this may have been the revival of the Hollywood epic via the film *Gladiator* that has been followed by *Troy* (2004), *Clash of the Titans* (2010), as well as HBO's *Rome* series (2005–7). Like the films, the TV documentary is not new. There are examples stretching back to Mortimer Wheeler's *Animal, Vegetable, Mineral?* in the 1950s. However, what is new is perhaps a greater sense of re-animation and recreation of the lives of those who lived in the past – docu-dramas that present not the evidence of archaeology but a vision of what it was like. The viewers of these programmes are sophisticated enough to realize that it is a presentation, but are left to wonder how this information is known. In contrast to the films made by Hollywood, which are defined as entertainment, the docu-drama seeks authenticity through interviews with academics.

The process of the making of a docu-drama begins with the sale of an idea for a programme by a production company to a network, or the commissioning of a programme on a certain subject by a network. A script is developed with locations sought out and experts consulted. The script then is adjusted – again and again and again – until it does not really resemble the original version but engages with the idea for the programme. Typically, a programme on Pompeii ends with the eruption – carefully recreated with detailed consultation on size of particles. National Geographic seems to commission a Pompeii programme from a different production company every two years. This reveals something about television – it is incredibly conservative and tends to replicate earlier programmes that have worked. In effect, television has created a Pompeii brand, a mad emperor brand, a Roman army brand, a sex-mad empress brand and so on. These are recognized in TV listings in the way viewers might also recognize Man United versus Liverpool. The Roman brand is far stronger than the Greek brand for reasons that seem far from clear apart from the fact that Rome is the most intensely popularized.

Re-animation is also present in museum displays beginning in the 1980s (see Chapter 10) and reveals the objective as the production of a visual image of the past. Re-animation creates a look that shows how the objects from the past were used and creates an image from which viewers can imagine their own Roman world. For television, the look may be linked more to cinematic experience than to archaeology. For instance, the producers of the 2005 SkyOne series *When in Rome* explained to me their desire for a programme based on the film *Lock, Stock and Two Smoking Barrels* set in Rome with a plot line that mirrored some of the plot lines of the film. The result was violence from Vigiles, an insula block that was burnt down, an insulted patron, a rebuild that made them money, and a programme that embraced many of the themes of urban living that we might find in Alex Scobie's 1986 article on life in Rome. Yet the look comes from the cinema. A similar process can be found in the development of a look by re-enactors involved in the docu-dramas of the first decade of the 21st century. Those involved in the staged dinner party at the beginning of the *Worst Xmas Jobs in History* (2005) were animated young adults in the pub discussing their next role as Messalina, but once on set adopted the posture and gesture of Hollywood epics, more recently found in HBO's *Rome*.

The limits of television led Alex Butterworth and myself to devise a book *Pompeii: The Living City* (Butterworth and Laurence 2005) that included re-animation. We had worked together on the development of the script for Channel 4's *Private Lives of Pompeii*. Alex saw re-animation as a means of developing a narrative that could compensate for the point at which archaeological evidence (combined with textual evidence) no longer provided an effective narrative and revealed instead the limits of the evidence. These fictional re-animations were evidence-based but identified by the use of an italic font as distinct from the rest of the book. Simply put, we invented characters who experienced aspects of the city of Pompeii. They could have thoughts, experience smell and so on, but they did not speak. This was a limitation that was self-imposed and made the book different from Robert Harris' *Pompeii* (2004).

The state, democracy and archaeology

Across Europe in 2012, there is a financial crisis that is affecting the delivery of archaeology as a discipline. Perhaps this is not a new phenomenon but we are today more acutely aware of the effects that it will have than we were before. The collapse of a building in Pompeii in late 2010 has demonstrated to all, if such a demonstration were necessary, that archaeology is fundamentally underfunded. The ongoing debate over the future of Pompeii is reported on *Blogging Pompeii* (http://bloggingpompeii.blogspot.com/). The involvement of a UNESCO inspection has resulted in a report that can be found at http://bloggingpompeii.blogspot.com/2011/07/unesco-committee-results.html. However, it seems that there first needs to be a real crisis – a collapse of a building in this case or a closure of a museum. The situation is not unique to Italy. It is a crisis that causes archaeologists to debate the very central tenet of the discipline – should we excavate? The results of this discussion were published in the Dutch journal *Archaeological Dialogues* in 2011 and conclude that excavation lies at the core of the discipline, but financially it will be difficult to support this core activity.

The UK has experienced sweeping cuts across the public sector since summer 2010 that have included the abolition of the Museums, Libraries and Archives (MLA) Council and massive cuts to the funding of English Heritage. What is perhaps less visible, in terms of news headlines, are the cuts to local government. The public sector lives in a world that has to see a reduction in spending and how that is achieved is often quick and lethal, rather than being considered and assuring the long-term future of heritage. The Institute for Archaeologists provides news of how local issues are being faced (www.archaeologists.net/news?page=1). Michael Fulford

(2011) has set out in a British Academy report the situation with regard to the rise of 'commercial' or developer-funded archaeology that has not empowered the communities in which developers have built new structures. For the most part, archaeology has been done as part of development but the results of the work have been ineffectively disseminated to the benefit of the community – who, in many cases via local taxation, fund museums and other points of access to the past. At the same time, museums are becoming less the repository of the past and much more a place in which social interaction allows access to the past. Museums, like university libraries, are developing cafés and other venues that draw people to them (for example, Westgate Towers and Gaol Café, www.canterburywestgatetowers. com). What is clear though is archaeology will not be the same in the future.

There is a sense in which the media spotlight or Facebook protests are required before politicians in democracies begin to value archaeology. After all, no politician can go to the hustings saying they are not pro-cultural heritage; instead there is a quiet slicing of budgets that results in the decline and slow demise of cultural resources before anyone really notices that archaeology is not in the greatest shape after all. A crisis can be of benefit and can cause a re-assessment of policy. In 2010, it was almost certain the Canterbury Roman Museum would close but with protest and lobbying by voters comes re-evaluation of policy within democracies. Whether the current re-evaluation will secure a future for the museum and the possibility of the public viewing a remarkable collection of objects will be subject to future policy-makers. A sense of unease does prevail across the sector that jobs are disappearing without protest, without clear advocacy – nowhere is this more clearly felt than in developer-funded archaeology, which due to a lack of development has resulted in a shrinking skill base as redundancies inevitably occur.

Archaeology after re-animation: a history of objects?

Plans are afoot, at the time of writing, for the Cultural Olympiad in 2012 in London. The Mayor, Boris Johnson, has announced an intention that primary school children should gain greater access to Latin and both secondary and primary school children should have talks on key topics relating to the classical world: the Olympic Games, Latin in English, famous Greeks and Romans, Athenian democracy and gladiators. There is, however, no mention of archaeology. The Olympics are taking place in a city founded by Rome and developed as a capital city in the Roman period, but there would seem to be less interest in valuing the history of London that might include recognition of our knowledge of the city's

Roman past – as seen for example in the Museum of London. Instead, the list of topics suggested to date appears not dissimilar to those re-animated for TV, plus an overlay of Latin. In anticipation of 2012, gladiator re-enactors are already appearing at London's Guildhall – admittedly a site of a Roman amphitheatre (www.durolitum.co.uk/gladhome.html). However, there is the obvious question: what have gladiators got to do with the Olympics? The means to engage the young is replicating the images from films and docu-dramas to create a view of the Romans that depends on re-animation rather than archaeology.

Archaeology needs to produce spectacle as much as crisis. A trawl through newspapers of the past will reveal that the discipline has consistently done this through the 20th century, for example with Amedeo Maiuri's presentation of the new excavations via articles in *The Times* newspaper (that can be located via the *Times Digital Archive*). In a situation in which the public does not know what has been found by archaeologists, there needs to be an explanation of what has been found, its importance and its significance for the past lives of people who had lived in a place. The means to do this need not be via print media, but through social networking to produce new virtual communities with whom archaeologists may communicate directly. This may seem obvious, but looking around at the audience at public lectures the age group by far in the majority is of those who are not young. This might be an inevitable demographic fact, but it is clear that those in their third age (or later years of life) tend to be more engaged with archaeology. The challenge is to engage those rather younger than the Friends group or the local archaeology society members who attend lectures. Only with further engagement can a case for archaeology be made to politicians – who may be inclined to see cultural heritage mainly as a line in the budget.

Pompeii, of course, continues to be archaeology's spectacle, even in the face of crisis. Yet, even in the study of Pompeii, we find a sense that archaeology may have lost its value in the face of a critic in the form of Mary Beard. Her book on Pompeii (Beard 2008), described by some as an extension of her blog, has focused on the interpretation by archaeologists of the past and taken apart the interpretations put forward by others, while at the same time resisting the act of interpretation. The book is an undoubted success. The critique found within the book is not just about the interpretation of Pompeii, but also of archaeology as a discipline (see Laurence 2009b). At the same time, Beard writes to reassure readers that common-sense functionalist empiricism will prevent us from simply reading off the interpretations of the data – but the expectation of an understanding of the past is shattered with no alternative view presented, so that archaeology is found to be a discipline of endeavour with no meaning.

In re-reading *Roman Archaeology for Historians*, I was struck how much archaeology has permeated into ancient history in the last decade, with the result that we find archaeology represented alongside textual evidence to create a fuller image of life in the past. The evidence being represented (and presented in this book) is selective. The relevance for ancient historians is that archaeology enriches a text-led interpretation by bringing into sharper focus the spatial and the visual and more importantly how objects are part of human experience and should find their place in history. The selection of material of itself presents some of the evidence for wider consumption, while not addressing problems of the study of the total assemblage and representativeness of the selection – a problem also found in the study of epigraphy. This is not unlike complaints of literary scholars who see ancient historians using passages in isolation. Ancient history, especially social history, does have a tendency to endeavour to discover structures of society and the experience of individuals with a view to creating a model. In so doing, social history endeavours to re-animate the Roman past and within that past there should be a history of objects. That history is about far more than Romanization: it is about the recovery of the human experience in relation to the senses of touch, smell and sight (and potentially taste) that underpins a cultural cognition of what an object was for or could be used for. There is a new history to be written that allows for a better understanding of the objects that fill museums, while enabling a past to be presented that resists the current genres of re-animation to present what it was to be human and to use the objects discovered by archaeologists. All objects, wherever they are found, can contribute to this form of history that can be built locally via research and that can then be disseminated locally, nationally and internationally. It would also place the museum at the very heart of a new idea of history that was specific and local – which could be built upon participation (volunteering) and the creation of a knowledge community or a knowledgeable community. Students of ancient history have a part to play in this process that has yet to be defined. All will have to become advocates for museums and for archaeology, but also in voluntary work – when it can be undertaken (through university volunteering schemes, dissertations and so on). The alternative is to accept that we live in a post-archaeology era, where the subject is no longer of sufficient significance to matter. Hopefully, if you have reached this point, you will not accept the premise and will realize that action needs to be taken and that means by you with a view to ensuring we do not slip into a post-archaeology era.

Hybridization

Much ink and hot air is produced in the definition of archaeology as a discipline that need not include the textual record. To put it crudely, the need to define a discipline and its degree course as distinct from either history or classics (including in both cases ancient history) creates both of these subjects as 'other' – as distinct or different from archaeology. The preservation of the central integrity of archaeology's self-identity is put into question when interaction with other subjects comes into play or ancient historians begin to pay attention to archaeology. Ancient historians tend to create, for want of a better expression, 'an archaeology of their own', which is a hybrid form that pays a close attention to texts, but includes material culture. This could be described as a twin-tracked approach to the past, but it is actually quite distinct from a single-tracked approach – it is a hybrid form, which need not value the things that archaeology says it values above all else in terms of education of students on degree courses (see www.qaa.ac.uk/Publications/InformationAndGuidance/Pages/Subject-benchmark-statement-Archaeology.aspx). The dialogue with ancient historians conducted by archaeologists also causes archaeology to alter its position, or to assert its identity as distinct from ancient history and see a need for the reinforcement of the central core identity. All those who have studied theories of cultural change that underpin the debates over Romanization (see Chapter 5) will know that the two subjects, ancient history and archaeology, in dialogue with one another will produce an alteration to both disciplines or create a hybrid form. There exists, in fact, an archaeology for Roman historians that joins together text and material culture. This means the strong assertive boundaries between the two disciplines are pulled apart and intermingling of the two disciplines happens, mostly not in a disciplined way, but in a less organized even post-modern format to create an intersection between two disciplinary positions – it is a hybrid and is evolving. Like other edge phenomena, it holds an exciting position that in some ways refuses definition and it is in a continual state of hybridization as new participants engage with both archaeology and ancient history.

Bibliography

Abascal, J. M., Alföldy, G. and Cebrián, R. (2001) 'La inscripcíon con letras de bronce y otros documentos epigráficos del foro de Segobriga', *Archivo Español de Arqueologia* 74: 117–30.

Abascal, J. M., Almagro-Gorbea, M. and Cebrián, R. (2002) 'Segobriga 1989–2000. Topografia de la ciudad y trabajos en el foro', *Madrider Mitteilungen* 43: 123–61.

Abbasoğlu, H. (2001) 'The founding of Perge and its development in the Hellenistic and Roman periods', in D. Parrish (ed.) *Urbanism in Western Asia Minor*, Portsmouth RI: 172–88.

Adam, J. P. (1994) *Roman Building: Materials and Techniques*, London.

Adams, J. N. (1994) 'Latin and Punic in contact? The case of the Bu Njem Ostraca', *Journal of Roman Studies* 84: 87–112.

——(1999) 'The poets of Bu Njem: Language, culture and the centurionate', *Journal of Roman Studies* 89: 109–34.

——(2003) *Bilingualism and the Latin Language*, Cambridge.

——(2007) *The Regional Diversification of Latin 200 BC–AD 600*, Cambridge.

Aldhouse-Green, M. (1976) *A Corpus of Religious Material from the Civilian Areas of Roman Britain*, BAR 24, Oxford.

——(1978) *Small Cult-Objects from the Military Areas of Roman Britain*, BAR 52, Oxford.

——(1989) *Symbol and Image in Celtic Religious Art*, London.

——(2003) 'Poles apart? Perceptions of gender in Gallo-British cult-iconography', in S. Scott and J. Webster (eds) *Roman Imperialism and Provincial Art*, Cambridge: 95–118.

Allason-Jones, L. (1999) 'Women and the Roman army in Britain', in A. Goldsworthy and I. Haynes (eds) *The Roman Army as a Community* (*Journal of Roman Archaeology* Suppl.34), Portsmouth RI: 41–51.

Allison, P. M. (2001) 'Using the material and written sources: Turn of the millennium approaches to Roman domestic space', *American Journal of Archaeology* 105: 181–208.

——(2004) *Pompeian Households: An Analysis of Material Culture*, Berkeley.

——(2006) 'Mapping for gender: Interpreting artefact distribution inside 1st and 2nd century AD forts in Roman Germany' (with responses by N. Ascherson, A. Baines, T. Becker, K. Brophy, E.C. Casella), *Archaeological Dialogues* 13: 1–47.

Ammerman, A. J. (1990) 'On the origins of the Forum', *American Journal of Archaeology* 94: 627–45.

——(1996) 'The Comitium in Rome from the beginning', *American Journal of Archaeology* 100: 121–36.

——(1998) 'Environmental archaeology in the Velabrum, Rome: An interim report', *Journal of Roman Archaeology* 11: 213–24.

——(2006) 'Adding time to Rome's *imago*', in L. Haselberger and J. Humphrey (eds) *Imaging Ancient Rome: Documentation – Visualization – Imagination* (*Journal of Roman Archaeology* Suppl.61), Portsmouth RI: 297–308.

Ammerman, A. J. and Filippi, D. (2004) 'Dal Tevere all'Argileto: nuove osservazioni', *Bullettino della Commissione Archeologia Comunale di Roma* 105: 7–28.

Ammerman, A. J., Iliopoulos, I., Bondioli, F., Filippi, D., Hilditch, J., Manfredini, A., Pennisi, L. and Winter, N. A. (2008) 'The clay beds in the Velabrum and the earliest tiles in Rome', *Journal of Roman Archaeology* 21: 7–30.

Anderson, M. (2011) 'Disruption or continuity? The spatio-visual evidence of post earthquake Pompeii', in E. Poehler, M. Flohr and K. Cole (eds) *Pompeii: Art, Industry and Infrastructure*, Oxford: 74–87.

Andrén, A. (1998) *Between Artifacts and Texts: Historical Archaeology in Global Perspective*, New York.

Angelucci, S., Baldassarre, I., Bragantini, I., Lauro, M. G., Mannucci, V., Mazzoleni, A., Morselli, C. and Taglietti, F. (1990) 'Sepolture e riti nella necropolis dell'Isola Sacra', *Bollettino di Archeologia* 5–6: 49–113.

Ashby, T. (1902) 'Classical topography of the Roman Campagna I', *Papers of the British School at Rome* 1: 125–285.

——(1903) 'Classical topography of the Roman Campagna II', *Papers of the British School at Rome* 3: 3–212.

——(1935) *The Aqueducts of Ancient Rome*, Oxford.

Audouze, F. and Buchenschutz, O. (1991) *Towns, Villages and Countryside of Celtic Europe*, London.

Aurigemma, S. (1940) *Velleia*, Rome.

Baddeley, S. C. (1904) *Recent Discoveries in the Forum 1898–1904*, London.

Baldassarre, I. (1990) 'Nuove ricerche nella necropolis dell'Isola Sacra', *Quaderni del Centro di Studio per l'Archeologia Etrusco-Italica* 18: 164–72.

Bang, P. F. (1998) 'Antiquity between "Primitivism" and "Modernism"', www.hum.aau.dk/dk/ckulturf/DOCS/PUB/pfb/antiquity.htm.

——(2008) *The Roman Bazaar. A Comparative Study of Trade and Markets in a Tributary Empire*, Cambridge.

Bang, P. F., Ikeguchi, M. and Ziche, H. G. (2006) *Ancient Economies, Modern Methodologies. Archaeology, Comparative History, Models and Institutions*, Bari.

Barrett, J. C. (1989) 'Afterword: Render unto Caesar … ', in J. C. Barrett, A. P. Fitzpatrick and L. Macinnes (eds) *Barbarians and Romans in North-West Europe from the Later Republic to Late Antiquity*, Oxford: 235–41.

——(1990) 'Sciencing archaeology – a reply to Lewis Binford', in F. Baker and J. Thomas (eds) *Writing the Past in the Present*, Lampeter.

——(1997a) 'Theorising Roman archaeology', in K. Meadows, C. Lemke and J. Heron (eds) *TRAC 96: Proceedings of the Sixth Annual Theroretical Roman Archaeology Conference*, Oxford: 1–7.

——(1997b) 'Romanization: A critical comment', in D. J. Mattingly (ed.) *Dialogues in Roman Imperialism*, Ann Arbor: 51–66.

Beard, M. (2008) *Pompeii: A Life of a Roman Town*, London.

Beaumont, P. (2008) 'Water supply at Housesteads Roman Fort, Hadrian's Wall: The case for rainfall harvesting', *Britannia* 39: 59–84.

Bénabou, M. (1976) *La résistance africaine à la romanisation*, Paris.

Bidwell, P. (1985) *The Roman Fort of Vindolanda*, London.

——(2009) 'The earliest occurrences of baths at auxiliary forts', in W. Hanson (ed.) *The Army and Frontiers (Journal of Roman Archaeology* Suppl.74), Portsmouth RI: 55–62.

Binazzi, G. (1981) 'Iscrizione pavimentale nel C.D. Foro di Assisi', in L. Gasperini (ed.) *Scritti sul mondo antico in memoria di Fulvio Grosso*, Rome: 29–35.

Birley, A. (2001) *Vindolanda's Military Bath Houses*, Hexham

——(2002) *Garrison Life at Vindolanda: A Band of Brothers*, Stroud.

——(2007) 'The frontier zone in Britain: Hadrian to Caracalla', in L. de Blois and E. Lo Cascio (eds) *The Impact of the Roman Army*, Leiden: 355–70.

Birley, A. and Blake, J. (2005) *Vindolanda Excavations 2003–2004*, Hexham.

——(2007) *Vindolanda Excavations 2005–2006*, Hexham.

Birley, B. and Greene, E. (2006) *The Roman Jewellery from Vindolanda*, Durham.

Birley, R., Blake, J. and Birley, A. (1999) *Vindolanda: 1997 Excavations – Praetorium Site – Interim Report*, Haltwhistle.

Blagg, T. (1995) 'The Marlowe excavations: An overview', in J. Elder (ed.) *Excavations in the Marlowe Car Park and Surrounding Areas*, Canterbury: 7–26.

Black, S., Browning, J. L. and Laurence, R. (2009) 'From quarry to road: The supply of basalt for road paving in the Tiber Valley', in F. Coarelli and H. Patterson (eds) *Mercator Placidissimus – The Tiber Valley in Antiquity*, Rome: 705–30.

Bland, R. and Orna-Ornstein, J. (1997) *Coin Hoards from Roman Britain Volume 10*, London.

Boatwright, M. T. (1991) 'Plancia Magna of Perge: Women's roles and status in Roman Asia Minor', in S. B. Pomeroy (ed.) *Women's History and Ancient History*, Chapel Hill: 249–72.

——(1993) 'The city gate of Plancia Magna at Perge', in E. D'Ambra (ed.) *Roman Art in Context*, Englewood Cliffs: 189–207.

Boni, G. (1901) 'Nuove scoperte nella città e nel suburbio', *Notizie degli Scavi* 1900: 291–340.

Bowman, A. K. (1994) *Life and Letters on the Roman Frontier: Vindolanda and its People*, London.

Bowman, A. K. and Thomas, J. D. (1983) *Vindolanda: The Latin Writing Tablets*, London.

——(1991) 'A military-strength report from Vindolanda', *Journal of Roman Studies* 81: 62–73.

——(1994) *The Vindolanda Writing-Tablets (Tabulae Vindolandenses II)*, London.

Bradley, K. R. (1991) *Discovering the Roman Family*, Oxford.

Bradley, R. (1990) 'Thirty years of Roman Britain', *Britannia* 21: 393–96.

Breeze, D. J. (2000) 'Supplying the army', in G. Alföldy, B. Dobson and W. Eck (eds) *Kaiser, Heer, und Gesellschaft in der Römischen Kaiserzeit*, Stuttgart: 59–64.

Brent, J. (1861) 'Roman cemeteries in Canterbury with some conjecture concerning the earliest inhabitants', *Archaeologia Cantiana* 4: 27–42.

Brogan, O. and Smith, D. J. (1984) *Ghirza, A Libyan Settlement of the Roman Period*, Tripoli.

Brunt, P. (1980) 'M. W. Frederiksen', *Journal of Roman Studies* 70: 1.

Bruun, C. (2010) 'Water, oxygen, isotopes and immigration to Ostia-Portus', *Journal of Roman Archaeology* 23: 109–32.

Bull, M. and Black, L. (2003) *The Auditory Culture Reader*, Oxford.

Burleigh, G. R., Fitzpatrick-Matthews, K. J. and Aldhouse-Green, M. J. (2006) 'A Dea Nutrix figurine from a Romano-British cemetery at Baldock, Hertfordshire', *Britannia* 37: 273–94.

Burnham, B. C. and Wacher, J. (1990) *The 'Small Towns' of Roman Britain*, London.

Burton-Brown, E. (1905) *Recent Excavations in the Forum Romanum 1898–1905*, London.

Butterworth, A. and Laurence, R. (2005) *Pompeii: The Living City*, London.

Campbell, B. (1996) *The Roman Army 31 BC–AD 337: A Sourcebook*, London

Carandini, A., D'Alessio, M. T. and Di Giuseppe, H. (2006) *La Fattoria e la Villa dell'Auditorium nel Quartiere Flaminio di Roma*, Rome.

Carlucci, C., De Lucia Brolli, A. M., Keay, S., Millett, M. and Strutt, K. (2007) 'An archaeological survey of the Faliscan settlement at Vignale, *Falerii Veteres* (Province of Viterbo)', *Papers of the British School at Rome* 75: 39–122.

Carrington, R. C. (1931) 'Studies in Campanian "Villae Rusticae"', *Journal of Roman Studies* 21: 110–30.

Chenery, C., Eckardt, H. and Müldner, G. (2011) 'Cosmopolitan Catterick? Isotope evidence for population mobility on Rome's northern frontier', *Journal of Archaeological Science* 38: 1525–36.

Chenery, C., Müldner, G., Evans, J., Eckardt, H. and Lewis, M. (2010) 'Strontium and stable isotope evidence for diet and mobility in Roman Gloucester', *Journal of Archaeological Science* 37: 150–63.

Cho, H. and Stout, S. D. (2005) 'Bone remodelling and age-associated bone loss in the past: An histomophometric analysis of the Imperial Roman skeletal population of Isola Sacra', in S. C. Agarwal and S. D. Stout (eds) *Bone Loss and Osteoporosis: An Anthropological Perspective*, New York: 207–28.

Cianfarani, V. (1959) 'Vecchie e nuove iscrizioni Sepinati', in *Atti del terzo congreso internazionale di epigrafia Greca e Latina* (Rome 4–8 September 1957), Rome: 371–80.

Clarke, S. (1999) 'In search of a different Roman period: The finds assemblage of the Newstead military complex', in G. Fincham, G. Harrison, R. Holland and L. Revell (eds) *TRAC 99. Proceedings of the Ninth Annual Theoretical Roman Archaeology Conference*, Oxford: 22–29.

Clarke, S. and Jones, R. (1996) 'The Newstead Pits', *Journal of Military Equipment Studies* 5: 109–24.

Classen,C. (1993) *Worlds of Sense: Exploring the Senses in History and Across Cultures*, Oxford

——(2005) *The Book of Touch*, Oxford.

Classen, C., Howes, D. and Synnott, A. (1994) *Aroma: The Cultural History of Smell*, London.

Coarelli, F. (1983) *Il foro Romano: Periodo Arcaico*, Rome.

——(1987) *I santuari del Lazio in etá Repubblicana*, Rome.

——(1988) *Il foro Boario*, Rome.

——(2005) 'Pits and *fora*: A reply to Henrik Mouritsen', *Papers of the British School at Rome* 60: 23–30.

——(2007) *Rome and its Environs: An Archaeological Guide*, Berkeley.

Collins, R. (2008) 'Identity in the frontier: Theory and multiple community inter-facing', in C. Fenwick, M. Wiggins and D. Wythe (eds) *TRAC 2007. Proceedings of the Seventeenth Annual Theoretical Roman Archaeology Conference*, Oxford: 31–44.

Collis, J. R. (1984) *Oppida: Earliest Towns North of the Alps*, Sheffield.

Coppola, M. R. (1984) 'Il Foro Emiliano di Terracina: Rilievo, annalisi tercnica, vicende storiche del monumento', *MEFRA* 96(1): 325–77.

Cornell, T. J. (1995) *The Beginnings of Rome: Italy and Rome from the Bronze Age to the Punic Wars*, London.

Corsi, C. and Vermeulen, F. (2011) *Changing Landscapes: The Impact of Roman Towns in the Western Mediterranean*, Bologna

Creighton, J. (2000) *Coins and Power in Late Iron Age Britain*, Cambridge.

——(2006) *Britannia: The Creation of a Roman Province*, London.

Crowe, F., Sperduti, A., O'Connell, T. C., Craig, O. E., Kirsanow, K., Germoni, P., Macchiarelli, R., Garnsey, P. and Bondioli, L. (2010) 'Water-related occupations and diet in two Roman coastal communities (Italy, first to third century AD): Correlation between stable carbon and nitrogen isotope values and auricular exostosis prevalence', *American Journal of Physical Anthropology* 142: 355–66.

Cumont, F. (1914) *Comment la Belgique fut Romanisée: Essai Historique*, 2nd edition, Brussels.

Cunliffe, B. W. and Rowley, T. (1976) *Oppida: The Beginnings of Urbanisation in Barbarian Europe*, Oxford.

Dark, P. (1997) *The Landscape of Roman Britain*, Stroud.

——(2000) *The Environment of Britain in the First Millennium AD*, London.

Dasen, V. (2009) 'Roman birth rites of passage revisited', *Journal of Roman Archaeology* 22: 199–214.

Davies, P. (2011) *Museums and the Disposals Debate*, London.

Day, J. (1932) 'Agriculture in the life of Pompeii', *Yale Classical Studies* 11: 167–203.

De Callataÿ, F. (2005) 'The Graeco-Roman economy in the super-long run: Lead, copper and shipwrecks', *Journal of Roman Archaeology* 18: 361–72.

De Caro, S. (1994) *La villa rustica in località Villa Regina a Boscoreale*, Rome.

De Cou, H.F. (1912) *Antiquities from Boscoreale in Field Museum of Natural History*, Field Museum of Natural History Publications 152, Anthropology Series vol. 7, Chicago.

De La Blanchère, M. R. (1887) 'Découverte d'une place à Terracine', *MEFR* 7: 414–18.

DeLaine, J. (1995) 'The supply of building materials to the city of Rome', in N. Christie (ed.) *Settlement and Economy in Italy 1500 BC to AD 1500*, Oxford: 555–62.

——(1996) 'The insula of the paintings: A model of the economics of construction in Hadrianic Ostia', in A. Gallina Zevi and A. Claridge (eds) *Roman Ostia Revisited*, London: 165–84.

——(2004) 'Designing for a market: "*Medianum*" apartments at Ostia', *Journal of Roman Archaeology* 17: 146–76.

DeLaine, J. and Wilkinson, D. (1999) 'The house of Jove and Ganymede', *Mededelingen van het Nederlands Instituut te Rome, Antiquity* 58: 77–79.

Derks, T. and Roynams, N. (2002) 'Seal-boxes and the spread of Latin literacy in the Rhine delta', in A. E. Cooley (ed.) *Becoming Roman, Writing Latin? Literacy and Epigraphy in the Roman West*, (*Journal of Roman Archaeology* Suppl.48), Portsmouth RI: 87–134.

——(2006) 'Returning auxiliary veterans: Some methodological considerations', *Journal of Roman Archaeology* 19: 121–35.

Deyts, S. (1992) *Images des Dieux de la Gaule*, Paris.

Dobney, K. (2001) 'A place at the table: The role of vertebrate zooarchaeology within a Roman research agenda', in S. James and M. Millett (eds) *Britons and Romans: Advancing an Archaeological Agenda*, York: 36–45.

Dobson, B. (2009) 'The role of the fort', in W. Hanson (ed.) *The Army and Frontiers* (*Journal of Roman Archaeology* Suppl. 74), Portsmouth RI: 25–32.

Dowker, G. (1887) 'Roman remains recently found at Canterbury', *Archaeologia Cantiana* 17: 34–37.

Draper, J. A. (2004) *Orality, Literacy, and Colonialism in Antiquity*, Atlanta.

Drobnick, J. (2006) *The Smell Culture Reader*, Oxford.

Dudley, D. (1967) *Urbs Roma: A Sourcebook of Classical Texts on the City and its Monuments*, Aberdeen.

Dumayne, L. (1994) 'The effect of the Roman occupation on the environment of Hadrian's Wall: A pollen diagram from Fozy Moss, Northumbria', *Britannia* 25: 217–24.

Dyson, S. L. (1993) 'From new to new age archaeology: Archaeological theory and classical archaeology – a 1990s perspective', *American Journal of Archaeology* 97: 195–206.

——(1995) 'Is there a text in this site?', in D. B. Small (ed.) *Methods in the Mediterranean: Historical and Archaeological Views on Texts and Archaeology* (*Mnemosyne* Suppl.135), Leiden: 25–44.

Eckardt, H. (2002) *Illuminating Roman Britain*, Montagnac.

——(2008) 'Technologies of the body: Iron Age and Roman grooming and display', in D. Garrow, C. Gosden and J. D. Hill (eds) *Rethinking Celtic Art*, Oxford: 113–28.

——(2010) 'Introduction: Diasporas in the Roman World', in H. Eckardt (ed.) *Roman Diasporas*, Portsmouth RI: 7–12.

Eckardt, H., Chenery, C., Booth, P., Evans, J. A., Lamb, A. and Müldner, G. (2009) 'Oxygen and strontium isotope evidence for mobility in Winchester', *Journal of Archaeological Science* 36: 2816–25.

Eckardt, H., Chenery, C., Leach, S., Lewis, M., Müldner, G. and Nimmo, E. (2010) 'A long way from home: Diaspora communities in Roman Britain', in H. Eckardt (ed.) *Roman Diasporas*, Portsmouth RI: 99–130.

Elsner, J. and Rutherford, I. (2005) *Pilgrimage in Graeco-Roman and Early Christian Antiquity*, Oxford.

Esmonde Cleary, S. (2008) *Rome in the Pyrenees. Lugdunum and the Convenae from the First Century BC to the Seventh Century AD*, London.

Evans, D. M., Shaw, C. and James, R. (2003) *Rebuilding the Past: A Roman Villa*, London.

Evans, J. (1987) 'Graffiti and the evidence of literacy and pottery use in Roman Britain', *Archaeological Journal* 144: 191–204.

Fabbricotti, E. (1976) 'I bagni nelle prime ville romane', *Cronache Pompeiane* 2: 29–111.

Faulkner, N. (2008) 'Roman archaeology in the epoch of neoliberalism and imperialist war', in C. Fenwick, M. Wiggins and D. Wythe (eds) *TRAC 2007. Proceedings of the Seventeenth Annual Theoretical Archaeology Conference*, Oxford: 63–74.

Fincham, G. (2002) *Landscapes of Imperialism: Roman and Native Interaction in the East Anglian Fenland*, Oxford.

Fink, R. O. (1971) *Roman Military Records on Papyrus*, Princeton.

Finley, M. I. (1973) *The Ancient Economy*, London.

——(1985) *Ancient History: Evidence and Models*, London.

FitzGerald, C., Saunders, S., Bondioli, L. and Macchiarelli, R. (2006) 'Health of infants in an Imperial Roman skeletal sample: Perspective from dental micro-structure', *American Journal of Physical Anthropology* 130: 179–89.

Forcy, C. (1997) '"Beyond Romanisation": Technologies of power in Roman Britain', in K. Meadows, C. Lemke and J. Heron (eds) *TRAC 96: Proceedings of the Sixth Annual Theroretical Roman Archaeology Conference*, Oxford: 15–21.

Forte, M. (2007) *La Villa di Livia: Un percorso di ricerca archeologia virtual*, Rome.

Foss, P. (1997) 'Watchful *Lares*: Roman household organization and the rituals of cooking and dining', in R. Laurence and A. Wallace-Hadrill (eds) *Domestic Space in the Roman World: Pompeii and Beyond*, Portsmouth RI.

Foxhall, L. (2004) 'Field sports: Engaging Greek archaeology and history', in E. W. Sauer (ed.) *Archaeology and History: Breaking Down the Boundaries*, London: 76–84.

Frank, T. (1918) 'The economic life of an ancient city', *Classical Philology* 13: 225–40.

——(1923) *A History of Rome*, New York.

——(1927) *An Economic History of Rome*, 2nd edition, London.

——(1940) *An Economic Survey of Ancient Rome Volume V: Rome and Italy of the Empire*, Baltimore.

Frederiksen, M. (1970–71) 'The contribution of archaeology to the Agrarian problem in the Gracchan period', *Dialoghi di Archeologia* 4–5: 330–57.

Frederiksen, M. and Ward-Perkins, J. (1957) 'The ancient road systems of the central and northern Ager Faliscus (notes on Southern Etruria 2)', *Papers of the British School at Rome* 25: 67–209.

Freeman, P. (1991) 'The study of the Roman period in Britain: A comment on Hingley', *Scottish Archaeological Review* 8: 102–8.

——(2007) *The Best Training-Ground for Archaeologists: Francis Haverfield and the Invention of Romano-British Archaeology*, Oxford.

Frere, S. (1947) *Roman Canterbury: The City of Durovernum*, London.

——(1978) *Britannia: A History of Roman Britain*, 3rd edition, London.

Fulford, M. (1989) 'The economy of Roman Britain', in M. Todd (ed.) *Research on Roman Britain 1960–89*, London.

——(1991) 'Britain and the Roman Empire: The evidence of regional and long-distance trade', in R. F. J. Jones (ed.) *Britain in the Roman Period: Recent Trends*, Sheffield.

——(2001) 'Links with the past: Pervasive "ritual" behaviour in Roman Britain', *Britannia* 32: 199–218.

——(2004) 'Economic structures', in M. Todd (ed.) *A Companion to Roman Britain*, Oxford: 309–26.

——(2010) 'Roman Britain: Immigration and material culture', in H. Eckardt (ed.) *Roman Diasporas*, Portsmouth RI: 67–78.

——(2011) 'The impact of commercial archaeology on the UK heritage', in B. Cunliffe (ed.) *History for the Taking: Perspectives on Material Heritage*, London: 33–54.

Fulford, M. and Timby, J. (2000) *Late Iron Age and Roman Silchester: Excavations on the Site of the Forum Basilica*, London.

Fyfe, R. M., Brown, R. M. and Rippon, S. J. (2004) 'Characterising the late prehistoric, "Romano-British" and Medieval landscapes and dating the emergence of a regionally distinct agricultural system', *Journal of Archaeological Science* 31: 1699–1714.

Gabriel, M. M. (1955) *Livia's Garden Room at Prima Porta*, New York.

Gaffney, V. L., White, R. H. and Goodchild, H. (2007) *Wroxeter, the Cornovii and the Urban Process: Volume 1 Researching the Hinterland*, Portsmouth RI.

Gardner, A. (2003) 'Debating the health of Roman archaeology: A review of "Whither Roman Archaeology"', *Journal of Roman Archaeology* 16: 435–41.

——(2006) 'The future of TRAC', in B. Croxford, H. Goodchild, J. Lucas and N. Ray (eds) *TRAC 2005. Proceedings of the Fifteenth Annual Theoretical Roman Archaeology Conference*, Oxford: 128–35.

——(2007) *An Archaeology of Identity: Soldiers and Society in Late Roman Britain*, Walnut Creek.

George, M. (2011) 'Slavery and Roman material culture', in K. Bradley and P. Cartledge (eds) *The Cambridge World History of Slavery, Volume 1: The Ancient Mediterranean World*, Cambridge: 385–413.

Giddens, A. (1984) *The Constitution of Society: Outline of a Theory of Structuration*, Cambridge.

Giuliani, C. F. and Verduchi, P. (1987) *L'Area Centrale del Foro Romano*, Florence.

Gjerstad, E. (1941) 'Il comizio Romano dell'età repubblicana', *Opuscula Archaeologica* 2: 97–158.

——(1952a) 'Scavi stratigrafici nel Foro Romano e problem ad essi relativi', *Bullettino della Commissione Archeologica Comunale di Roma* 83: 13–29.

——(1952b) 'Stratigraphic excavations in the Forum Romanum', *Antiquity* 26: 60–64.

Gordon, M. L. (1927) 'The *ordo* of Pompeii', *Journal of Roman Studies* 17: 165–83.

——(1931) 'The freedman's son in municipal life', *Journal of Roman Studies* 21: 65–78.

Gowland, R. (2001) 'Playing dead: Implications of mortuary evidence for the social construction of childhood in Britain', in G. Davies, A. Gardner and K. Lockyear (eds) *TRAC 2000: Proceedings of the Tenth Annual Theoretical Roman Archaeology Conference*, Oxford: 152–68.

——(2006) 'Ageing the past: Examining age identity from funerary evidence', in R. Gowland and C. Knüsel (eds) *Social Archaeology of Funerary Remains*, Oxford: 143–54.

Gowland, R. and Chamberlain, A. (2002) 'A Bayesian approach to ageing perinatal skeletal material from archaeological sites: Implications for the evidence of infanticide in Roman Britain', *Journal of Archaeological Science* 29: 677–85.

Gowland, R. and Garnsey, P. (2010) 'Skeletal evidence for health, nutritional status and malaria in Rome and the empire', in H. Eckardt (ed.) *Roman Diasporas*, Portsmouth RI: 131–56.

Graham, E. J. (2006) *The Burial of the Urban Poor in Italy in the Late Roman Republic and Early Empire*, BAR Int. Ser. 1565, Oxford.

Graham, S. (2005) 'Networks, agent-based modelling and the Antonine Itineraries', *Journal of Mediterranean Archaeology* 19: 45–64.

——(2006) 'Who's in charge? Studying social networks in the brick industry of central Italy', in C. Mattusch, A. Donohue and A. Bauer (eds) *Common Ground: Archaeology, Art, Science, and Humanities (Proceedings of the XVIth International Congress of Classical Archaeology)*, Oxford: 359–62.

——(2008) 'The space between: The geography of social networks in the Tiber Valley', in F. Coarelli and H. Patterson (eds) *Mercator Placidissimus: The Tiber Valley in Antiquity*, Rome.

Grahame, M. (2000) *Reading Space: Social Interaction and Identity in the Houses of Roman Pompeii*, BAR Int. Ser. 886, Oxford.

Greene, K. (1986) *The Archaeology of the Roman Economy*, London.

——(2000) 'Technological innovation and economic progress in the ancient world: M. I. Finley re-considered', *Economic History Review* 53: 29–59.

——(2005) 'The economy of Roman Britain: Representation and historiography', in J. Bruhn, B. Coxford and D. Grigoropoulos (eds) *TRAC 2004. Proceedings of the Fourteenth Annual Theoretical Roman Archaeology Conference*, Oxford: 1–15.

Groeneman-Van Waateringe, W. (1978) 'Shoe sizes and palaeodemography', *Helinum* 28: 184–89.

Groot, M. (2008) *Animals in Ritual and Economy in a Roman Frontier Community*, Amsterdam.

Harris, R. (2004) *Pompeii*, London.

Harris, W. V. (1994) 'Child exposure in the Roman Empire', *Journal of Roman Studies* 84: 1–22.

——(2005) 'Some reflections about Martin Frederiksen and his work', in W. V. Harris and E. Lo Cascio (eds) *Noctes Campanae. Studi di storia antica ed archeologia dell'Italia preromana e romana in memoria di Martin W. Frederiksen*, Bari: VII–XV.

Haselberger, L., Romano, D. G. and Dumser, E. A. (2002) *Mapping Augustan Rome (Journal of Roman Archaeology Suppl.50)*, Portsmouth RI.

Häussler, R. and King, A. C. (2007–8) *Continuity and Innovation in Religion in the Roman West Volume 1 and 2*, Portsmouth RI.

Häussler, R. and Pearce, J. (2007) 'Towards an archaeology of literacy', in K. Lomas, R. D. Whitehouse and J. B. Wilkins (eds) *Literacy in the Ancient Mediterranean*, London: 219–38.

Haverfield, F. (1906) *The Romanization of Roman Britain*, Oxford.

——(1911a) 'An inaugural address delivered before the first annual general meeting of the society, 11th May, 1911', *Journal of Roman Studies* 1: xi-xx.

——(1911b) 'Town planning in the Roman world', in *Transactions of the RIBA Town Planning Conference, 1910*, London: 123–32.

——(1913) *Ancient Town Planning*, Oxford.

——(1915) *The Romanization of Roman Britain*, 3rd edition, Oxford.

Haynes, I. (1999a) 'Introduction: The Roman army as a community', in A. Goldsworthy and I. Haynes (eds) *The Roman Army as a Community (Journal of Roman Archaeology* Suppl.34), Portsmouth RI: 7–14.

——(1999b) 'Military service and the cultural identity in the *auxilia*', in A. Goldsworthy and I. Haynes (eds) *The Roman Army as a Community (Journal of Roman Archaeology* Suppl.34), Portsmouth RI: 165–74.

——(2002) 'Britain's first information revolution: The Roman army and the transformation of economic life', in P. Erdkamp (ed.) *The Roman Army and the Economy*, Amsterdam: 111–26.

Helttula, A., Gestrin, T., Kahlos, M., Pentti-Tuomisto, R., Tuomisto, P., Vainio, R. and Valjus, R. (2007) *Le iscrizioni sepolcrali Latine nell'Isola Sacra* (Acta Insitituti Romani Finlandiae 30), Rome.

Henig, M. (1975) *Vindolanda Jewellery*, Newcastle-upon-Tyne.

——(2004) 'A house divided: The study of Roman art and the art of Roman Britain', in E. W. Sauer (ed.) *Archaeology and History: Breaking Down the Boundaries*, London: 134–50.

Hill, J. D. (2001) 'Romanisation, gender and class: Recent approaches to identity in Britain and their consequences', in S. James and M. Millett (eds.) *Britons and Romans: Advancing an Archaeological Agenda*, York.

Hillier, B. and Hanson, J. (1986) *The Social Logic of Space*, Cambridge.

Hingley, R. (1982) 'Roman Britain: The structure of Roman imperialism and the consequences of imperialism on the development of a peripheral province', in D. Miles (ed.) *The Romano-British Countryside: Studies in Rural Settlement and Economy*, BAR Brit. Ser. 103(i), Oxford: 17–52.

——(1991) 'Past, present and future – the study of the Roman period in Britain', *Scottish Archaeological Review* 8: 90–101.

——(1993) 'Attitudes to Roman imperialism', in E. Scott (ed.) *Theoretical Roman Archaeology: First Conference Proceedings*, Aldershot: 23–28.

——(1997) 'Resistance and domination: Social change in Roman Britain', in D. J. Mattingly (ed.) *Dialogues in Roman Imperialism*, Ann Arbor: 81–100.

——(2000) *Roman Officers and English Gentlemen: The Imperial Origins of Roman Archaeology*, London.

——(2005) *Globalizing Roman Culture: Unity, Diversity and Empire*, London.

——(2008) *The Recovery of Roman Britain 1586–1906*, Oxford.

——(2009) 'The indigenous population', in M. F. A. Symonds and D. J. P. Mason (eds) *Frontiers of Knowledge: A Research Framework for Hadrian's Wall Volume I: Resource Assessment*, Durham: 149–52.

Hodder, I. (1989) 'Writing archaeology: Site reports in context', *Antiquity* 63: 268–74.

Hodges, R. (2000) *Visions of Rome: Thomas Ashby Archaeologist*, London.

Hoffmann, B. (1995) 'The quarters of legionary centurions of the principate', *Britannia* 26: 107–52.

Holder, P. A. (1982) *The Roman Army in Britain*, London.

Hope, V. (1997) 'A roof over the dead: Communal tombs and family structure', in R. Laurence and A. Wallace-Hadrill (eds) *Domestic Space in the Roman World* (*Journal of Roman Archaeology* Suppl.22), Portsmouth RI: 69–90.

Hopkins, K. (1978) *Conquerors and Slaves*, Cambridge.

——(1980) 'Taxes and trade in the Roman Empire', *Journal of Roman Studies* 70: 101–25.

——(1983) *Death and Renewal*, Cambridge.

Horden, P. and Purcell, N. (2000) *The Corrupting Sea*, Oxford.

Hurcombe, L. M. (2007) *Archaeological Artefacts as Material Culture*, London.

Hurst, H. (1999) *The Coloniae of Roman Britain*, Portsmouth RI.

James, S. (2001) 'Soldiers and civilians: Identity and interaction in Roman Britain', in S. James and M. Millett (eds) *Britons and Romans: Advancing an Archaeological Agenda*, York: 77–89.

——(2003) 'Roman archaeology: Crisis and revolution', *Antiquity* 77: 178–84.

Jansen, G. E. M. (1999) 'Ancient hydraulic engineering and the raising of Ostia', *Mededelingen van het Nederlands Instituut te Rome, Antiquity* 58: 93–96.

Jashemski, W. F. (1979) *The Gardens of Pompeii Volume 1*, New York.

——(1987) 'Recently excavated gardens and cultivated land at Boscoreale and Oplontis', in E. B. Macdougall (ed.) *Ancient Roman Villa Gardens*, Washington.

——(1993) *The Gardens of Pompeii Volume 2*, New York.

Jashemski, W. F. and Meyer, F. (2002) *The Natural History of Pompeii*, New York.

Jenkins, F. (1953) 'The genius Cucullatus in Kent', *Archaeologia Cantiana* 66: 86–91.

——(1956) 'Nameless or Nehallania', *Archaeologia Cantiana* 70: 192–200.

——(1957) 'The cult of Dea Nutrix in Kent', *Archaeologia Cantiana* 71: 38–46.

——(1958) 'The cult of the "pseudo-Venus" in Kent', *Archaeologia Cantiana* 72: 60–76.

Jiménez, A. (2008) 'A critical approach to the concept of resistance: New "traditional" rituals and objects in funerary contexts of Roman Baetica', in C. Fenwick, M. Wiggins and D. Wythe (eds) *TRAC 2007. Proceedings of the Seventeenth Annual Theoretical Roman Archaeology Conference*, Oxford: 15–30.

Johns, C. (2003) 'Art, Romanization and competence', in S. Scott and J. Webster (eds) *Roman Imperialism and Provincial Art*, Cambridge: 9–23.

Johnstone, C. (2008) 'Commodities or logistics? The role of equids in Roman supply networks', in S. Stallibrass and R. Thomas (eds) *Feeding the Roman Army: The Archaeology of Production and Supply in NW Europe*, Oxford: 128–45.

Jones, C. P. (1999) 'Old and new in the inscriptions of Perge', *Epigraphica Anatolica* 31: 8–17.

Jones, G. B. D. (1962) 'Capena and the Ager Capenas Part I', *Papers of the British School at Rome* 30: 116–207.

——(1963) 'Capena and the Ager Capenas Part II', *Papers of the British School at Rome* 31: 100–158.

Jongman, W. (1988) *The Economy and Society of Pompeii*, Amsterdam.

Jouffroy, H. (1986) *La construction publique en Italie et dans l'Afrique Romaine*, Strasburg.

Kahane, A., Threipland, L. M. and Ward-Perkins, J. B. (1968) 'The Ager Veientanus, north and east of Rome', *Papers of the British School at Rome* 36: 1–218.

Kähler, H. (1964) *Das Funfsäulendenkmal für die Tetrarchen auf dem Forum Romanum*, Cologne.

Kaiser, A. (2011a) 'What was a *via*? An integrated archaeological and textual approach', in E. Poehler, M. Flohr and K. Cole (eds) *Pompeii: Art, Industry and Infrastructure*, Oxford: 115–30.

——(2011b) *Roman Street Networks*, New York.

Keay, S., Millett, M., Poppy, S., Robinson, J., Taylor, J. and Terrenato, N. (2000) 'Falerii Novi: A survey of the walled area', *Papers of the British School at Rome* 68: 1–94.

Kellum, B. A. (1994) 'The construction of landscape in Augustan Rome: The Garden Room at the *Villa ad Gallineas*', *The Art Bulletin* 76: 211–24.

Killgrove, K. (2010) 'Identifying immigrants to Imperial Rome using strontium isotope analysis', in H. Eckardt (ed) *Roman Diasporas*, Portsmouth RI: 157–74.

King, A. (1984) 'Animal bones and the dietary identity of military and civilian groups in Roman Britain, Germany and Gaul', in T. Blagg and A. C. King (eds) *Military and Civilian in Roman Britain* (BAR 137), Oxford: 187–217.

——(1999a) 'Animals and the Roman army: The evidence of animal bones', in A. Goldsworthy and I. Haynes (eds) *The Roman Army as a Community*, Portsmouth RI: 139–49.

——(1999b) 'Diet in the Roman world', *Journal of Roman Archaeology* 12: 168–202.

——(2005) 'Animal remains from temples in Roman Britain', *Britannia* 36: 329–69.

Kleiner, D. E. E. (1992) *Roman Sculpture*, New Haven.

Klynne, A. and Liljenstolpe, P. (2000a) 'Where to put Augustus? A note on the placement of the Prima Porta Statue', *American Journal of Philology* 121: 121–28.

——(2000b) 'Investigating the gardens of the Villa of Livia', *Journal of Roman Archaeology* 13: 221–33.

Kokinidou, D. and Nikolaidou, M. (2000) 'A sexist present, a human-less past: Museum archaeology in Greece', in M. Donald and L. Hurcombe (eds) *Gender and Material Culture in Archaeological Perspective*, Basingstoke: 33–55.

Koolhaas, R., Attati, J., Boutang, M., Kwinter, S., Grether, R., Boeri, S., Rozenblat, C., Sassen, S., Simefords, Y., Tazi, N., Wark, M., Chaslin, F., Llotsma, B., Obrist, H.-U. (2001) Harvard Project on the City, *Mutations*, New York.

Laes, C. (2011) *Children in the Roman Empire*, Cambridge.

Lanciani, R. (1988) *Notes from Rome*, London.

La Regina, A. (2001–6) *Lexicon Topographicum Urbis Romae: Suburbium*, Rome.

Larsson Lovén, L. (2002) *The Imagery of Textile Making: Gender and Status in the Funerary Iconography of Textile Manufacture in Roman Italy and Gaul*, Gothenburg.

Launaro, A. (2011) *Peasants and Slaves: The Rural Population of Roman Italy (200 BC to AD 100)*, Cambridge.

Laurence, R. (1994) *Roman Pompeii: Space and Society*, 1st edition, London.

——(1996) 'Ritual, landscape and the destruction of place in the Roman imagination', in J. Wilkins (ed.) *Approaches to the Study of Ritual*, London: 111–21.

——(1999a) 'Theoretical Roman archaeology', *Britannia* 30: 387–90.

——(1999b) *The Roads of Roman Italy: Mobility and Cultural Change*, London.

——(2000) 'Metaphors, monuments, and texts: The life course in Roman culture', *World Archaeology* 31: 442–55.

——(2001) 'Roman narratives: The writing of archaeological discourse – a view from Britain?' (with responses by A. Snodgrass, M. J. Versluys, D. Krausse and R. Hingley), *Archaeological Dialogues* 8: 90–164.

——(2004) 'The uneasy dialogue between ancient history and archaeology', in E. W. Sauer (ed.) *Archaeology and History: Breaking Down the Boundaries*, London: 99–113.

——(2005) 'Health and the life course at Herculaneum and Pompeii', in H. King (ed.) *Health in Antiquity*, London: 83–96.

——(2006) '21st Century TRAC: Is the Roman battery flat?', in B. Croxford, H. Goodchild, J. Lucas and N. Ray (eds) *TRAC 2005. Proceedings of the Fifteenth Annual Theoretical Roman Archaeology Conference*, Oxford: 116–27.

——(2007) *Roman Pompeii: Space and Society*, 2nd edition, London.

——(2009a) *Roman Passions: A History of Pleasure in Imperial Rome*, London.

——(2009b) 'Observing Pompeii and its archaeologists in a re-invented guidebook', *Journal of Roman Archaeology* 22: 584–86.

——(2011) 'Investigating the emperor's toga – privileging images on Roman coins', in M. Harlow (ed.) *Approaches to Dress in the Past*, Oxford: 71–84.

Laurence, R. and Newsome, D. J. (2011) *Rome, Ostia and Pompeii: Movement and Space*, Oxford.

Laurence, R., Esmonde Cleary, E. C. and Sears, G. (2011) *The City in the Roman West*, Cambridge.

Lauwerier, R. C. G. M. (2009) 'Animal husbandry and fishing', in W. J. H. Willems, and H. van Enckevort (eds) *Ulpia Noviomagus – Roman Nijmegen: The Batavian Capital at the Imperial Frontier*, Portsmouth RI: 158–64.

Leach, N., Eckardt, H., Chenery, C., Müldner, G. and Lewis, M. (2010) 'A Lady of York: Migration, ethnicity and identity in Roman Britain', *Antiquity* 84: 131–45.

Leach, N., Lewis, S., Chenery, C., Müldner, G. and Eckardt, H. (2009) 'Migration and diversity in Roman Britain: Multi-disciplinary approach to identification of migrants in Roman York, England', *American Journal of Anthropology* 140–61.

Legge, A., Williams, J. and Williams, P. (2000) 'Lambs to the slaughter: Sacrifice at two Roman temples in southern England', in P. Rowley-Conwy (ed.) *Animal Bones, Human Societies*, Oxford: 152–57.

Lewis, M. E. (2007) *Biological and Forensic Archaeology*, Cambridge.

Liljenstolpe, P. and Klynne, A. (1997) 'The imperial gardens of the Villa of Livia at Prima Porta', *Opuscula Romana* 22–23: 127–47.

Lintott, A. W. (1994) 'Political history 146–95 BC', in *Cambridge Ancient History Volume IX: The Last Age of the Roman Republic 146–43 BC*: 40–103.

Lloyd, J. A. (1986) 'Why should historians take archaeology seriously?', in J. L. Bintliff and C. F. Gaffney (eds) *Archaeology at the Interface: Studies in Archaeology's*

Relationships with History, Geography, Biology and Physical Science BAR Int. Ser. 300, Oxford: 40–49.

Lo Cascio, E. (2006) 'The role of the state in the Roman economy: Making use of the new institutional economics', in P. F. Bang, M. Ikeguchi and H. G. Ziche (eds) *Ancient Economies – Modern Methodologies*, Bari: 215–34.

——(2007) 'L'approvigionamento dell'escerto romano: Mercato libero o'commercio amministrato', in L. de Blois and E. Lo Cascio (eds) *The Impact of the Roman Army*, Leiden: 195–206.

Lomas, K. (2007) 'Introduction: Literacy and the state in the ancient Mediterranean and Near East', in K. Lomas, R. D. Whitehouse and J. B. Wilkins (eds) *Literacy in the Ancient Mediterranean*, London: 11–24.

Macdonald, G. (1924) 'Biographical notice', in G. Macdonald (ed.) *The Roman Occupation of Britain Being Six Ford Lectures Delivered by F. Haverfield*, Oxford: 15–37.

MacDonald, W. L. (1986) *The Architecture of the Roman Empire II: An Urban Appraisal*, New Haven.

Mackinnon, M. (2001) 'High on the hog: Linking zooarchaeological, literary and artistic data for pig breeds in Roman Italy', *American Journal of Archaeology* 105: 649–73.

——(2004) *Production and Consumption of Animals in Roman Italy*, Portsmouth RI.

——(2006) 'Supplying exotic animals for the Roman amphitheatre games', *Museion* 6: 137–61.

——(2007a) 'Peopling the mortuary landscape of North Africa: An overview of the human osteological evidence', in D. L. Stone and L. M. Stirling (eds) *Mortuary Landscapes of North Africa*, Toronto: 204–40.

——(2007b) 'Osteological research in classical archaeology', *American Journal of Archaeology* 111: 473–504.

Maltby, M. (2010a) *Feeding a Roman Town: Environmental Evidence from Excavations in Winchester 1972–1985*, Winchester.

——(2010b) 'Zooarchaeology and the interpretation of deposition in shafts', in J. Morris and M. Maltby (eds) *Integrating Social and Environmental Archaeologies: Reconsidering Deposition*, BAR Int. Ser. 2077, Oxford: 24–32.

Mann, J. (1985) 'Two *Topoi* in the Agricola', *Britannia* 16: 21–24.

Manzi, G., Sperduti, A. and Passarello, P. (1991) 'Behavior-induced auditory exostoses in imperial Roman society: Evidence from coeval urban and rural communities near Rome', *American Journal of Physical Anthropology* 85: 253–63.

Martin, A. (1999) 'The rises in level at Ostia, Regio I, *Insula* x 3', *Mededelingen van het Nederlands Instituut te Rome, Antiquity* 58: 74–77.

Martinón-Torres, M. (2008) 'Why should archaeologists take history and science seriously?', in M. Martinón-Torres and T. Rehren (eds) *Archaeology, History and Science: Integrating Approaches to Ancient Materials*, Walnut Creek CA: 15–36.

Mattingly, D. J. (1997) 'Introduction: Dialogues of power and experience in the Roman Empire', in D. J. Mattingly (ed.) *Dialogues in Roman Imperialism*, Portsmouth RI: 7–26.

——(2003) 'Family values: Art and power at Ghirza in the Libyan pre-desert', in S. Scott and J. Webster (eds) *Roman Imperialism and Provincial Art*, Cambridge: 153–70.

——(2004) 'Being Roman: Expressing identity in a provincial setting', *Journal of Roman Archaeology* 17: 5–25.

——(2006) *An Imperial Possession: Britain and the Roman Empire, 54 BC–AD 409*, London.

Mattusch, C. C. (2005) *The Villa dei Papiri at Herculaneum: Life and Afterlife of a Sculpture Collection*, Los Angeles.

Mays, S. (2003) 'Comment on "A Bayesian approach to ageing perinatal skeletal material from archaeological sites: Implications for the evidence for infanticide in Roman Britain"', *Journal of Archaeological Science*, 30: 1695–1700.

Mays, S. and Eyers, J. (2011) 'Perinatal infant death at the Roman Villa Site at Hambledon, Buckinghamshire, England', *Journal of Archaeological Science* 38: 1931–38.

Meiggs, R. (1973) *Roman Ostia*, Oxford.

Melikian, M. and Sayer, K. (2007) 'Recent excavations in the "Southern Cemetery" of Roman Southwark', in S. R. Zakrzewski and W. White (eds) *Proceedings of the Seventh Annual Conference of the British Association for Biological Anthropology and Osteology*, BAR Int. Ser. 1712, Oxford: 14–23.

Mennella, G. and Lastrico, L. (2008) 'Le *Matronae-Iunones* nell'Italia sententrionale: Anatomia delle dediche', in R. Haeussler and A. C. King (eds) *Continuity and Innovation in Religion in the Roman West Volume 2*, Portsmouth RI: 119–30.

Messineo, G. (2001) *Ad Gallinas Albas: Villa di Livia*, Rome.

Miles, D. (1982) *The Romano-British Countryside: Studies in Rural Settlement and Economy*, BAR Brit. Ser. 103(i), Oxford.

Millett, M. (1990a) *The Romanization of Britain*, Cambridge.

——(1990b) 'Romanization: Historical issues and archaeological interpretation', in T. Blagg and M. Millett (eds) *The Early Roman Empire in the West*, Oxford: 35–44.

——(2007a) 'Epilogue: Beyond Romanization', in M. Millett (ed.) *Shiptonthorpe, East Yorkshire: Archaeological Studies of a Romano-British Roadside Settlement*, Leeds: 325–26.

——(2007b) 'Urban topography and social identity in the Tiber Valley', in R. Roth and J. Keller (eds) *Roman by Integration: Dimensions of Group Identity in Material Culture and Text*, Portsmouth RI: 71–82.

——(2011) 'Town and country in the early Roman West – a perspective', in C. Corsi and F. Vermeulen (eds) *Changing Landscapes: The Impact of Roman Towns in the Western Mediterranean*, Bologna: 17–26.

MLA (2010) *Museums Libraries and Archives (MLA) Light Touch Peer Review – Canterbury City Council Museums and Galleries*, www.scribd.com/doc/47280073/MLA-Light-Touch-Peer-Review-CCC-Museums-and-Galleries-Service-Oct-2010.

Moeller, W. O. (1976) *The Wool Trade of Ancient Pompeii*, Leiden.

Mols, S. T. A. M. (1999) *Wooden Furniture in Herculaneum: Form, Technique and Function*, Amsterdam.

Momigliano, A. (1989) 'The origins of Rome', in F. W. Walbank, A. E. Astin, M. W. Frederiksen and R. M. Ogilvie (eds) *The Cambridge Ancient History Volume VII: The Rise of Rome to 220 BC*, 2nd edition, Cambridge: 52–112.

Moore, J. P. (2007) 'The "Mausoleum Culture" of Africa Proconsularis', in D. L. Stone and L. M. Stirling (eds) *Mortuary Landscapes of North Africa*, Toronto: 75–109.

Moreland, J. (2001) *Archaeology and Text*, London.

Morley, N. (1996) *Metropolis and Hinterland*, Cambridge.

Morris, I. M. (2000) *Archaeology as Cultural History: Words and Things in Iron Age Greece*, Oxford.

Mouritsen, H. (2004) 'Pits and politics: Interpreting colonial *fora* in Republican Italy', *Papers of the British School at Rome* 59: 37–67.

——(2005) 'Freedmen and decurions: Epitaphs and social history in Imperial Italy', *Journal of Roman Studies* 95: 38–63.

Newsome, D. J. (2009) 'Traffic, space and legal change around the Casa del Marinaio at Pompeii' (VII 15.1–2), *Babesch* 84: 121–42.

Nicolay, J. (2007) *Armed Batavians: Use and Significance of Weaponry and Horse Gear from Non-military Contexts in the Rhine Delta (50 BC to AD 450)*, Amsterdam.

Noy, D. (2000) *Foreigners at Rome: Citizens and Strangers*, London.

——(2010) 'Epigraphic evidence for immigrants at Rome and in Roman Britain', in H. Eckardt (ed.) *Roman Diasporas*, Portsmouth RI: 13–26.

Ortloff, C. R. and Crouch, D. P. (2001) 'The urban water supply and distribution system of the Ionian city of Ephesus in the Roman Imperial period', *Journal of Archaeological Science* 28: 843–60.

Owens, E. J. (1991) *The City in the Greek and Roman World*, London.

Özgür, M. E. (1996) *Sculptures of the Museum in Antalya I*, 2nd edition, Ankara.

Öztürk, A. (2009) *Die Architecktur der Scaenae Frons des Theaters in Perge*, Berlin.

Parkin, T. (1992) *Demography and Roman Society*, Baltimore.

Pasqui, A. (1897) 'La villa Pompeiana della Pisanella presso Boscoreale', *Monumenti Antichi* 7: 398–579.

Patterson, H., Di Giuseppe, H. and Witcher, R. (2004) 'Three south Etrurian "crises": First results of the Tiber Valley Project', *Papers of the British School at Rome* 72: 1–36.

Patterson, H. and Millett, M. (1998) 'The Tiber Valley Project', *Papers of the British School at Rome* 66: 1–20.

Patterson, J. R. (2006) *Landscapes and Cities: Rural Settlement and Civic Transformation in Early Imperial Italy*, Cambridge.

Patterson, T. C. (1995) *Toward a Social History of Archaeology in the United States*, Orlando FL.

Pearce, J. (2010) 'Burial, identity and migration in the Roman world', in H. Eckardt (ed.) *Roman Diasporas*, Portsmouth RI: 79–98.

Pena, J. T. (2007) *Roman Pottery in the Archaeological Record*, Cambridge.

Phang, S. E. (2007) 'Military documents, languages and literacy', in P. Erdkamp (ed.) *A Companion to the Roman Army*, Oxford: 286–305.

Pinto-Guillaume, E. M. (2002) 'Mollusks from the Villa of Livia at Prima Porta, Rome: The Swedish Garden Archaeological Project 1996–99', *American Journal of Archaeology* 106: 37–58.

Platner, S. B. and Ashby, T. (1929) *A Topographical Dictionary of Ancient Rome*, Oxford.

Poehler, E. E. (2006) 'The circulation of traffic in Pompeii's *Regio* VI', *Journal of Roman Archaeology* 19: 53–74.

——(2011) 'Practical matters: Infrastructure and the planning of the post-earthquake forum at Pompeii', in E. Poehler, M. Flohr and K. Cole (eds) *Pompeii: Art, Industry and Infrastructure*, Oxford: 149–63.

Potter, T. W. (1979) *The Changing Landscape of South Etruria*, London.

Prowse, T. L., Barta, J. L., von Hunnius, T. E. and Small, A. M. (2010) 'Stable isotope and mitochondrial DNA evidence for geographic origins on a Roman estate at Vagnari (Italy)', in H. Eckardt (ed.) *Roman Diasporas*, Portsmouth RI: 175–97.

Prowse, T. L., Saunders, S. R., Schwarcz, H. P., Garnsey, P., Macchiarelli, R. and Bondioli, L. (2007) 'Isotopic evidence for age-related immigration to Rome', *American Journal of Physical Anthropology* 132: 510–19.

Prowse, T. L., Schwarcz, H. P., Saunders, S., Macchiarelli, R. and Bondioli, L. (2004) 'Isotropic paleo-diet studies of skeletons from the imperial age cemetery at Isola Sacra, Rome, Italy', *Journal of Archaeological Science* 31: 259–72.

Prowse, T. L., Schwarcz, H. P., Saunders, S., Macchiarelli, R. and Bondioli, L. (2005) 'Isotropic evidence for age-related variation in diet from Isola Sacra, Italy', *American Journal of Physical Anthropology* 128: 2–13.

Rankov, B. (2004) 'Breaking down boundaries: The experience of the multi-disciplinary *Olympias* project', in E. W. Sauer (ed.) *Archaeology and History: Breaking Down the Boundaries*, London: 49–61.

Rautman, M. L. (1990) 'Archaeology and Byzantine studies', *Byzantinische Forschungen* 15: 137–65.

Rawson, B. (2003) *Children and Childhood in Roman Italy*, Oxford.

——(2011) *A Companion to Families in the Greek and Roman Worlds*, Chichester.

Redfern, R. (2010) 'A regional examination of surgery and fracture treatment in Iron Age and Roman Britain', *International Journal of Osteoarchaeology* 20: 443–71.

Redfern, R. and DeWitte, S. N. (2010) 'A new approach to Romanization in Britain: A regional perspective of cultural change in late Iron Age and Roman Dorset using the Siler and Gompertz-Makeham models of mortality', *American Journal of Physical Anthropology* 144: 269–85.

Reece, R. (1989) 'Review of *Research on Roman Britain*', *Archaeological Journal* 147: 445–47.

——(2002) *The Coinage of Roman Britain*, Stroud.

Reeder, J. C. (2001) *The Villa of Livia Ad Gallineas Albas*, Providence RI.

Revell, L. (2007) 'Military bath-houses in Britain – a comment', *Britannia* 38: 230–37.

——(2009) *Roman Imperialism and Local Identities*, Cambridge.

Richardson, L. (1992) *A New Topographical Dictionary of Rome*, Baltimore.

Rigsby, K. J. (1996) *Asylia. Territorial Inviolability in the Hellenistic World*, Berkeley.

Rinaldi, M. R. (1956) 'Ricercher sui giocattoli nell'antichità: A proposito di un'iscrizione di Brescello', *Epigraphica* 18: 104–29.

Rivet, A. L. F. (1964) *Town and Country in Roman Britain*, London.

Rodgers, R. (2003) 'Female representation in Roman art: Feminising the provincial other', in S. Scott and J. Webster (eds) *Roman Imperialism and Provincial Art*, Cambridge: 69–93.

Rogers, G. (1991) *The Sacred Identity of Ephesos: Foundation Myths of a Roman City*, London.

Romanelli, P. (1965) 'l'iscrizione di L. Nevio Surdino', in *Gli archeologi Italiani in onore di Amedeo Maiuri*, Cava di Tirreni: 379–90.

Rostovtzeff, M. I. (1926) *The Social and Economic History of the Roman Empire*, Oxford.

Roth, J. P. (1999) *The Logistics of the Roman Army at War (264 B.C. – A.D. 235)*, Brill.

Roueché, C. (1989) 'Floreat Perge', in M. M. Mackenzie and C. Roueché (eds) *Images of Authority*, Cambridge: 206–28.

Ruffini, G. (2008) *Social Networks in Byzantine Egypt*, Cambridge.

Rushworth, A. (2009) *Housesteads Roman Fort – The Grandest Station: Excavation and Survey at Housesteads, 1954–95, by Charles Daniels, John Gillam, James Crow and Others*, Swindon.

Saller, R. P. (2002) 'Framing the debate over economic growth in the ancient economy', in W. Scheidel and S. Von Reden (eds) *The Ancient Economy*, Edinburgh: 251–69.

Salomies, O. (2002) 'People in Ostia: Some onomastic observations and comparisons with Rome', *Acta Instituti Romani Finlandiae* 27:135–59.

Salway, P. (1965) *The Frontier People of Roman Britain*, Cambridge.

——(1981) *Roman Britain*, Oxford.

Sauer, E. W. (2004a) 'The disunited subject: Human history's split into "history" and "archaeology"', in E. W. Sauer (ed.) *Archaeology and History: Breaking Down the Boundaries*, London: 17–46.

——(2004b) 'A matter of personal preference? The relevance of different territories and types of evidence for Roman history', in E. W. Sauer (ed.) *Archaeology and History: Breaking Down the Boundaries*, London: 114–33.

Scheidel, W. (2001) 'Progress and problems in Roman demography', in W. Scheidel (ed.) *Debating Roman Demography*, Leiden: 1–81.

——(2003) 'Germs for Rome', in C. Edwards and G. Woolf (eds) *Rome the Cosmopolis*, Cambridge: 158–76.

——(2004) 'Human mobility in Roman Italy, I: The free population', *Journal of Roman Studies* 94: 1–26.

——(2007) 'Marriage, families and survival: Demographic aspects', in P. Erdkamp (ed.) *A Companion to the Roman Army*, Oxford: 417–34.

Scheidel, W., Morris, I. M. and Saller, R. P. (2007) *The Cambridge Economic History of the Greco-Roman World*, Cambridge.

Scheidel, W. and Von Reden, S. (2002) *The Ancient Economy*, Edinburgh.

Scobie, A. (1986) 'Slums, sanitation and mortality', *Klio* 68: 399–433.

Scott, E. (1989) 'In search of Roman Britain: Talking about their generation', *Antiquity* 64: 953–56.

——(1993) 'Writing the Roman Empire', in E. Scott (ed.) *Theoretical Roman Archaeology: The First Conference Proceedings*, Aldershot: 5–22.

——(2006) '15 Years of TRAC: Reflections of a journey', in B. Croxford, H. Goodchild, J. Lucas and N. Ray (eds) *TRAC 2005. Proceedings of the Fifteenth Annual Theoretical Roman Archaeology Conference*, Oxford: 111–15.

Scott, S. (2003) 'Provincial art and Roman imperialism: An overview', in S. Scott and J. Webster *Roman Imperialism and Provincial Art*, Cambridge: 1–7.

Scott, S. and Webster, J. (2003) *Roman Imperialism and Provincial Art*, Cambridge.

Seetah, K. (2005) 'Butchery as a tool for understanding the changing views of animals: Cattle in Roman Britain', in A. Pluskowski (ed.) *Just Skin and Bone? New Perspectives on Human-Animal Relations in the Historical Past*, BAR Int. Ser. 1410, Oxford: 1–8.

Smith, P. and Kahlia, G. (1992) 'Identification of infanticide at archaeological sites: A case study from the late Roman–early Byzantine periods at Ashkelon, Israel', *Journal of Archaeological Science* 19: 667–75.

Sofaer, J. R. (2006) 'Gender, bioarchaeology and human ontogeny', in R. Gowland and C. J. Knüsel (eds) *Social Archaeology of Funerary Remains*, Oxford: 155–67.

Sogliano, M. (1925) 'Il foro di Pompei', *Memorie della Classe di Scienze Morali, Soriche, e Filogiche (Atti della Reale Accademia Nazionale dei Lincei)* 322: 221–72.

Somner, C. S. (1984) *The Military Vici of Roman Britain* (BAR 129), Oxford.

Speidel, M. P. (1989) 'The soldiers' servants', *Ancient Society* 20: 239–47.

Stallibrass, S. (2000) 'Dead dogs, dead horses: Site formation processes at Ribchester Roman fort', in P. Rowley-Conwy (ed.) *Animal Bones, Human Societies*, Oxford: 158–65.

——(2009a) 'The way to a Roman soldier's heart: A post-medieval model for cattle droving to the Hadrian's Wall area', in M. Driessen, S. Heeren, J. Hendriks, F. Kemmers and R. Visser (eds) *TRAC 2008. Proceedings of the Eighth Annual Theoretical Roman Archaeology Conference*, Oxford: 101–12.

——(2009b) 'Fauna', in M. F. A. Symonds and D. J. P. Mason (eds) *Frontiers of Knowledge: A Research Framework for Hadrian's Wall. Volume I: Resource Assessment*, Durham: 142–45.

Steinby, M. (1993–2000) *Lexicon Topographicum Urbis Romae* (6 volumes), Rome.

Stokes, P. (2000) 'A cut above the rest? Officers and men at South Shields Roman fort', in P. Rowley-Conwy (ed.) *Animal Bones, Human Societies*, Oxford: 145–51.

Stray, C. (2010) '"Patriots and professors": A century of Roman studies 1910–2010', *Journal of Roman Studies* 100: 1–31.

Sykes, N. J., Baker, K. R., Carden, R. F., Higham, T. F. G., Hoelzel, A. R. and Stevens, R. E. (2011) 'New evidence for the establishment and management of the European fallow deer (Dama dama dama) in Roman Britain', *Journal of Archaeological Science* 38: 156–65.

Symonds, M. F. A. and Mason, D. J. P. (2009) *Frontiers of Knowledge: A Research Framework for Hadrian's Wall Volume II: Agenda and Strategy*, Durham.

Taglietti, F. (2002) 'Ancore su incinerazione e inumazione: La necropolis dell'Isola Sacra', *Palilia* 8: 149–58.

Terrenato, N. (2001) 'A tale of three cities: The Romanization of northern coastal Etruria', in S. Keay and N. Terrenato (eds) *Italy and the West: Comparative Issues in Romanization*, Oxford: 54–67.

Tocheri, M. W., Dupras, J. L., Sheldrick, P. and Molto, J. E. (2005) 'Roman period fetal skeletons from East Cemetery (Kellis 2) of Kellis, Egypt', *International Journal of Osteology* 15: 326–41.

Todd, M. (1989) *Research on Roman Britain*, Britannia Monograph Series 11, London.

Tudot, E. (1860) *Collection des figurines en Argile: Oeuvres premiers de l'art gaulois*, Paris.

Vaglieri, D. (1903) 'Gli scavi recenti del Foro Romano', *Bullettino della Commissione Archeologica Communale di Roma* 31: 3–239.

Van Bremen, R. (1996) *The Limits of Participation: Women and Civic Life in the Greek East in the Hellenistic and Roman Periods*, Amsterdam.

van Buren, E. D. (1918) 'Studies in the archaeology of the Forum at Pompeii', *Memoirs of the American Academy at Rome* 2: 67–76.

——(1925) 'Further studies in Pompeian archaeology', *Memoirs of the American Academy at Rome* 5: 103–13.

Van Deman, E. B. (1922) 'The Sullan Forum', *Journal of Roman Studies* 12: 1–31.

van Driel-Murray, C. (1993) 'The Leatherwork', *Vindolanda Research Reports* 3: 1–75.

——(1998) 'A question of gender in a military context', *Helinium* 34: 342–62.

——(1999) 'And did those feet in ancient time … Feet and shoes as a material projection of the self', in P. Baker, C. Forcey, S. Jundi and R. Witcher (eds) *TRAC 98. Proceedings of the Eighth Annual Theoretical Roman Archaeology Conference*, Oxford: 131–40.

——(2001) 'Vindolanda and the dating of Roman footwear', *Britannia* 32: 185–97.

van Tilburg, C. (2007) *Traffic and Congestion in the Roman Empire*, London.

Vann, R. L. (1992) 'The harbor Herod built, the harbor Josephus saw', in B. J. Little (ed.) *Text-Aided Archaeology*, London: 103–22.

Verboven, K. (2007) 'Good for business: The Roman army and the emergence of a "business class" in the north western provinces of the Roman empire', in L. de Blois and E. Lo Cascio (eds) *The Impact of the Roman Army*, Leiden: 295–314.

Wacher, J. (2000) *A Portrait of Roman Britain*, London.

Waldron, T., Taylor, G. M. and Rudling, D. (1999) 'Sexing of Romano-British baby burials from the Beddington and Bignor Villas', *Sussex Archaeological Collections* 137: 71–79.

Wallace-Hadrill, A. (1991) 'Introduction', in J. Rich and A. Wallace-Hadrill (eds) *City and Country in the Ancient World*, London: ix–xviii.

——(1994) *Houses and Society in Pompeii and Herculaneum*, Princeton.

——(2001) *The British School at Rome: One Hundred Years*, London.

——(2008) *Rome's Cultural Revolution*, Cambridge.

Ward-Perkins, J. (1955) 'Notes on Southern Etruria and the Ager Veientanus', *Papers of the British School at Rome* 23: 44–72.

——(1961) 'Veii: The historical topography of the ancient city', *Papers of the British School at Rome* 29: 1–123.

——(1974) *Cities of Ancient Greece and Italy: Planning in Classical Antiquity*, London.

Webster, J. (1994) 'The Just War: Graeco-Roman texts as colonial discourse', in S. Cotan, D. Dungworth, S. Scott and J. Taylor (eds) *TRAC 94: Proceedings of the Fourth Annual Theoretical Roman Archaeology Conference*, Oxford: 1–10.

——(1999) 'At the end off the world: Druidic and other revitalization movements in post-conquest Gaul and Britain', *Britannia* 30: 1–20.

——(2001) 'Creolizing the Roman provinces', *American Journal of Archaeology* 105: 209–25.

——(2003) 'Art as resistance and negotiation', in S. Scott and J. Webster (eds) *Roman Imperialism and Provincial Art*, Cambridge: 24–52.

Weilguni, M. (2011) *Streets, Spaces and Places: Three Pompeian Movement Axes Analysed*, Uppsala.

Welch, K. (2007) *The Roman Amphitheatre from its origins to the Colosseum*, Cambridge.

Wells, P. S. (1984) *Farms, Villages and Cities: Commerce and Urban Origins in Late Prehistoric Europe*, Ithaca.

——(2001) *Beyond Celts, Germans and Scythians*, London.

Whittaker, C. R. (1990) 'The consumer city revisited: The *vicus* and the city', *Journal of Roman Archaeology* 3: 110–18.

——(2002) 'Supplying the army: Evidence from Vindolanda', in P. Erdkamp (ed.) *The Roman Army and the Economy*, Amsterdam: 204–34.

Wild, J. P. (2002) 'The textile industries of Roman Britain', *Britannia* 33: 1–42.

Wilkes, J. J. (1983) 'John Bryan Ward-Perkins 1912–81', *Proceedings of the British Academy* 69: 631–55.

Willis, S. (2005) *Samian Pottery, a Resource for the Study of Roman Britain and Beyond*, http://intarch.ac.uk/journal/issue17/willis_index.html.

Witcher, R. (2005) 'The extended metropolis: *Urbs*, *suburbium* and population', *Journal of Roman Archaeology* 18: 120–38.

——(2006a) 'Settlement and society in early Imperial Etruria', *Journal of Roman Studies* 96: 88–123.

——(2006b) 'Broken pots and meaningless dots? Surveying the rural landscapes of Roman Italy', *Papers of the British School at Rome* 74: 39–72.

Woodward, P. and Woodward, A. (2004) 'Dedicating the town: Urban foundation deposits in Roman Britain', *World Archaeology* 36: 68–86.

Woolf, G. (1990) 'World-systems analysis and the Roman Empire', *Journal of Roman Archaeology* 3: 44–58.

——(1992) 'The unity and diversity of Romanisation', *Journal of Roman Archaeology* 5: 349–52.

——(1993) 'Rethinking the Oppida', *Oxford Journal of Archaeology* 12: 223–34.

——(1997) 'Beyond Romans and natives', *World Archaeology* 28: 339–50.

——(2003) 'The present state and future scope of Roman archaeology: A comment', *American Journal of Archaeology* 108: 417–28.

Zanker, P. (1988) *The Power of Images in the Age of Augustus*, Ann Arbor.

Index